Heather
Sowards

Nov 2010

ALL IS ONE

How the pieces of
life's puzzle fit together

Joop van Montfoort

AuthorHouse™ UK Ltd.
500 Avebury Boulevard
Central Milton Keynes, MK9 2BE
www.authorhouse.co.uk
Phone: 08001974150

First published by AuthorHouse   6/30/2010

ISBN: 978-1-4490-9526-0 (sc)

This book is printed on acid-free paper.

Socrates and Plato taught the perennial Gnostic philosophy that **all is one** ...[1]

He made this world to match the world above, and whatever exists above has its counterpart below ... and **all is one**.

Zohar, Book 2, 20a

Therefore I give you still another thought, which is yet purer and more spiritual: In the Kingdom of Heaven all is in all, **all is one** and all is ours.[2]

Meister Eckhart

If only we could move towards a mystical state of consciousness where **all is one**. ... Now what I say of Zen is also true of Christian mysticism. It also leads to an altered state of consciousness where **all is one** in God.[3]

William Johnston

This letter is written to you [readers of *Exploration into God*] who are feeling your way into the new understanding that **all is One**.[4]

George Trevelyan

Literally all things are connected. **All is One**.[5]

Lawrence LeShan

Thus the chant '**All is One**,' if repeated enough, will from this viewpoint, bring you closer to the knowledge that this is true.[6]

Lawrence LeShan

Acknowledgements

As life is all about learning, I must acknowledge 'the wise old people' who over the years taught me many lessons, especially my grandfather Elis van den Berg who taught me so much when I was still called Jopie. Also the 'feminine', exemplified by my partner, Emmy de Groot, who tripped me up when I had become 'Joop' and still believed that science would ultimately be able to produce all the answers to life's problems. I am also very grateful for her sketches and general support.

Furthermore I would like to thank my family, friends, teachers, colleagues and pupils, and all those who have contributed to imparting the many lessons I had to learn. And the ones who have sometimes made life difficult for me, because by their actions they stopped me in my tracks so that I was forced to look around.

I am grateful to Satish Kumar for being the catalyst for my embarking on this book project, because when we discussed some of my ideas a very long time ago he asked me to write them down.

To emphasize that the message I'm trying to convey is an ancient and widespread one, I have used quotations from many sources. For quotations taken unwittingly out of their proper context, I do apologise.

I am very grateful to Emmy de Groot for her drawing of figures 10.2, 11.2 and 11.4. And to Rupert Sheldrake, Dan

Wolaver and NASA, for permission to use their illustrations as my figures 5.2, 8.1 and 8.3 respectively.

The rest of the illustrations were done by Pat Mohan converting my simple sketches into the polished drawings you will find in the book. This is a special dedication to him, because before its publication he returned to the light.

Finally I must thank Charlie Shand, who obviously had so much confidence in me that when he heard that I was writing this book ordered the first copy without any hesitation.

Croyde, Devon, 2010

CONTENTS

LIST OF FIGURES

LIST OF TABLES

1 INTRODUCTION

1.1 WHY DID IT TAKE SO LONG?

All things are one

Heraclitus

The universe and I exist together, and all things and I are one.[1]

Chuang Tzu

All are one, and the One is all.[2]

Sri Nisargadatta Maharaj

Who knows himself, knows the All.

Hermes Trismegistus

Everything in the Godhead is one.

Meister Eckhart

The image of God is found essentially and personally in all mankind. Each possesses it whole, entire and undivided, and all together not more than one alone. In this way we are all one ...[3]

Ruysbroeck

Electrical engineers are notorious for their wild ideas.

John Polkinghorne

It was over thirty years ago that I had a number of experiences, which could not be fitted into any framework that I was then aware of. Instead of following the advice of a colleague at the scientific research institute where I was employed at that time to just ignore them, I did not give up, desperately wanting to find an explanation; because just letting go is so very much against my investigative nature.[4]

Unexpectedly and powerfully, an insight came to me that undermined everything that I had been taught to consider as established fact. This breakthrough led to an urge to explore further, and to my surprise I found that what I thought was a completely new discovery had been described over the ages by many people from very different traditions; even going back to what I, in my arrogant ignorance, had considered to be primitive times and tribes.

After this brief introduction, I will describe in the following chapters my journey of discovery, and because it was so very much based on personal experiences, I will start with describing my background in chapter 2, not because I am in any way special, but rather to illustrate that it could have happened to anyone.

Chapter 3 describes the events that led to me being 'tripped up' and the 'aha' experience which suddenly made the pieces of the jigsaw puzzle fit together. And to illustrate that my experiences were not at all novel, I will summarise an ancient Greek tale and a nineteenth century one, both telling the same story using completely different imagery.

In chapter 4, I will use a different metaphor, employing an 'ocean' model, perhaps because that appealed so much to me after my Mediterranean scuba diving experiences. Using that model, I will explore the consequences of looking horizontally over the ocean's spacetime surface or vertically exploring its hidden depths.

This leads directly to describing in chapters 5 and 6 what can now be classified as typically 'horizontal' or 'vertical' pursuits.

Science comes to mind as representative of the former, while religion (in the true sense of the word: *re-ligare,* translating as *to re-connect*) is representative of the latter. This exploration leads to the conclusion that the founders of our many religions have all expounded a strikingly simple message, namely that—using the language of our model—priority should be given to vertical pursuits over horizontal ones.

Amazingly, with only few exceptions, we have never taken their recommendations seriously and that is exactly why mankind is in such a mess. Of course we need to make sure that everyone's basic needs are fulfilled, but after that goal has been reached, we should abandon our horizontal materialistic pursuits of more and more material possessions, and give priority to exploring our inner (vertical) spiritual depths instead.

Chapter 7 outlines how there are fortunately several much less drastic methods, than—for instance having a near-death experience—to initiate our inner exploration. Because we are all so very different, there really is no one method superior to any of the others, but it is very important to keep in mind that if one method does not work for you, not to lose courage but to keep trying! There are indeed many different paths to choose from, but all are leading to the top of the same mountain, in the words of Ramana Maharshi: 'All spiritual teachings are only meant to make us retrace our steps to our Original Source'.[5]

Because the message is indeed so very basic and important, its essentials are recapitulated in chapter 8, followed by applications of our model to experiences such as paranormal phenomena and near-death experiences (NDEs). The enormous progress in our medical capabilities has made the revival of patients who would previously have died now a fairly common occurrence, and for many of these, their NDE has proven to be a very drastic method for opening up a whole new dimension to their lives. And while this message that we should give priority to exploring our inner (vertical) realm has been proclaimed over and over again from the very beginnings of—and probably from much before—recorded history, why we have never really listened to that essential message is explored in chapter 9.

After describing a few examples of trying to live in accordance with our message, chapter 10 points out that we need to change to a completely new orientation for our society, leading to a review and conclusions from our exploration in chapter 11.

As I have cast my net over a very wide area indeed, I will undoubtedly have made errors in specialist fields, so if you come across these mistakes, apart from letting me know, do not concentrate on my errors but do keep the general framework of my argument in mind. I have tried to keep the main text brief by relegating side remarks to the extensive notes at the end of the book. And you might very well think that these notes are over the top, but I have done that deliberately because I am very well aware of what I am up against, as so many very learned people deny forcibly that there is anything beyond the horizontal realm, which is the only one subject to scientific investigation.

I remember years ago during a coffee break discussion, when I was arguing a point of view rather along the lines presented in this book, that one of my colleagues—who until then had obviously taken me seriously—looked at me with horror on his face as if I had really lost my marbles, exclaiming: 'Joop, you're not serious, are you?' However, a few years later I met him again and he then remarked: 'When you told us about the importance of spiritual pursuits, I thought you had gone around the bend, but now I am beginning to think that you were right after all'.

I have deliberately provided many quotations and references to books and articles, so that if you want to explore the subjects I mention in greater depth, there is really no end in sight. And if you do think that I have overdone references to the experiences of others, consider this book as an anthology of universal and timeless wisdom told by many others and here embedded in my personal story; or see it simply as an ancient tale retold by an engineer using some of the tools of his trade. It may come as a relief that I can assure you that what I have quoted and referred to, represents only a small fraction of the books, articles and notes I have collected over the years; but I had to force myself to put a firm line under my researches, because otherwise the book would never have gone to the printers.

Aldous Huxley's calls this common wisdom 'The Perennial Philosophy' and in his book of the same title, he summarised the quest for insight as follows: 'The Perennial Philosophy is primarily concerned with the one, divine Reality substantial to the manifold world of things and lives and minds'. And I do think that Huxley himself would consider this book to be his finest, although he became well known mainly because of his *Brave New World*.

In case you are really interested in further reading, there is a 65-page 'Guide to the Literature of Transformation' at the end of James Redfield, Michael Murphy and Sylvia Timbers' book, *God and the Evolving Universe*, published in London in 2002; and only after completing my manuscript, I became aware of the series of books written by John Davidson expounding a very similar message in considerably more detail.[6]

The simple model I am presenting in the following pages has certainly helped me, and several others, to have a better insight into what the sages and mystics throughout man's history have been talking and writing about. But do keep very much in mind the crucial warning Krishnamurti gave: 'One can go endlessly reading, discussing, piling up words upon words, without ever doing anything about it. It is like a man that is always ploughing, never sowing, and therefore never reaping'.[7]

It took me a very long time indeed to discover what the real purpose of being alive is, and I do hope that this book will be of some help to others to shorten that time of discovery. But—as Krishnamurti and so many others emphasise—you will only be able to ferret out what is important by exploring that other realm (beyond the limitations of the horizontal one) for yourself. And as experience is such a very personal thing, I will conclude this brief introduction with the profound advice given by Philipp Frank:

... reality in its fullness can only be experienced, never presented.

2 BACKGROUND

2.1 WHY SHOULD I WRITE A BOOK AT ALL?

The more we learn about the universe the more humble we should be, realizing how ignorant we have been in the past and how much more there is still to discover.[1]

John Templeton

Rationalism and doctrinairism are the diseases of our time; they pretend to have all the answers.[2]

Carl G. Jung

We feel that even if *all possible* scientific questions be answered, the problems of life have still not been touched at all.[3]

Ludwig Wittgenstein

I should like to speak like Nature, altogether in drawings.[4]

Wolfgang Goethe

You teach best what you need to learn most.[5]

Richard Bach

'I don't feel so alone anymore.'[6]

Tao and Physics Course participant

Why should anyone in his right mind want to write another book at all? Libraries and bookshops and our houses are full of them, while, even when that is not enough, the World Wide Web is a practically unlimited source of information. And isn't it true that, given sufficient correct information and using our rational intellect, we will be able to solve all of mankind's problems?

I had to learn the hard way that this belief is a fatal misconception and had to discover that throughout human history there have always been prophets, rishis, sages, etc. who have proclaimed a completely different message. Evidence of their teachings can be found all over the planet, from ancient India and China and the Middle East to what we used to dismiss as primitive tribal areas.[7] Unfortunately, not many of us have ever really listened to what they had to say, or at least we have not taken their recommendations seriously.

My radical change of insight was initiated by being tripped up by a number of personal experiences, and I am very grateful indeed that the woman who was instrumental in causing several of these, crossed my path. These experiences forced me to completely review my perspective of the world around us. Amongst others, this led to discovering that these experiences and the resulting insights were not unique at all, but similar ones had been described since antiquity.

Desiring to fit my experiences into some existing framework, I started to hunt for interesting books, usually avoiding the glossy shopping centres and making second hand bookshops, often in back streets, my first ports of call in any place I visited. This resulted in me filling over the last quarter century some thirty metres of bookshelves! Although not in a very systematic manner, to some extent I kept up with recently published books as well, with the fortunate result that I am now spared an enormous amount of work. Originally it was my intention to write a solidly researched book with impeccable references to other sources and to the many notes and copies of articles that fill another of my shelves.

That major effort has fortunately been carried out by several other writers, so that I can try to limit my text to an outline, quoting from others whose writings may be explored for further details and study. A special mention deserves the extensive book *Every One is Right* by the electrical engineer Roland Peterson.[8] Not only does he convey a very similar message to the one I am expressing here, but he also gives hundreds of quotations in support of that message. As an engineer myself, I especially appreciate his orderly tabular comparisons between the highly similar sayings that can be found in the various religious traditions.

When I occasionally expressed my changing views, these seemed to raise some interest, resulting in me being asked to give a couple of courses in Oxford over twenty years ago. I called these (with apologies to Fritjof Capra), 'The Tao and Physics', and they covered in outline the material presented in much more detail in this book.[9]

At the end of one of these courses, when asking for comments, one of the participants reacted by saying: 'I don't feel so alone anymore'. I have never forgotten that cry from the heart, and I do realise that there are many people like her feeling desperately alone because their experiences do not seem to fit within the framework of our so-called 'normal' materialistic society. For those people this book has been written!

So if you think that your religious faith or science gives you all the answers you need, then this book is definitely not for you. And in the event that you are convinced that science will eventually provide all the answers, you would be much better off reading for instance, Victor J. Stenger's book, *Physics and Psychics*.[10] He summarises his belief as follows: 'At this writing, neither the data gathered by our external senses, the instruments we have built to enhance those senses, nor our innermost thoughts require that we introduce a nonmaterial component to the universe. No human experience, measurement, or observation forces us to adopt fundamental hypotheses or explanatory principles beyond those of the Standard Model of physics and the chance process in evolution'.

I very much like the manner in which he condenses the theme of his book in one formula: $\Psi = \mathbf{0}$, or in words: 'psi is zero', in which Ψ (the Greek letter psi) stands for the 'nonmaterial component of the universe'; and with this formula he wants to express that no phenomena exist beyond the physical universe. If you are indeed a convinced materialist and someone tells you a story that does not fit the materialistic framework, the easiest solution is to declare that obviously the story cannot be true and the storyteller is either a crank or a liar. I cannot blame anyone for having that attitude, because there are an enormous number of storytellers and very credulous people around who will believe anything, but I can assure you that I am not one of them.

Some thirty years ago, I would have largely been in agreement with Stenger's beliefs, and if a friend had told me then about some of the 'paranormal' events that I am describing in this book, I would have shrugged my shoulders with the thought, 'Poor chap, he certainly has lost his critical faculties'. However, as these events are part of my own personal experience, they could not be dismissed so easily and I persisted until I could fit them into a framework that made sense for me.

This implied that I had to change my views of the world dramatically, and had to find a framework that would encompass those 'paranormal' experiences as well. It would certainly have been easier (but less interesting), to have followed the advice of a colleague, who commented (when I was persevering to find an intermittent, not easily reproducible fault in some complicated piece of electronic equipment): 'Joop, you have to learn to look the other way and just give up; that will make your life much easier'. But that attitude is very much against my character and when I persisted, I eventually found and repaired the intermittent fault, and that same attitude is behind the writing of this book.

That I reached a very different conclusion from the materialistic one expressed by Stenger should now not come as a surprise, and following his example, I could condense my message in a formula as well: $\Psi = \infty$, standing for: 'psi is infinite'. My aim is not to open an offensive against materialism, but rather to expound what I now consider to be a more complete view of reality. For me, Stenger's formula says very much about him, but nothing about reality!

Of course, I fully understand the reluctance of allowing psi to be anything other than zero ($\Psi \neq \mathbf{0}$), because that admission opens the floodgates to all the cranks of the world claiming that they have (usually for a significant fee) the solution to all of our problems, and that can indeed prove to be a true opening up of a Pandora's box. But without taking that risk we can be sure to have thrown the baby out will the bath water.

The message that I will expound in this book should be considered as a way to stand up in defence of those sensitive people who are so often crushed under the weight of materialistic argumentation. They are usually made to think that there must be something wrong with them because they do not seem to fit in our so-called 'normal' society. Young people in particular desperately want to be considered 'normal' and will avoid anything that makes them stand out from the crowd. However, I have now come to the conviction that, while I desperately wanted to be considered normal when I was young, the 'abnormal' label should be very much appreciated as a compliment. Indeed I now think that it should be considered very worrying to be considered normal! And if you have any doubts about that statement, you only have to look around you to register what our so-called 'normal' society is up to.

Moreover, you will find out that you are often in excellent company if you are being labelled as abnormal. Wayne Dyer exposes society's lawful behaviour as: 'When we stop to consider most of the evils that have been perpetrated on humanity, they have virtually all been accomplished under the protective custody of society's laws. Socrates was murdered because the law said it was proper to so dispose of intellectual dissidents. St Joan of Arc was burned at the stake because it was the law'.[11] And his two cases could be extended easily with many other painful examples. Indeed, if we take a careful look at human history, we will find that it has often been the 'abnormal' ones who ended up very badly, but in hindsight have contributed most to the progress of mankind. Just to drop a few more names, think of Socrates, Lao Tzu, the Buddha, Jesus, Muhammad, Guru Nanak, William Blake, Baha'u'llah, Simon Kimbangu, Gandhi, Martin Luther King, Nelson Mandela, etc.

Socrates, for example, dismissed the notion that madness should be simply considered an evil: "... for it is the cause of many blessings: the ancients will bear witness that 'madness which comes from god is a finer thing than the moderation which is from men'".[12] So you should consider it to be a compliment, rather than denigration, if you are considered to be 'abnormal'.

In his book *The Soul's Religion,* Thomas Moore calls these outsiders 'holy fools': 'An image is a powerful thing. The non-Romantics among us may prefer numbers and abstractions, but those who live from the soul know the importance of images and know not to reduce them to ideas and interpretations. Being a romantic in the age of rationalism and technology requires that you be eccentric, outside the circle, a holy fool'.[13] I am also on his wavelength regarding the use of images, and will be using many pictures in this book. Not because I am an artist, but because (circuit) diagrams are very much an essential part of my electronics engineering background, and as mentioned before, I want to keep the text as brief as possible—and isn't a picture worth a thousand words? Hence I asked Patrick Mohan and my partner Emmy de Groot to convert my rough sketches into the skilful illustrations you will find further on.

So if I have succeeded in making you curious, exercise some patience and stay with me so that we can explore the meaning of several of my life-changing experiences together. All the described events are authentic; the only elements I have sometimes changed are the names of the other people involved. I realise that observational detachment is highly prized in scientific circles, but as my life-changing happenings are of such a personal nature, there is no other way than to build my narrative around details of my personal background and experiences.

2.2 I USED TO BE QUITE NORMAL

A normal middle class neurotic.

Woody Allen

The Christian should welcome scientific discoveries as new steps in man's domination of nature.[14]

World Council of Churches

"Afterwards I did a lot of thinking. All those religious people, all that carefully measured out adherence to minute details of minute laws ... And then they just miss the big, enormous challenges of their lives, their opportunities to show G-d, to show themselves, how much they love, how much they believe. ..." [15]

Jenni

The religious geniuses of all ages have been distinguished by the kind of religious feeling which knows no dogma and no God conceived in man's image, so that there can be no church whose central teachings are based on it. Hence it is precisely among the heretics of every age that we find men who were filled with this highest kind of religious feeling and were, in many cases, regarded by their contemporaries as atheists, sometimes also as saints. Looked at it in this light men like Democritus, Francis of Assisi and Spinoza are closely akin to one another.[16]

Albert Einstein

Whoso would be a man, must be a nonconformist. ... Nothing is at last sacred but the integrity of our own mind.[17]

Ralph Waldo Emerson

I will illustrate my 'normality' by going quickly through an outline of my personal background: I entered the world above a grocery shop in the central Dutch city of Utrecht as my parents' firstborn. They were members of a fundamentalist Calvinist church, and I grew up in that very well protected environment. Not only did I go to pre-school, primary and secondary schools with the correct denominational labels, but also to similarly confined clubs.

But in my teens, during catechism instruction, I refused to accept the teaching, expounded by our minister that everyone who was not a Christian would go to hell.[18] Although the other churches were according to him clearly mistaken in their teachings, for their members the gates of heaven might still be opened when they arrived there. But for those who had not been saved by the 'Blood of the Lamb', there was only eternal damnation in the fires of hell.[19] I remember vividly that I challenged him with: 'You do not seriously believe that a baby born in the jungle of Papua New Guinea, on dying of an infant disease, will go to hell because she has never heard of Jesus?'[20] When he answered that there was indeed no other possibility, the break with my family's religious tradition was unavoidable, adding to the statistics of what is cynically described by church administrators as 'leakage'.[21]

Much later I discovered that I was certainly not the first one to make the point about the unacceptability of a loving God condemning sinners to hell, because already the Christian philosopher Origen (living around 200 CE) '... could not believe that a just and compassionate God would condemn any soul to eternity in hell, but thought that all souls would be saved through experiencing repeated human incarnations'. In fact he argued '... that the literal terrors of hell were false, but they ought to be publicised in order to scare simple believers'.[22] Hell was indeed intended to keep the flock together and obedient to the Church hierarchy. And it was only many years later that I understood that these rules, regulations, prohibitions and threats are like a protective barbed wire fence preventing blind people falling over a cliff edge. However, the whole point of being alive is to get your eyes open!

Gandhi illustrated his difficulties with Christian dogma as well, when he wrote: 'It was more than I could believe, that Jesus was the only incarnate son of God and that only he who believed in him would have everlasting life. If God could have sons, all of us were his sons'.[23]

And I was certainly not alone in the twentieth century either, because so many others have left their churches in anger or pain. Take for instance what Miranda MacPherson (Holden) related in an interview with Steve Wright concerning one of 'The Interfaith Seminary' (chapter 10) sessions: 'Ray Gaston, the Anglican vicar from Leeds, spent hours listening to all the pain and the anger of so many in the group of students whose early experiences of Christianity had been so negative. I remember how he moved so many when he stood there and three times said, "I am sorry", "I am sorry for what has been done to you in the name of the church and Christianity", "That is not what Jesus' message is all about and these things should not have happened to you and I am sorry on behalf of the church"'.[24]

Hence, like so many others, I became an agnostic and I would to a large extent have agreed with, the materialist's standpoint earlier referred to, that 'psi is zero'. Like so many people in our materialistic society, I was not broadly educated, but was trained rather efficiently to perform as a useful cog in our technological society. In my case I went to technical college, studying electronic engineering, a direction following quite logically from my childhood hobby of building and repairing radios.

It may sound like a dream for present day students, but those were the days in the early 1950s that even before having finished my education, I had the luxury of being able to choose between three firm job offers. So after having fulfilled my National Service obligations as a radar specialist in the Royal Dutch Air Force, I joined the staff of the research laboratories of the biggest electronics company in the Netherlands; where I not only worked on very interesting projects but was given the opportunity to study physics as well. This study confirmed me in my belief that with sound reasoning mankind would be able to solve all its problems intellectually. Wasn't everything subject to the power of our brains? Religion I considered very much as a—now fortunately harmless—leftover from a primitive phase in mankind's evolution (much later, I discovered that Sigmund Freud had come to the same conclusion).

It was a very interesting job, designing all kind of electronic solutions for research and manufacturing problems.[25] After some five years of this, I was invited to join a techno-commercial team and I accepted, as I anticipated to experience in that job a bit more of the real action. Hence I became one of the first digital engineers and travelled around Europe to inform our sales organisations and customers about our range of digital 'Circuitblocks'.[26] They were the forerunners of the integrated circuits, which made amongst others the present personal computer, mobile phone and Internet revolutions possible.

I married and we had two sons and everything seemed perfectly normal. I had become very much what Woody Allen so poignantly describes as, 'A normal middle class neurotic'. However I completely ignored the clear warning signals, such as my stuttering, nail biting and irregular migraine attacks, as signs that all was not well.[27]

2.3 LISTEN AND LEARN

... the really important thing is not to live, but to live well.[28]

Socrates

When a civilization lacks rites of passage, its soul is sick. The evidence for this sickness is threefold: first, there are no elders; second, the young are violent; third, the adults are bewildered.[29]

Meladoma Some

Whoso would be a man, must be a nonconformist.

Ralph Waldo Emerson

Where is the wisdom that was lost in knowledge?
Where is the knowledge that was lost in information?

T.S. Eliot

Understanding is the essence obtained from information intentionally learned and from all kinds of experiences personally experienced.[30]

Father Giovanni

Learning continues until death and only then does it cease.[31]

Hsün Tzu

My commercial department job environment, which had superficially seemed so interesting and challenging, turned out to be very stressful as well. People were always under pressure, trying to meet deadlines or increased turnover objectives. Hence memories resurfaced of the tales that older colleagues had told me when I was working with them at the research laboratories. Some had been floored by a heart attack, stomach ulcer, nervous breakdown or similar affliction. As their misfortune fortunately happened in the days when firms still felt a social responsibility for their workers, they had not been kicked out, but were allowed to spend the remaining years up to their retirement in the more relaxed environment of the research laboratory; where with their widely ranging experience, they often made significant contributions, sometimes indeed resulting in completely new product ranges. They also told me that when young, they had been just such eager beavers as I obviously was, and that I should listen to them and heed their warnings. Fortunately their remarks stuck in my mind to counter the 'normal' attitude that 'you should not listen to old scientists because their brains have gone soft'.

Another very valuable message came from the company psychologist Dr de Graaf, when I consulted him in order to be cured of my stuttering. At the end of our discussion and his assessment, he gave me the following advice: 'The only one who can solve that problem are you yourself'. Now I know that he was absolutely right, but at the time I considered it a very unhelpful comment, hadn't I consulted him as the specialist trained to 'repair' my defect? Imagine a car mechanic saying the same thing to a customer bringing his car in for repair. But taken together, all these wise counsels most probably contributed to my decision to apply for other jobs, preferably in better climes, using the miserable summer of 1961 in the Netherlands as a valid excuse.

My job applications resulted in a job offer at a research laboratory in Frascati, just south of Rome in Italy. When I informed my boss at Philips that I was moving on, he reacted with amazement that someone with such 'bright future prospects' could possibly leave. I countered that when I scrutinised the occupants of the higher levels in our hierarchy, I could easily list their stress-related health problems: one of them was recovering from a heart attack, another was eating pills for his stomach ulcer, a third had just returned from a half-year's 'rest' in a psychiatric institution, etc. Hence my obvious conclusion was that it was high time that I started looking for a healthier work environment. That must have resonated somehow, because he stopped arguing with me.[32]

Subsequently I worked for a number of years in a very satisfying job in a beautiful and sunny environment (where the wine was cheaper by the litre than petrol), but had to return to Holland because of family problems. After having worked there initially in applied research, I became head of the electronics group and enjoyed very much the design and development, both of instrumentation and interfacing hardware together with the software for the early days computers that I was then involved in.

I will never forget that once, after I had shown our head of personnel around our rooms and explained to him what we were involved in, he remarked at the door when leaving: 'And you're getting paid for this as well?'

I have indeed been blessed that I have always found fulfilment in my work and the fact that I was paid well for it, was an added bonus. Kahlil Gibran expressed my experience so beautifully in *The Prophet* that indeed, 'Work is Love made visible'.

However, in the personal sphere all was not well, and a few years later my wife told me that she wanted a divorce, resulting in me receiving a letter from her lawyer that I had to leave our house (which in effect I was still working on) on Saturday 15 February 1975. The evening before (I didn't then know that it was St Valentine's Day, because observing it was not part of the Dutch tradition), I went to a talk by a Dutch sociologist, where I met my present partner Emmy.[33] From my side it was not just meeting a new acquaintance, but meeting someone I seemed to know already. Obviously, I was so overwhelmingly convincing that we started to live together within a fortnight and have never looked back... Emmy was very much instrumental in waking me up to the realisation that there is another, complementary dimension to the one dominated by intellectual and materialistic pursuits, and that leads to the next significant episode in my life's adventure at Lac Noir, which will be covered in the next chapter. There I learned what Jung intended when he wrote:

Experiences cannot be *made.* They happen—...[34]

3 HOW I WAS TRIPPED UP

3.1 LAC NOIR

Still, he could not deny the concrete nature of these experiences. All of it presented the scientist in him with a very serious conflict; everything he was experiencing went against everything he "knew." Then a solution to the conflict presented itself to him and everything became very clear: It was necessary to revise his present scientific beliefs—something that he knew had happened many times to others in the course of history—rather than to question the relevance of his own experience.[1]

Stanislav Grof

Woman is equally equipped with man to tread the spiritual path. No nation can be built strong and stable except on the spiritual culture of its women.[2]

Sathya Sai Baba

The intellect, of course, would like to ... write the whole thing off as a violation of the rules. But what a dreary world it would be if the rules were not violated sometimes![3]

C. G. Jung

If anyone claims to have seen a vision or heard voices, he is not treated as a saint or as an oracle. It is said he is mentally disturbed.[4]

Joseph L. Henderson

The fact that we do not understand precisely how these mechanisms operate can no longer be used as evidence that they do not exist.[5]

Vernon Coleman

In 1975 Emmy and I went with our campervan on a short skiing holiday in the area northwest of Colmar in the French Vosges. While cross-country skiing through the woods there, we realised that this area had obviously been World War I front line, because the slopes of the mountains were still gouged with the remains of what had been trenches and in the woods we came across several cemeteries, ranging in size from hundreds of victims to well over ten thousand. Emmy did not want to visit these cemeteries because 'it did not feel right' for her to enter their gates, as the young people lying there had been killed so unprepared and violently. As I didn't feel anything anomalous, I found her behaviour rather incomprehensible, muttering, 'Women!' under my breath. I then visited several of these sorrowful memorials to our collective madness without further ado.

On one of our expeditions, we saw a couple standing in the middle of a woodland track studying a map, and as I thought this might be a more detailed map of the area than we had ourselves, I approached them and in my best French asked if I could please have a look. The woman replied in Dutch, recognising my accent immediately, as she turned out to be a teacher of French at a secondary school in Amsterdam. I introduced myself as 'Joop van Montfoort', whereupon they looked at each other, exclaiming: 'That's what it was!' Of course I wanted to know what the meaning of this remark was, and they explained that the name 'Montfoort' had for several days somehow come up in their conversations. Because 'Montfort' is a closely related French version[6], they had studied wine and cheese labels to determine where this rather uncommon name came from, and now concluded with relief that it must have been me. I found all of this rather strange, but as they seemed to be very nice people, we invited them for a cup of coffee in our campervan. We got along so well that they invited us for an evening meal with a glass of wine in the small inn where they were staying.

Hence in the evening, we went there and found that the inn was on the shore of a lake called Lac Noir, which looked very much like the flooded crater of an ancient volcano. While we supped and shared a bottle of wine, the subject of our conversation turned to dreams. They talked about Jung and told us that they recorded their dreams and tried to learn lessons from their contents. For me all this was very much gobbledygook, as I was then still very much a straight and tunnel-visioned engineer, and what they were doing seemed to me very much like a useless waste of time and energy.

However, we agreed to go skiing together the next morning, and parted company for the night; they going upstairs to their bedroom and we to our campervan standing on a bit of land jutting out in the lake in front of the inn. In the meantime it had started to snow, and a howling wind turned it into a blizzard. I wanted to dive into bed immediately, but Emmy objected. She did not want to sleep there and asked if we could go somewhere else. I resisted because I liked the place, and wasn't here as good as anywhere else? In this blizzard it was surely a much better idea to get as quickly as possible inside our king-size down sleeping bag. But as a compromise, I moved the van the short distance to the lee of the steep crater wall next to the inn, and went to sleep shrugging my shoulders about this enigmatic female behaviour.

The next thing I knew was that I woke up from a very realistic 'dream'. It wasn't really like a dream at all because it was so real and happened right there in our bed in the campervan. In the 'dream', a soldier in a greyish uniform and kepi was trying to pull open the rear flap of our Citroën HY van, and I was desperately hanging onto the inside handle to prevent him from pulling it upwards.[7] When I woke up, tense from the struggle, I noticed that Emmy was sitting bolt upright in bed and I asked why she wasn't asleep. She replied that it was impossible for her to sleep in this place, and please could I move the van to another location. Normally I would have scoffed at such a clear symptom of female foolishness and would have argued, as before, about how could one place be any different from another. But the experience of my realistic 'dream' had softened me up considerably and in my pyjamas I got behind the steering wheel, started the engine and drove off.

Fortunately I had snow chains on the front drive wheels, so ascending the snow-covered road with its hairpin bends along the wall of the old crater did not cause any difficulty. I asked Emmy to tell me when it would be all right to stop so that we could get the rest of our night's sleep. As soon as the road levelled out when we came over of the crater's edge, she said that it felt all right now, so I pulled off the road at the first opportunity and we slept there without further events.

The next morning I wanted to know what could be the possible explanation for this strange adventure that was unlike anything I had ever experienced before. So after having driven down again, I started to explore the area around the inn. Near our first parking place there was a plaque fixed to the rock face commemorating a group of people who had died in a flooding accident in a nearby electric power station.[8]

The parking place where I had had my 'dream' was next to the inn and examining the steep slope above it, I noticed an opening in the rock face. Obviously this had once served a military purpose, because regimental Roman numbers were still visible on the rock face next to it, while a door was still hanging by one hinge. Further along the road there was a row of large buildings obviously used for children's summer holidays, which was then a widespread practice in southern European countries.

After these investigations, everything that had happened remained still very much an obscure mystery, and I asked Emmy what was the particular feeling she experienced in this place. Her answer was, *'doodsangst'* (mortal fear), and she added that she could not understand how anybody in his right mind could possibly build a children's holiday centre in a place like this.[9] She also remarked that it was inconceivable how sensitive people such as our new friends could sleep there at all but she insisted that I should not say a word to them about what had happened to us.

Somewhat later than agreed, our new friends Etty and Paul came out of the inn's front door and we went on our way and had a lovely cross-country skiing tour. For lunch we stopped at a small farmhouse and the old farmer told us interesting stories of how it was like of being completely snowed under, and once even having to climb through one of the roof skylights to get out of their house at all. After our meal I could not resist asking Etty and Paul if they had slept well. They looked at each other and Etty replied: 'We haven't slept at all'.

When I wanted to know why, she said that it sounded ridiculous in broad daylight, but that they were convinced that a soldier had been trying to get into their bedroom by trying to push open its door. They had only succeeded in keeping the door shut by dragging the bed against it and had tried to get some sleep by pulling the mattress onto the floor in the middle of the room. When I asked her if she had had any particular feeling during this experience, she replied with exactly the same word as Emmy had used: '*doodsangst*'.

When I then told them about our so very similar experience, good old Carl Jung must have chuckled in his grave.[10] But of course at that time I had hardly heard of Jung and certainly hadn't read any of his books, so that his idea of 'synchronicity' was completely alien to me. Hence I was completely unable to fit our vivid shared experience into any framework known to me, or even imaginable.[11]

However, over the following weeks I kept brooding it over very much, until I had a spontaneous 'eureka!' experience, exclaiming, 'There must be a ninety degree phase shift!' Unless you are an electrical or electronics engineer, this exclamation will not make any sense to you,[12] so I will try to demystify what is so crucial about my insight by using a *Gedankenexperiment* (thought experiment) in the Albert Einstein tradition. After that, I will use an outline of Edwin A. Abbot's entertaining description of life in *Flatland* to illustrate the use of a model.

Many years later I discovered that our experience was indeed not unique at all. For instance, the British poet Robert Graves describes a similar event with a dead soldier appearing to him during the First World War. He remarks that 'Ghosts were numerous in France at the time'.[13] And Anthony North lists in his book *The Paranormal* many examples of people who 'usually do not know they are dead, or are reluctant to leave, feeling themselves robbed of life'.[14] While Gary Schwartz explains that: 'It is our fervent hope that future research will enable us to establish definitely that some of the people who call themselves mediums are neither frauds nor freaks but may actually be among humankind's greatest friends by providing confirmed evidence of the existence of a larger spiritual family'.[15]

These observations are underlined by Joan Grant, who writes about her wartime experiences while caring for wounded soldiers: 'But I was now becoming closely concerned with people who had so recently been killed that they had not yet realised they were safely dead'.[16]

3.2 NINETY DEGREE PHASE SHIFT?

We see what we expect not what there is.

Patagonia Dossey

In particular, the conditions of analysis and synthesis of so-called psychic experiences have always been an important problem in philosophy. It is evident that words like thoughts and sentiments, referring to mutually exclusive experiences, have been used in a typically complementary manner since the very origin of language.[17]

Niels Bohr

A voyage of discovery does not start with new vistas but with new eyes.

Proust

It had all begun at the end of the 1950s. It was still a time when most scientists were loath to concede the possibility that ESP existed. Many people didn't talk about their ESP experiences, and some even feared that they would be considered symptoms of mental illness. The general attitude in the scientific community was skepticism.[18]

Douglas Dean et al.

Unfortunately the statistical evidence, at least for telepathy, is overwhelming. It is very difficult to rearrange one's ideas [about the 'thinking machine'] to fit these new facts in.[19]

Alan Turing

Imagine a house with an electricity consumption meter located—as is now common here in the UK—in a box on an external wall. It shows in kilowatt-hours the amount of electricity that has been consumed. This meter is watched by Jill, while Jack is inside, watching an ampere meter wired in series with a wall socket measuring the electrical current, as sketched in figure 3.1. On this meter Jack can see how much current is flowing, and he remembers from his school days that he can arrive at the electricity consumption in kilowatts by multiplying the known mains voltage by the current reading on his meter.

After these preparations, I go into the house with three identical looking boxes, marked A, B and C respectively; each box having an electrical cable with mains plug connected to it. I plug the boxes into our socket one after another, and ask Jill and Jack to read their instruments.

Figure 3.1 Experimental set-up

From their readings I ask them to conclude whether box B is equal to box A or to box C. To their amazement Jack concludes that boxes A and B are the same, while Jill concludes that B and C are.

As insiders, we know that all three boxes are different: box A contains a resistor, box B contains a capacitor, so chosen that it draws the same current from the mains as the resistor, while box C is empty. The reason for Jack and Jill's differing conclusions is that Jack has observed that boxes A and B draw the same current, while box C draws no current at all, and concludes from this observation that they are equal.

Jill is watching a more sophisticated instrument that takes into account the phase shift angle between voltage and current as well. Although the capacitor draws exactly the same current from the mains as the resistor, no power is consumed because a (loss-free) capacitor causes a ninety degree phase shift between voltage and current. And therefore Jill concluded correctly from her reading of the kilowatt-hour meter that boxes B and C behaved identically (at least their lack of measured power consumption was identical), while Jack came to a wrong conclusion because the instrument he was using was not sophisticated enough and did not reveal the full picture; he was simply fooled by lack of information.

The only way Jill will be able to convince Jack that she is right, is to take him outside and show him the result that her more sophisticated instrument reveals when they repeat the experiment. Alternatively we could have given Jack an elementary course in electrical engineering and an oscilloscope displaying on a screen the voltage and current waveforms one below the other. Then from a correct interpretation of the pictures on his screen he would have arrived at the same conclusion as Jill.

This is not an electrical engineering textbook, and unless you know exactly what you are doing, do not try this experiment at home. Do also not think that the ninety degree phase shifted current is just a harmless phantom that has no practical relevance, because in mains power distribution systems it generates real heat in electrical power cables, so that electricity companies have to take appropriate compensatory measures to reduce these losses.

Translating the result of this experiment into psychological terminology, we could explain its outcome as Jill experiencing the world at a higher level of consciousness than Jack. His limited perspective caused him to come to a completely erroneous conclusion; what seemed at first sight so obvious is not necessarily true.

Having sketched what my exclamation about the ninety degrees phase shift after the Lac Noir experience entails, I will now illustrate how the use of a model can be very helpful in coming to grips with an experience that for most of us does not fit in with our 'normal' day to day experience. Subsequently I will combine the two representations.

3.3 FLATLAND

In the last analysis, the psychological roots of the crisis humanity is facing on a global scale seem to lie in the loss of the spiritual perspective.[20]

Stanislav Grof

Belief is no substitute for inner experience.[21]

C. G. Jung

In particular, the conditions of analysis and synthesis of so-called psychic experiences have always been an important problem in philosophy. It is evident that words like thoughts and sentiments, referring to mutually exclusive experiences, have been used in a typically complementary manner since the very origin of language.[22]

Niels Bohr

The beginning of knowledge is the discovery of something we do not understand.

Frank Herbert

Without a theory facts are a mob, not an army.[23]

W. F. Barrett

Edwin A. Abbot's book *Flatland,* first published at the end of the nineteenth century, is still in print and really worth reading, so here I will give a very brief outline only.[24] Abbot describes in great detail the happenings in a two-dimensional world. His protagonist is a Mr Square who, in the second half of the book, while sitting inside his house with all the doors shut, sees that something is passing through his living room. It starts as a point, becoming a line, which then contracts into a disappearing point again. When he challenges the intruder, a voice answers: 'I am a sphere'.

Although in a dream Mr Square has been in a similar discussion with the king of one-dimensional Lineland, his immediate reaction is that a sphere is impossible because 'everybody knows that the third dimension does not exist'. He simply is unable to envisage a higher than two-dimensional world. Moreover, in Flatland it is considered a serious crime to even mention the possibility of a third dimension. After much to-ing and fro-ing, the sphere ends up pulling Mr Square out of Flatland, which lies suddenly completely open to his amazed eye. He witnesses top-secret government deliberations because, although all Flatland doors are guarded very carefully, it lies completely open to the third dimension from where nothing can be hidden. After his 'out-of-Flatland' experience, Mr Square becomes a prophet of the third dimension and I will leave you curious about how that works out.

Because it is for us easy to understand how Mr Square was imprisoned in his two-dimensional world, his example might make it more acceptable that we are in a similar way imprisoned in a four-dimensional one. And although we firmly exclaim, backed up by science, that 'the third dimension does not exist' (remember $\Psi = 0$, in chapter 2), there have always been people, such as those of some of the quotations I opened this chapter with, who extolled a different message. As happened in my case, the message often comes from the feminine, in line with what Richard Feynman experienced: '... husbands always like to prove their wives wrong—and he found out as husbands often do, that his wife was quite right'.[25]

Before we start examining the message that there is more to life than reason can explain, I will use the above preparation to develop a model in the next chapter.

4 THE 'OCEAN' MODEL

4.1 OUR FOUR-DIMENSIONAL UNIVERSE

... the universe begins to look more like a great thought than like a great machine.[1]

James Jeans

There is no place in this new kind of physics both for the field and matter, for the field is the only reality.[2]

Albert Einstein

Rationalism and doctrinarism are the diseases of our time; they pretend to have all the answers.[3]

Carl G. Jung

Nowhere, my Beloved, will world be but within us.

Rainer Maria Rilke

What can be done? You never change things by fighting the existing reality. To change something, build a new model that makes the existing model obsolete.

Buckminster Fuller

Since Einstein's general theory of relativity, we know that the three dimensions of space are intrinsically linked with time, so that the resulting four-dimensional universe is usually referred to as a spacetime one.[4] That space and time are firmly bound together is demonstrated in seemingly absurd results of experiments, such as that a moving clock runs slower than a stationary one.[5] Extrapolating this result leads to the famous twin paradox, proclaiming that if one of a pair of twins embarked on a fast exploration of the universe, upon his return he would be younger than his twin brother who had stayed at home.

As we are unable to envision a four-dimensional space-time universe, Abbot's trick (chapter 3) is extended to reducing the three dimensions of space to one. James Jeans and Richard Feynman come to mind, having done this very successfully to illustrate the interactions between elementary particles.[6]

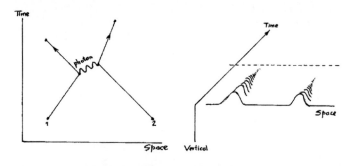

Figure 4.1 Four-dimensional worlds

The sketch on the left illustrates the interaction between two particles, while I ask you to imagine the wavy line on the right to be the surface of an 'ocean' representing our four-dimensional universe.[7] Its three dimensions of space are reduced to one and the other dimension represents time; the waves illustrating that the presence of matter distorts the space-time surface of our ocean, waves coming and going with time, as well as moving along the space dimension.

That this four-dimensional surface is distorted by the presence of mass follows from general relativity. An example of a practical application of knowing about this distortion is the solution to the so called perihelion precession problem of the planet Mercury, whose orbit does not obey the predictions derived from Newton's laws of motion. Now we know that spacetime so near the sun is distorted to such an extent that this distortion has a measurable effect on Mercury's orbit. In fact, not only galaxies, stars and planets can be represented as distortions on the surface of the spacetime 'ocean', but so can our bodies and everything physical around us. With a lot of artistic licence, we can now depict a very small part of the ocean's surface (i.e. on a very large scale) of us and our environment, as in figure 4.2.

Figure 4.2 We and our world

Already in the 1930s, James Jeans gave a very appropriate description, calling our 'ocean' a 'soap-bubble': 'To sum up, a soap-bubble with irregularities and corrugations on its surface is perhaps the best representation, in terms of simple and familiar materials, of the new universe revealed to us by the theory of relativity. The universe is not the interior of the soap-bubble but its surface, and we must always remember that, while the surface of the soap-bubble has only two dimensions, the universe-bubble has four—three dimensions of space and one of time'.[8]

The life-giving energy to everything on our planet comes from our sun, which is, compared to us, a huge wave on the same ocean surface, a very long horizontal distance away. Everything on earth derives its energy and life from our glorious sun.

Right?   No, wrong!

4.2 THE SOURCE OF ALL

... the healing of the inner eye of man if it is to behold its true Sun—not that image of the Sun in the sky which you know, but that Sun of which it is written, "The Sun of Righteousness is risen upon me".[9]

Saint Augustine

... the eternal sun in the realm of spirits.[10]

Friedrich von Schelling

A cinema audience may look up and see that all screen images are appearing through the instrumentality of one imageless beam of white light. The colourful universal drama is similarly issuing from the single white light of a Cosmic Source.[11]

Paramahamsa Yogananda

We cannot tell whether God and the unconsciousness are two different entities.[12]

C. G. Jung

God is not in you in the same sense that a raisin is in a bun. That is not unity. God is in you as the ocean is in a wave. The wave is nothing more nor less than the ocean expressing as a wave.[13]

Eric Butterworth

All that is visible corresponds to an invisible source.[14]

African Elder

Joop van Montfoort

The sun is of course very much the source of physical, measurable energy falling on our planet, but 'life' derives its energy from somewhere else.[15] To illustrate that point, I will complete figure 4.2 on a much smaller scale, because in that figure only a tiny part of the 'surface' of our four-dimensional universe has been depicted. If it would be possible to observe our universe from the outside, it could (remembering Jeans' image of the 'soap-bubble'), again with much artistic freedom be represented as in figure 4.3. This picture also makes clear that, when Einstein speculated that the spacetime surface curved back on itself, one of the consequences would be—if you were able to see as far as you would like—that you would see the back of your own head.

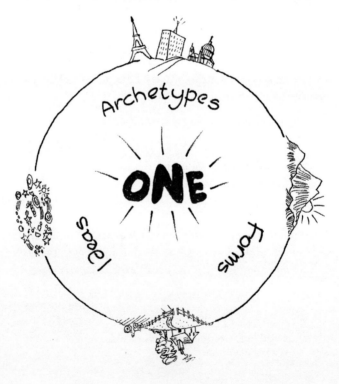

Figure 4.3 The universe and the 'One'

So, by representing our four dimensional universe as the (horizontal) surface of a spherical ocean, we can depict at its centre another 'sun' which is the source of all (vertical) energy. George Trevelyan uses the same image in the following quotations:

Space is filled with an endless ocean of Living Energy. Visible forms and bodies of any sort are coagulations [on the ocean's surface] of this energy.

There is a huge ocean of thought filling all ethereal space, infinite and eternal. It is the primal thought of God, from which all matter and form is derived, for substance is indeed frozen spirit.

Behind the physical sun that we see with our eyes and which warms our bodies is the Spiritual Sun ...[16]

The above depiction is of course, only to be interpreted as symbolic for the source of our 'life' energy irradiating the surface of our ocean from 'within'. Although this spiritual sun has been given many different names, such as personalising it as 'God', Spinoza made it clear that 'God is not He who is, but That which is'. As there is indeed only one such a 'sun', I will call it—like Plotinus did a long time ago— the 'One'.[17] Also I use this description of the 'indescribable' to honour Giordano Bruno, who was burned at the stake for expressing ideas similar to those I hold; he called it the 'Infinite One'.

At the ocean's surface, the energy flow emanating from the One 'coagulates' into matter, forming the material substance of our universe.[18] As the One is well outside the spacetime prison of the ocean's surface, we should in reality not try to locate it anywhere; it is both 'outside' and 'inside' both of space and time.[19] One of the subjects of Michael Newton's hypnotherapy sessions described it very well thus: 'There really is no center. The source is all around us as if we were ... inside a beating heart'.[20] And I will illustrate that this 'outside time' concept is used by scientists, as well as by poets, with quotations from Albert Einstein: 'To us who are committed scientist, the past, present and future are only illusions, however persistent'; Sigmund Freud: 'Unconscious mental processes are in themselves timeless. In the id there is nothing corresponding to the idea of time'; and T. S. Eliot: 'To be conscious is not to be in time'.[21]

That 'sun' representing the One, is the source of the 'light' that was created on the first day in the ancient creation tale in Genesis, and the prophet Isaiah explains in the same vein that 'the Lord shall be unto thee an everlasting light'.[22] (Similar 'light' imagery we find in many other traditions, for instance Plutarch refers to the Egyptian Osiris as having white vestments '... symbolizing the Intelligible Light beyond the cosmos',[23] which I have tried to illustrate in figure 4.3 as the light radiating from the One energising the 'cosmos'.)

In subsequent chapters we will see that not only the 'One', but its 'light' as well, has been given many different names, and that this basic model can be used to clarify many issues. I will just mention here that already Socrates made use of the same simile of the 'sun', which we can identify with our One, as the 'Idea of the Good'.[24] After explaining that we need the sun to illuminate objects to make them visible to our eyes, he draws parallels with our inner realm. Plato puts into Socrates' mouth these words: 'The good has begotten [this 'sun'] in its own likeness, and it bears the same relation to sight and visible objects in the visible realm that the good bears to intelligence and intelligible objects in the intelligible [vertical] realm'.[25]

Indeed the 'light' image is widely used for this transcendent source of all being; take for instance the *Gospel of Thomas*, in which Jesus is reported to have said, 'If they say to you: "Where did you come from?", say to them: "We have come from the Light, where the light came into being by itself."' While Plotinus wrote in the *Enneads*: 'We may think of the Divine as a fire whose outgoing warmth pervades the Universe'.

And developing Socrates' succinct remark that 'we are thoughts in the mind of god', he wrote elsewhere: 'Since from the Supreme God Mind arises, and from Mind, Soul, and since this in turn creates all subsequent things and fills them all with life, and since this single radiance illumines all and is reflected in each, ... the attentive observer will discover a connection of parts, from the Supreme God down to the last dregs of things, mutually linked together and without a break'.[26]

So when we call that what is below our ocean's surface mind, we see that it condenses at the ocean's surface as matter, which insight was expressed succinctly by Arthur Eddington: 'To put the conclusion crudely—the stuff of the world is mind-stuff'.[27]

Centuries after Socrates, the 'sun' image was also used by Thomas Aquinas: 'For as our sun, not by choosing or taking thought but by merely being, enlightens all things, so the Good ... by its mere existence sends forth upon all things the beams of goodness'.[28]

And Marsillio Ficino followed him in his turn in the fifteenth century, writing: 'Nothing reveals the nature of the Good more fully than the light [of the sun]. ... The sun can signify God himself to you...'[29]

We have to keep very much in mind that over the ages many people have used these similes trying to express in words, experiences from outside our spacetime prison that really cannot be described at all. Take this apparent nonsense from Jung, for instance: 'I begin with nothing. Nothing is the same as fullness. ... That which is endless and eternal has no qualities, because it has all qualities'.[30]

Running ahead of our story, and calling with Ficino the source of light, or the One, 'God', it may seem odd to locate 'him' at the bottom of our ocean, as traditionally god is looking down upon us from the heavens above. But remember again that the One, the source of all being, is not imprisoned in the spacetime surface of our ocean at all. So we can really locate 'it' anywhere, and because the ocean model appeals to me particularly, I have located the One at the 'bottom' of our bottomless ocean, keeping in mind that that 'bottom' is the 'centre' of it all, as was depicted in figure 4.3.

The energy flow from the One to the ocean's surface has been given many names as well. In the Christian tradition it is known as the 'Holy Ghost/Spirit', in which spirit translates as 'breath'. And that this is a universal idea we can see, for example in Richard Wilhelm's translation of the ancient Chinese text *The Secret of the Golden Flower,* illustrating that in a far eastern tradition the word 'breath' is used for the all-enveloping life-giving energy flow from the 'One' as well: 'Heaven created water through the One. That is the true energy of the great One. If man attains this One he becomes alive; if he loses it he dies. But even if man lives in the energy (vital breath, *prana*) he does not see the energy (vital breath), just as fishes live in water but do not see the water. Man dies when he has no vital breath, just as fishes perish when deprived of water'.[31] It is certainly very interesting to end this section with the observation that in the latest developments towards understanding our universe, there are '...speculative string theory models in which our [four dimensional] universe is confined to the surface of a membrane, or brane, floating in a higher dimensional space known as the "bulk".[32]

In chapter 6, in the section on religion, we will explore in more detail the different names that have been given in diverse religious traditions to the source, its energy flow and its manifestation at the ocean's surface.

4.3 BELOW THE OCEAN'S SURFACE

Every drop of the ocean shares its glory but is not the ocean.[33]

Mohandas Gandhi

Our soul we call it; properly speaking, it is not ours, but we are its. It is not a part of us, but we are a part of it.[34]

Frederic Hedge

We are like islands in the sea, separate on the surface but connected in the deep.

William James

Ninety-nine percent of who you are is invisible and untouchable.

R. Buckminster Fuller

This [J. B. Rhine's experimental evidence] indicates that our conceptions of space and time, and therefore of causality also, are incomplete. A complete picture of the world would require the addition of still another dimension; only then could the totality of phenomena be given a unified explanation.[35]

C. G. Jung

The good therefore may be said to be source not only of the intelligibility of the objects of knowledge, but also of their being and reality; yet it is not itself that reality, but is beyond it, and superior to it in dignity and power.[36]

Socrates

For me the appeal of using an oceanic model most probably originates in one of my Italian scuba-diving experiences.[37] I remember vividly that, back in the 1960s when I was living near Rome, we went for a diving exploration of an ancient wreck site off the Mediterranean coast not far from Anzio. A steady force four wind was blowing, and the Mediterranean was speckled with 'white horses'. We boarded our inflatable craft at the beach and at full throttle rattled across the surface to our destination. The experience was like travelling inside a washing machine, and several of us saw white around our noses when we finally arrived at our diving location. We geared up, and after entering the water we were still tossed about by the waves. But after submerging, the tossing about became less and less, until at the bottom all was delightfully silent and still. Looking upwards, you could still see the frantic activity on the surface gradually petering out to the peacefulness at greater depth. Indeed, all was so peaceful and quiet here, that little fish would gather around your fingers in the hope that you would stir up something edible from the sediment.

Similarly, in our model our ego is the top of the wave, battered around by all the world's problems, while our soul/higher-self resides in the stillness of the ocean's depths below.[38] The ocean's surface is the hectic realm (prison) of space and time (spacetime), which—like the wave turmoil at the surface of the Mediterranean described above—peters out gradually to the stillness below. Many different images have been used for this experience, and I will just take as an example the illustration Pir Vilayat Khan uses of 'a pendulum in which the point from where the line is suspended represents the eternal pole of our being, and the pendulum is our personal notion of ourselves moving in spacetime'.[39] Only at that still point of suspension are we completely outside the agitation of the spacetime realm, and from there looking up/down, neither time nor space exists, everything just 'is'.

Our consciousness is not imprisoned in the ocean's surface. During dreaming, for instance, 'it is as if the observing ego had stepped outside the time line. It can survey the past, the present, and the future in one single moment. ...' And according to Freud, 'there is nothing corresponding to the idea of time...'[40]

Like Mr Square in Abbot's story during his 'out of Flatland' experience (chapter 3); during my Mediterranean dive I had from below a panoramic view of everything that was happening at the surface. I saw the boat and other divers still being tossed about, and would have been able to clearly see a shark attacking them, to which they, caught up in the middle of the wave turmoil, would have been completely oblivious. In other words I could, from my viewpoint outside their 'prison of space and time', have predicted their likely future. And this is exactly what is reported by people having an 'out of the body' experience, as sometimes occurs during a near-death experience (chapter 8).

Looking back on their lives, they describe that you are not seeing it in a time sequence as in a film, but seeing everything panoramically, seemingly happening all at the same time. The composer Mozart describes a similar experience in the realm of music when he writes about how his muse inspires him: 'Nor do I hear in my imagination the parts *successively*, but I hear them, as it were, all at once [gleich alles zusammen]. What a delight this is I cannot tell! ... and this is perhaps the best gift I have my Divine Maker to thank for'.[41] Brian Inglis' book *The Unknown Guest*—from which I have taken this quotation—is a treasure trove of many well-documented similar experiences.

By having again run ahead of my story, I trust you can now better understand my affinity to the 'ocean' model because I find the diving experience very similar to what can happen during a meditation session; the aim of which is to leave the madhouse of our hectic 'surface' life behind and enter into the stillness of the depths of the 'ocean' of the One. This experience of diving into the stillness of the watery depths is indeed similar to the description by Meister Eckhart of the immobility beyond surface categories: '... that eternal Unity which was mine before all time, when I was what I would, and would what I was ...a state above all addition or diminution ... the Immobility whereby all is moved'.[42]

Later we will see that thoughts arise in these depths of our ocean. And that there simply is no possibility of going beyond the One, is made very clear in this translation by Richard Wilhelm of the ancient Chinese text, *The Secret of the Golden Flower*: 'Nothing is gained by pushing reflection further. One must be content to see where the thought arose, and not seek beyond the point of origin; for to find the heart (consciousness, to get behind consciousness with consciousness), that cannot be done'.[43]

My 'ninety degree phase-shift' exclamation, which was the result of our Lac Noir experience described in chapter 3, can now be clarified with the aid of this ocean model. Its 'horizontal' surface is the four-dimensional spacetime universe in which all matter and hence our bodies, are 'imprisoned'. The 'vertical' realm, at ninety degrees to its surface, is outside that prison, and as we will see later, not only has it been given many different names, but it can be explored as well.[44]

The vertical dimension has been called the fourth or the fifth dimension, but I think that one should really not give it a number, because we have seen how the nineteenth century fourth dimension became—after Einstein's four-dimensional spacetime, the fifth dimension in the twentieth century.[45] Therefore, as it is really beyond number, I have called it in this book deliberately the 'vertical' one.

Imagining for a moment that you are a wave and that your eyes are located at its top; when looking horizontally around you over the ocean's surface, you see the other waves as completely separate from yourselves. But if, for instance during dreaming, your awareness moves inwards in the 'vertical' direction and you roam around under the ocean's surface, this can sometimes result in clairvoyant experiences. Many people have expressed their awareness that they are one with all of creation, or translated into the language of our model, that they are part of the same ocean, and that in essence all waves are one. John Donne's 'No man is an island' comes to mind immediately, and I cannot resist to quote here an episode from Mitch Albom's moving book *Tuesdays with Morrie*.

Albom, an American sports journalist rushing around in the fast lane, had heard on the news that his old professor Morris (Morrie) Schwartz was dying from ALS.[46] This resulted in him visiting Morrie every Tuesday and writing down the life lessons he learnt during those visits. The book is full with wisdom fitting in beautifully with my story and I will quote Morrie's ocean story in full:

"I heard a nice little story the other day," Morrie says. He closes his eyes for a moment and I wait.

" Okay, the story is about a little wave, bobbing along in the ocean, having a grand old time. He's enjoying the wind and fresh air—until he notices the other waves in front of him crashing against the shore.

"'My God, this is terrible,' the wave says. 'Look what's going to happen to me!'

"Then along comes another wave. It sees the first wave, looking grim, and it says to him, 'Why do you look so sad?'

"The first wave says, 'You don't understand! We're all going to crash! All of us waves are going to be nothing! Isn't it terrible?'

"The second wave says, 'No, you don't understand. You're not a wave, you're part of the ocean'"

I smile. Morrie closes his eyes again.

"Part of the ocean," he says, "part of the ocean," I watch him breathe, in and out, in and out.[47]

Kabir used the same imagery in a beautiful poem:

The river and its waves are one surf:
Where is the difference between the river and its waves?
When the wave rises, it is the water;
and when it falls, it is the same water again.

Tell me, Sir, where is the distinction?
Because it has been named a wave,
Shall it no longer be considered as water?
Within the Supreme Brahma, the worlds are told like beads:
Look upon that rosary with the eyes of wisdom.[48]

While Eric Butterworth expresses it similarly: 'A wave is the ocean expressing itself as a wave. It has form and shape and movement. It has an identity, a uniqueness; yet it is nothing less and nothing more than the ocean'.[49]

Another of our modern day mystics, Dean Inge, expresses the mystical experience as: 'The mystical experience seems to those who have it to transport them out of time and place and separate individuality ... Those mystics who are also philosophers generally hold that neither space nor time is ultimately real'.[50] And regarding this experience of not being imprisoned in time, Jesus' saying comes to mind: 'Before Abraham was, I am'.

This wave model also illustrates clearly that the soul is not in the body (Descartes, for instance locating it in the pineal gland), but the soul is part of the divine 'ocean'. And as a 'wave upon that ocean' it encapsulates a body, which it uses to manifest itself at the surface; i.e. it incarnates to learn particular lessons in the spacetime realm. Suzuki expresses this as: 'We can conceive of the soul as not entering into a body ... ready to receive the soul, but as creating a body suitable for its habitation ... the soul comes first and the body is constructed by it'.[51] Or to put it very concisely: a human is not a body having a soul, but a soul having a body.

Another important characteristic is, that like a layer of seaweed, everything we do, think or suffer, is stored there in our unconscious, nothing is lost or forgotten. This layer is as Thomas Aquinas called it like a 'veil' between the 'light' and us.[52] But, unless we are 'enlightened', this layer, very appropriately called by a mediaeval writer 'The Cloud of Unknowing', also blocks the 'light' from below very efficiently. Going still deeper we come to the region where our collective (Akashic) memories and the laws of the universe are stored and deeper still we encounter the Platonic Ideas or Forms, which are the templates for everything that manifests itself on the spacetime surface. We can expect the Middle East to be aware of Plato's Forms, as witnessed for instance by Al-Ghazali, explaining that for 'everything that is in the world of the visible, there is a corresponding likeness in the world of the supreme nature'.[53] And Rumi expresses the same idea as: 'I look in your inmost self and see the universe not yet created'.[54]

Our worldwide interconnectedness is demonstrated by the fact that we find the same idea in Chinese tradition as well. For instance Chang Tsai expressing it concisely as: 'When the *ch'i* condenses, its visibility becomes apparent so that there are then the shapes (of individual things)'.[55] And that this ancient insight is corroborated by modern science as well should come as no surprise; for instance in *Grammatical Man*, Jeremy Campbell quotes B. G. Goodwin, who from his biology standpoint declares that: 'Aristotle was correct to insist that something like formative "ideas", different in some sense from ordinary physical matter, must guide the intricate and extraordinarily varied formative processes of organic nature'.[56] While further on he quotes from a conversation he had with Naom Chomski, who not only accepts that there is a deep memory lying at the origin of languages, but also expresses that these views apply to the field of biology as well: 'In my view, ... natural selection in itself does not provide anything near enough structure to account for what happens in evolution'.[57] I have illustrated this process of 'guided' evolution in figure 4.4. From top to bottom we see matter on the ocean's surface being guided vertically by the 'Forms' deep below to ever more intricate creations. At the animal level, consciousness awakens, culminating into self-consciousness at the human level.

Figure 4.4 Guided evolution

We will see further on that the few sources I have quoted from are not just odd exceptions to the horizontal slit vision of so many scientists, but that there are many others who have expressed similar ideas. And that this idea is very old indeed and dates at least back to ancient Egypt is illustrated by the famous statement, 'As above, so below', attributed to Hermes Trismegistus (in the 'upside down' ocean model, 'above' and 'below' have of course to be interchanged). Our model also makes clear what F. W. H. Myers meant when he stated that 'hidden in the deep of our being is a rubbish heap as well as a treasure house'.[58]

Declaring the influence on the surface of our spacetime ocean of these deep memories as being caused by 'morphogenetic fields', a modern exponent of this ancient idea is Rupert Sheldrake. In his courageous book *A New Science of Life* (see next chapter) he writes: '... morphogenetic fields are eternal. They are simply given, and are not explicable in terms of anything else. Thus even before this planet appeared, there already existed in a latent state the morphogenetic fields of all the chemicals, crystals, animals and plants that have ever occurred on the earth, or that will ever come into being in the future. This answer is essentially Platonic ...'[59]

Gary Lachman's comments on Sheldrake's ideas are worth noticing: 'Sheldrake's notion of the "presence of the past," the idea that life forms may possess a kind of "memory" not localised in the strict mechanics of DNA but perhaps housed in a nonphysical field—first presented more than a century ago by Samuel Butler—is ... reminiscent of what we have seen of the Akashic Record, as well as Bergson's idea that the past "still exists" and is still "present to consciousness," requiring but a slight adjustment on our part to be made available'.[60]

Descending from the surface of our ocean into its depths, we pass through regions that have been given many different names. For instance, Pierre Teilhard de Chardin describes these as the Biosphere, the Noosphere and the Theosphere,[61] while Jung names them the Personal Conscious, the Personal Unconscious and the Collective Unconscious. Stanislav Grof confirms Jung's views from his own experience: '... our observation of hundreds of people who have reported ancestral, racial and collective experiences support Carl Gustav Jung's assertion that our psyches are also deeply affected by a collective unconscious that gives us access to a vast warehouse of memories encompassing all of human experience from the beginning of time'.[62]

The ancient Hindus described everything that is stored in these deeper regions as the 'Akashic Chronicle'[63] ; while in the Tibetan tradition the realisation that all that is stored in the depths of our ocean is of our own making, is expressed in their *Book of the Dead* as, 'O nobly-born, whatever fearful and terrifying visions thou mayst see, recognize them to be thine own thought forms'. And a few lines further on, it warns very appropriately that '... if one recognize not one's own thoughtforms, however learned one may be in the Scriptures ... one obtains not Buddhahood'.[64] This ancient knowledge has been resurrected in modern garb by, for instance John A. Wheeler, when he proposed that the basic stuff of the universe is information; indeed, a transcendent ocean brimming with timeless information.

In many traditions we can recognise a layered progression when we proceed from lower to higher levels, of what I have called the vertical dimension, which in our ocean model corresponds to diving from the surface down to deeper levels. Although given different names, this layering can be recognised in many writings and traditions, of which I have just given a few indications in table 4.1.[65]

Frequency Range	Hinduism chakras	Healing colours	Bodies	Steiner 'planets'
mains	base	red	physical	Moon
long wave	sacral	orange	etheric	Mercury
medium wave	solar plexus	yellow	astral	Venus
short wave	heart	green	mind instinctive	Sun
FM radio	throat	Blue	mind intellectual	Mars
TV	third eye	Indigo	mind spiritual	Jupiter
UHF	crown	purple	spirit	Saturn

Table 4.1 Below the ocean's surface

To illustrate this idea with a practical example, I have indicated in the first column the electromagnetic spectrum, progressing from low frequency mains power to higher frequencies such as the UHF (Ultra High Frequency) band, with a corresponding increase in communication capabilities and information content. The second column gives a similar progression associated in Hinduism with the chakras, the spiritual energy centres along the human body, closely associated with the body's endocrine glands. Because diving deeper in the ocean's depths corresponds to attaining higher spiritual levels, in the table they are listed upside down compared to their usual representation. The chakras are often indicated with the same rainbow colours as given in the next column under healing.[66]

What appealed to me as an electronics engineer was how William A. Tiller compared the chakras with electronic tuning circuits to illustrate how each of them is tuned into a different level of the realm below our ocean's surface, similar to how radios, TVs, mobile phones, etc. are tuned in to the different frequency bands listed in the first column.[67] In this way the chakras act as transducers transforming the energies of the spiritual realm into biological signals that can amongst others be interpreted by their corresponding endocrine gland. Then in the next column the names associated with the various bodies that have been described as surrounding our physical bodies, each of them linked to a particular level in the vertical dimension. Finally, the last column gives the names given by Rudolf Steiner associated with similar levels using 'planetary' imagery.[68]

Tiller explains models in a similar stepwise vein and warns: '... models are like the rungs of a ladder from which one climbs from one level of understanding to another. Most models are eventually wrong in detail, but they serve the tremendous function of allowing one to climb from one position of understanding of the universe to a more enlightened position of understanding'.[69] And Frances Young expresses this idea of gradualism thus: '... the Platonic scheme avoided drawing a line between the divine and the created in its hierarchy of existence; there was a succession of descent'.[70] As you now will realise, this process is similar to what takes place when 'diving' in our ocean, going from the gross surface level to deeper and more potent levels, where the solution to life's problems can be discovered. Hence I will now make use of this model to explain briefly what happened at Lac Noir.

Obviously Emmy had been aware of the suffering and terror that had sunk below the spacetime surface of our ocean and become stored in the layer of 'seaweed'. You have to be intuitively sensitive to pick up these inner vibes, and I was completely oblivious to them because they were not at all evident to my horizontal physical senses (sight, hearing, etc.).[71] During my 'dream', I left my limited surface awareness behind and encountered the 'dead' soldier, who was still roaming around in the 'unconscious' depths below the ocean's surface. Freud's remark that 'dreams are the royal road to the unconscious' corresponds beautifully with my experience.

The soldier—seemingly ignorant of the fact that he was dead—was then still roaming around in the area, and I do hope that after so many years he has been able to move on. Others have described many similar experiences,[72] and when a haunting occurs it can often be stopped by an exorcism procedure designed to convince the dead person that it is really time to move on towards the 'light' at greater depths.

However, we have to keep very much in mind that when we want to dive into the ocean's depths, our possessions and hang-ups are like corks keeping us with their associated problems firmly at the surface. Therefore, to make spiritual progress easier, in many religions we see that seekers (monks, nuns, etc.) are advised to live without possessions and as simply as possible.

4.4 HORIZONTAL AND VERTICAL

Francis [of Assisi] had double vision—horizontal as well as vertical.[73]

Sallie McFague

The Cartesian Revolution has removed the vertical dimension from our "map of knowledge"; only the horizontal dimensions are left. To proceed in this flatland, science provides excellent guidance: it can do everything except lead us out of the dark wood of a meaningless, purposeless, "accidental" existence.[74]

E. F. Schumacher

Thus the integrity of living organisms and the characteristics of conscious individuals and human cultures present features of wholeness, the account of which implies a typical complementary mode of description.[75]

Niels Bohr

The world embraces not only a Newton, but a Shakespeare—not only a Boyle, but a Raphael—not only a Kant, but a Beethoven—not only a Darwin, but a Carlyle... They are not opposed, but supplementary—not mutually exclusive, but reconcilable.[76]

John Tyndall

He believes there is a world beyond the present three-dimensional world defined by physics, that this three-dimensional world is merely a shadow of a fourth-dimensional, non-material world.[77]

Dr Hashimoto

Let me now stress the explanatory power of our model incorporating a horizontal and a vertical dimension by referring to table 4.2 below. From its contents it will be clear that I had not discovered anything new, but that the same idea has been around for a very long time indeed.[78] Take these lines from Arthur Lovejoy for example when discussing Leibniz: 'Most non-materialistic philosophers of the seventeenth and eighteenth centuries still habitually thought in terms of two realms of being. The world of essences, 'natures' or Platonic Ideas, was to them as indubitably and objectively there to be reckoned with as the world of individual, temporal existents, physical or spiritual. The former, indeed, though it did not 'exist,' was the more fundamental and the more solid reality of the two'.[79] Or consider the lines written by Fritz Schumacher, which I quoted, on the previous page.

The table below is to be considered just as an indication of how this idea of two orthogonal dimensions can be applied to many different fields, the details of some of which I will enter into later.[80] In case you want to study the listed subjects further, the references given can widen your vista for many of these.

A baffling illustration of 'Synchronicity' was the fact that in the very week I was writing this chapter, I came across the following paragraph in one of Frithjof Schuon's books, which fits in very well indeed: '... in the sphere of the manifestations of Divine Power, one has to distinguish between "horizontal" and "vertical" dimensions, the vertical being supernatural and the horizontal natural; for the materialists, only the horizontal dimension exists, and that is why they cannot conceive of causes which operate vertically and which for that very reason are non-existent for them, like the vertical dimension itself'.[81]

Joop van Montfoort

Horizontal	Vertical	Who/where
Ψ = 0 (psi is zero)	Ψ = ∞ (psi is infinite)	
West	East	
yang	yin	China
Nile valley	kingdom of Osiris	ancient Egypt
lower knowledge	higher knowledge	Upanishads
relative knowledge	absolute knowledge	Buddhism
conditional truth	transcendental truth	Buddhism
Epimetus	Prometeus	Greek
Logos	Eros	
cave	outside world	Socrates/Plato [82]
visible realm	intelligible realm	Socrates/Plato
world	kingdom of God/heaven	Jesus
Martha	Mary	Luke 10: 38ff
wide gate	narrow gate	Matthew 7: 13
primary	secondary	Galileo
Machiavelli	St Francis of Assisi	
Athens	the wood	Shakespeare [83]
logic	mysticism [84]	
Roman Christianity	Celtic Christianity [85]	
Dominicans	Franciscans	RC Orders
morning people	evening people [86]	
solar	lunar	
science	art	

Table 4.2a Horizontal and vertical expressions

Horizontal	Vertical	Who/where
church	religion	
physics	psychology	
cognitive	affective	
individual	collective	
quantity	quality	
manifest	unmanifest	
to have	to be	
transpiration	inspiration	
ego	self, atman	
thing oriented	person oriented	
outer man	inner man	
phenomenal	noumenal	
pragmatism	mysticism	
noetic	poetic	
cognitive	affective	
causality	destiny	
intellect	feeling	
head	heart	
right brain	left brain	
reason	intuition	
rational	emotional	
realism [87]	idealism	
objective	subjective	

Table 4.2b Horizontal and vertical expressions (continued)

Horizontal	Vertical	Who/where
masculine	feminine	
mechanist	vitalist	
ponderable things	imponderable values	W. R. Inge [88]
res extensa	res cogitans	Descartes
particle	wave	Quantum Physics
I - it	anima	Carl Jung
extrovert	introvert	Carl Jung
Appolonian	Dionysian	Carl Jung
subject-object	subject-subjects	Sallie McFague [89]
matter	field	Albert Einstein [90]
world of the senses	world of the Spirit	Joel S. Goldsmith [91]
sensory reality	clairvoyant reality	Lawrence LeShan [92]
civilised	'primitive'	Laurens van der Post
explicate order	implicate order	David Bohm [93]
tangential	radial	P. Teilhard de Chardin [94]
natural	supernatural	Frithjof Schuon [95]
force	power	David R. Hawkins [96]
three-dimensional-	subjective-space	Peter Plichta [97]
doingness	beingness	Neale D. Walsch [98]
literalism	gnosticism	T. Freke & P. Gandy [99]
how	why	

Table 4.2c Horizontal and vertical expressions (continued)

Indeed, by studying table 4.2 we will become aware that the items in the horizontal and vertical columns are not as they are so often presented in opposition, but are indeed complementary to each other. Also do not take the various items listed in the same column as identities, but rather as similarities. This complementarity was beautifully illustrated by the Danish physicist Niels Bohr, who—when he was initiated into the Danish

'Order of the Elephant'—chose as his coat of arms the ancient Chinese yin/yang symbol surrounded by the motto: *Contraria sunt Complementa* (Opposites are Complementary), which I have reproduced in figure 4.5.[100] And his motto expresses in Latin very much what I, as an electronics engineer, recognised in the (for me) familiar behaviour of two ninety degree phase shifted electrical currents.

Figure 4.5 Not opposites, but complementary!

This so very essential point that the two dimensions in the table are complementary rather than in opposition cannot be stressed enough. That means that, because they have this ninety degree angle between them, they are never antagonistic and like chalk and cheese, you simply cannot add or subtract them. The very intuitive woman Gill Edwards makes the same point: 'What once seemed to be irreconcilable opposites—science and religion, analysis and synthesis, rationality and intuition, West and East, materialism and spirituality, yang and yin, conscious and subconscious, objective and subjective, individual and society—will be seen as complementary aspects of a greater whole. The old boundaries will dissolve. 'Either/or' limitations will be replaced by 'both/and' complementarity'.[101]

Stephen Jay Gould in his book subtitled, *Science and Religion in the Fullness of Life,* describes these two dimensions as NOMA (non-overlapping magisteria). He summarises that: '... the net, or magisterium, of science covers the empirical realm; what is the universe made of (fact) and why does it work this way (theory). The magisterium of religion extends over questions of ultimate meaning and moral value. These two magisteria do not overlap, nor do they encompass all enquiry (consider for example, the magisterium of art and the meaning of beauty). To cite the old clichés, science gets the age of rocks, and religion the rock of ages; science studies how the heavens go, religion how to go to heaven'.[102]

Indeed, we have to venture beyond the object/subject dualism and this should be obvious when later we make a more detailed study of the character of the subjects covered in the next chapters. I will just mention here the fact that these two magisteria are not independent; the horizontal one forms the surface layer of the vertical one, expressing in that spacetime dimension the Forms stored vertically below it, while everything that happens in the horizontal dimension will be stored below that surface layer in the depths of the vertical one.

However, I will not now embark upon further comment or explanation; that will come later when I tackle some applications of our ocean model. But we always have to keep very much in mind the very appropriate warning Ian Ramsey gave: 'Models, whether in theology or science, are not descriptive miniatures, they are not picture enlargements; in each case they point to mystery, to the need to live as best as we can with theological and scientific uncertainties. It is in these ways and for these reasons that we may say that theorizing by models is the understanding of a mystery whose depths are never sounded by man's plumb lines, however long and however diverse these lines may be, however far developed'.[103]

It has been my intention in this book to stress the point that the vertical dimension is the really important one; therefore I have great sympathy with what Percy Bysshe Shelley wrote: 'Titles are tinsel, power a corruption, glory a bubble and excessive wealth a libel on its possessor'.[104]And for that very reason I have deliberately refrained from labelling the people I quoted from; so you will not find impressive (horizontal) descriptions or titles, such as 'the famous Nobel prize winner', or 'His Excellency' or 'Her Holiness', 'Lord A to Z', etc., etc. If you happen to be interested in those horizontal labels you can find them on the Internet, in any *Who's Who* or encyclopaedia. But because my grandfather taught me that 'the exception confirms the rule',[105] I will make an exception for *Queen* Elisabeth of Austria, because she is making the very same point: 'Our innermost being is more valuable than are all titles and honors. Those are colored rags to hang on and with which we try to cover our nudities. Whatever is of value in us we bring from our spiritual pre-existences'.[106]

In the next chapter I will deal with typical horizontal pursuits, while the one after that will be dedicated to vertical ones; but please, when subjecting my categorising to a critical analysis, I repeat Philipp Frank's sound advice, that:

... reality in its fullness can only be experienced, never presented[107]

5 Horizontal pursuits

5.1 PHYSICS

The intellect has a sharp eye for methods and tools, but is blind to ends and values.[1]

Albert Einstein

... the more we know of particular things, the more we know of God.[2]

Spinoza

You know, many scientists I know tell me they became scientists because of the mystical experience they had with the night sky as children.[3]

Matthew Fox

The more we learn about the universe the more humble we should be, realizing how ignorant we have been in the past and how much more there is still to discover.

John Templeton

The Christian should welcome scientific discoveries as new steps in man's domination of nature.[4]

World Council of Churches

... geniuses are cranks who happen to be right...[5]

I. J. Good

In this chapter, I will deal with disciplines such as physics, biology and medicine which are supposedly subject to the power of the intellect only, and hence firmly subject to intellectual pursuits. Science should be exclusively based on hard facts, rigorously tested for the possibility of falsification, and in the Aristotelian tradition its domain is strictly limited to the horizontal dimension.[6] And as Laplace pointed out in the following quotation, there it rules supreme: 'We may conceive the present state of the universe as the effect of its past and the cause of its future. An Intellect who at any given instant knew all the forces that animate nature and the mutual position of the beings who compose it, were this Intellect but vast enough to submit his data to analysis, could condense into a single formula the movement of the greatest body in the universe and that of the lightest atom; to such an Intellect nothing would be uncertain, for the future, even as the past, would be ever present before his eyes'.[7]

Nowadays the Committee for the Scientific Investigation of Claims of the Paranormal (CSICOP) functioning as their unholy Inquisition, and the threat of the '... possible loss of camaraderie and respectability, loss of funding, and loss of scientific credibility with an inability to publish in mainstream journals; even a loss of one's position may result'.[8] These are the modernised versions of the dungeon and the gallows.

Physics is the 'hardest' of all the sciences, and for its practical application I completely agree with Stenger's formula $\Psi = 0$, which I mentioned in chapter 2. Also Fritz Schumacher made its restriction to the horizontal dimension quite clear: 'Physics cannot have any philosophical impact because it cannot entertain the qualitative notion of higher and lower levels of being. With Einstein's statement that everything is relative the vertical dimension disappeared from science and with it the need for any absolute standards of good and evil'.[9] Believing that the intellect rules supreme and that Mother Nature had no hidden secrets anymore; this attitude led in the second half of the nineteenth century to e.g. that Edwin Hall was advised against studying physics; because such a bright young man should look for challenge and fame in other fields, as in physics all major discoveries had been wrapped up already.[10]

A clear example of this attitude is, for instance, George Thomson (Lord Kelvin) who, when discoursing to the Royal Institute in April 1900, told his audience that '... physics knowledge is almost complete. Two small clouds remain on the horizon...' One of his small clouds was the Mercury perihelion problem, i.e. Mercury seemingly not obeying Newton's Laws of Motion (mentioned in chapter 4); the other was the so-called ultraviolet crisis in black body radiation. But even when we firmly limit our field of view to the horizontal dimension only, we can still be in for big surprises because precisely Thomson's 'two small clouds' would develop into the hurricanes of general relativity and quantum mechanics, sweeping all of the nineteenth century certitudes away. And this experience most certainly has made today's physicists much more careful, as exemplified by Leonard Susskind cautioning in a recent interview: 'I am pretty sure that physicists will go on searching for natural [horizontal] explanations of the world. But I have to say that if that happens, as things stand now we will be in a very awkward position. Without any explanation of nature's fine-tunings we will be hard pressed to answer the ID [Intelligent Design] critics. One might argue that the hope that a mathematically unique solution will merge is as faith based as ID'.[11]

I will explore a bit further the idea that even in physics all is not so horizontal as it seems. Take for example complex algebra, which is a very useful tool, especially in electronics and is widely used to calculate the value of components such as capacitors and inductances used in the tuning circuits that you find in every radio receiver and transmitter, ranging from the tiny circuits in mobile phones to the giant ones in broadcasting transmitters. Now this algebra uses real numbers: 1, 2, 3, etc., and so-called imaginary numbers; the real numbers can be depicted graphically along a horizontal 'real' axis and the imaginary ones along a vertical axis at ninety degrees to the first one. The unit along this last axis is the square root of minus one. It works fine, and in modern physics, calculations are successfully done even with many more dimensions. But the first thing that is pointed out when the subject of square roots is taught in mathematics, is that it is impossible to extract roots of negative numbers. So here at the very heart of horizontal physics, something 'impossible' finds a very useful application. This very fact made Gottfried W. Leibniz exclaim: 'The Divine Spirit found a sublime outlet in that wonder of analysis, that portent of the ideal world, that amphibian between being and not-being, which we call the negative root of negative unity'.[12]

Moreover, do not forget that several scientists—now considered with awe—were often ridiculed by their contemporaries; examples are Joule, because of his ideas on energy conversion; Jenner for his attempt to vaccinate; and the geologist Louis Agassiz who encountered great scepticism by the scientific community when he presented the idea of ice ages in 1837. Even Einstein became in the 1930s the butt of a Nazi campaign to discredit him and his theories, just because he was Jewish (the list of campaigners included a German Nobel Prize winner, who signed up for this despicable action).

Even more disconcerting for the 'dogmatic establishment' are the cases when progress in science is due to the intervention of 'impossible' outsiders. Some names of ostracised pioneers are: the monk Gregor Mendel in the field of genetics; Georg Ohm with his law of electrical resistance; Louis Pasteur and his germ theory; Ignaz Semmelweiss in his desperate fight to have doctors wash their hands between patients to prevent childbed fever (he ended up in a mental institution); Lister's subsequent promotion of antisepsis, and Alfred Wegener with his pioneering ideas of continental drift.[13]

So if your ideas are vilified, don't despair because you might be in very good company indeed. And if you think that this does not happen anymore today, take the recent case of Barry

Marshal and Robin Warren. Their idea that bacteria could cause stomach ulcers was vilified, but for that ridiculed idea they were awarded the 2005 Nobel Prize. Paul Lauterbur even goes as far as declaring: 'You could write the history of science of the last fifty years in terms of papers rejected by *Science* or *Nature*".[14]

Albert Einstein was a university graduate who also didn't fit the 'normal' mould at all; in his own words, he was '... a pariah, discounted and little loved'.[15] After graduation he was refused a place at his *Technische Hochschule* in Zürich and could only land a job as a patent examiner, 3rd class, in Berne. That did not prevent him from shocking the very dogmatic foundations of nineteenth century physics, first with his special and later with general relativity, both leading to completely new insights into the laws of the universe.

But because of heavy opposition, these brilliant new insights on the scale of the universe were in the end not the ones for which he was awarded the Nobel Prize.[16] That was for his explanation of the photoelectric effect, i.e. in the range of the extremely small. And as his clarification of that effect is directly linked to quantum theory, he can be considered as one of the founding fathers of that other twentieth century revolution in physics as well. As already mentioned, both theories together swept away the nineteenth century's 'certitudes' completely.

However, Einstein himself did not like the fuzzy consequences of quantum theory at all, and he entered into many arguments about its ramifications with Niels Bohr. By allowing 'spooky action at a distance', Einstein's argued that quantum theory is incomplete, but every time he had to submit to Bohr's arguments. One of Einstein's objections was directed against Heisenberg's uncertainty relation, which states that it is impossible to know both the position and momentum (mass times speed) of a particle at the same time. Einstein's argument—refined together with Boris Podolsky and Nathan Rosen—resulted in the so-called EPR paradox.

Basically this paradox means that, against the dictates of quantum mechanics, one could measure both the position and the momentum (speed) of a particle. To achieve this, they proposed to split a twin particle and letting the two halves fly off in opposite directions. Measuring the speed of the one and the position of the other would make it possible to calculate backwards to obtain both position and momentum of the original twin. John Bell expressed this problem in a mathematical formulation (Bell's inequality) that led to several experimental investigations.[17]

The most famous one (proving Einstein wrong), was done by Alain Aspect and his team measuring the polarisation angle of a pair of entangled photons emitted by a single atom. They proved not only that there is definitely action at a distance, but also that communication between these photons is faster than the speed of light.[18] Others have confirmed these findings, indicating that indeed 'there is no speed barrier in the universe'.[19] Einstein had acknowledged that 'If the correlations are real then I must believe in telepathy...' Paul Davies' and John Gribbin's comments are profoundly relevant and far-reaching: '... the quantum world possesses a kind of holism that transcends time, as well as space, almost as if the particle-waves seem to know ahead of time what decision the observer will make'.[20]

In our ocean model, these baffling results can be interpreted as elementary particles not being as firmly incarcerated inside our spacetime surface layer prison, as more substantial items are. They are closer to the oneness of our ocean, which Fritjof Capra clarifies with this significant statement: 'As we penetrate into matter, nature does not show us any isolated basic building blocks, but rather appears as a complicated web of relations between the various parts of a unified whole'.[21]

Another consideration is that what to us seems to be a vast distance, according to relativity theory for particles moving near the speed of light, the distance is much smaller, which might contribute to their sharing of experience. Or expressed differently, they are at the lower boundary of the ocean's surface and can communicate with their counterparts due to their intimacy with the oneness of the ocean's depths where spacetime peters out. A remark Arthur Eddington once made fits in our picture as well: 'There is only one electron'. His statement points again to the fact that the zillions we are aware of can be imagined to be manifestations of the underlying One, and another of his remarks that 'the stuff of the world is mind stuff' can be expressed in the language of our model as matter being a surface manifestation on the ocean of mind.

Light is another escapee from our spacetime prison. I have already mentioned the twin paradox, which has as ultimate consequence that if you could move at the speed of light, time would come to a complete standstill. So for our everyday light—that we can switch on or off with the flick of a switch—time does not exist at all. Although their actuality is now being doubted by some, the Big Bang and the end of the universe, whether that will be a Big Crunch or a Big Rip, are present in an all-encompassing now.[22]

Because the present expanding universe model has to be kept feasible with bolting on so many stopgap measures, some physicists are even expressing the unthinkable, namely to abandon the present standard model, which amongst others implies that the Big Bang never happened.[23] One of the interesting consequences of the new physics, as expressed by Paul Davies and John Gribbin in *The Matter Myth*, is that 'The universe has only been borrowed from the vacuum, after all; all that inflation has done is to delay the inevitable. In quantum physics, something can come out of nothing for a while, but eventually the debt has to be repaid.'[24] Not that the vacuum—which is the term physicists use for our ocean—will notice that there is any debt at all, because its energy content is infinite and it is in Davies' words '... not inert and featureless, but alive with throbbing energy and vitality'.[25]

Walter Sullivan expressed graphically what John Wheeler said about this subject in an address before the American Physical Society in 1967: '... what we naively call a vacuum. ... One can say that in a thimbleful of vacuum there is more of this energy than would be released by all the atomic bomb fuel in the universe...'[26]

And Jaffe cautioned that 'it [is considered] "disturbing" that our best theory of forces and fields predicts—even relies upon—something that is not currently measurable.'[27]

Just to illustrate that the use of models—as I did in the previous chapter—is widespread in modern physics, I have sketched in figure 5.1 how a tiny spontaneous quantum-effect disturbance on the 'surface' of the vacuum exploded with an almighty 'Big Bang' into our spacetime universe. Although highly abstract, similar illustrations can be found in many physics books.

In the ocean model, I have gone one step beyond this model by considering spacetime as the two dimensional 'horizontal' surface of the 'ocean of the vacuum', while its transcendent 'depths' are in the third, 'vertical' dimension.

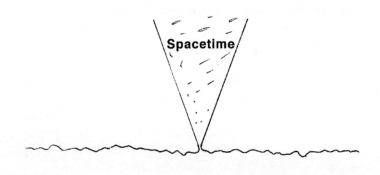

Figure 5.1 The origin of our universe

As a boy, Einstein was fascinated with light and tried to imagine what it would be like to travel, riding on a beam of light.

If that had been possible, he would have discovered that time would then not exist. The fact that light is not confined to our spacetime prison can be interpreted that it can move backwards in time as well. This principle was applied by Boris Ya. Zel'dovich and colleagues to get rid of atmospheric distortion when laser beams are aimed at satellites through a turbulent atmosphere. In an article describing this effect, they refer to a "time-reversed" beam of light.[28]

Another phenomenon that seems to demonstrate that photons are 'aware' is the fact that they seem to 'know' whether one or two slits are open in Thomas Young's classical double-slit interferometer experiment. This experiment was first performed at the beginning of the nineteenth century, but in the last century it was repeated at very low light intensities. This results in the fact that the photons traverse the interferometer at such long time intervals that they cannot possibly interact directly with previous ones. However, the characteristic banded interference pattern still appears. So each photon seems to 'know' individually whether the other slit is open or closed. And one of the latest experiments confirms that space and time are intimately linked, because instead of just via slits in space, the double-slit effect is seen over time as well.[29] There are many excellent books, such as the ones I already referred to, describing the details of these revolutionary new insights; here I will mention just a few other considerations to illustrate my story.

The Greek philosophers Leucippus and Democritus are at the origin of our concept that all matter ultimately consists of hard, indivisible 'atoms'. That notion has now changed to one in which the basic building materials are rather packets of condensed energy, quarks held together by gluons.[30] They come in threes or twos and their various combinations lead to the motley zoo of elementary particles.[31] Interference experiments with elementary particles lead to the baffling conclusion that they sometimes behave as if they were particles and sometimes as if they were waves. This led William Bragg to exclaim in despair 'Electrons seem to be waves on Mondays, Wednesdays and Fridays and particles on Tuesdays, Thursdays and Saturdays'.[32]

In our ocean model, that baffling experience corresponds to favouring a horizontal or vertical orientation for your experiment. If you look horizontally you will find your particle as a well-defined wave top, but looking vertically you realise that they are just a manifestation of a wave on the ocean of energy. Indeed, modern physics has progressed to such an extent that Gerald Holton commented on this gigantic paradigm shift: 'In particle physics today one no longer believes that there are one or two or three very simple laws at the bottom of all this turmoil of spontaneous disintegration and creation of particles. On the contrary, a more correct view is that at the bottom of our simple laws there is a vast sea, a flux of chaotic disorder in which these particles continually change and rearrange, a whole zoo of "virtual" particles that for small intervals of time disobey all the classical laws. A nineteenth-century physicist would find this view ... intolerable'.[33]

David Bohm uses the same ocean image: 'The present state of theoretical physics implies that empty space has all this energy and that matter is a slight increase of that energy and therefore matter is like a small ripple on the tremendous ocean of energy, having some relative stability and being manifest'.[34] You may comment that if you are hit on the head with a hammer, it definitely does not feel at all like the effect of just a 'small ripple', but it helps to compare the hammer blow's effect rather with that of an aeroplane propeller rotating at high speed, which considered in its plane of rotation, is mostly empty space as well.

I find it very revealing that several of the famous physicists of that belief-shattering early twentieth century period took up the study of ancient Eastern wisdom. For instance in the previous chapter I mentioned the Danish physicist Niels Bohr with his yin/yang coat of arms, but many other physicists have expressed this complementarity view as well. Take for instance Robert Oppenheimer—the father of the USA's atom bomb—commenting: 'We can't find anything wrong with it so we will just have to ignore it.'[35] But he also wrote: 'These two ways of thinking, the way of time and history and the way of eternity and timelessness, are both part of man's effort to comprehend the world in which he lives. Neither is comprehended in the other nor reducible to it. They are, as we have learned to say in physics, complementary views each supplementing the other, neither telling the whole story'.[36] And just to name two others: Wolfgang Pauli collaborated with Carl Jung in the psychological field,[37] while Erwin Schrödinger studied Buddhism extensively.

Because he uses the same ocean image, I will quote more extensively from one of the earlier physicists, namely Oliver Lodge, who stated: 'My thesis is that the spiritual world is the reality, and this life only a temporary episode'.[38] He was so sure of this: 'I know for a fact that as individuals we survive the death of the body', because of paranormal experiences relating to his son, who was killed during the First World War.[39]

He ends the quotation I took from one of his books, by quoting in his turn from Tennyson's 'Ancient Sage': 'The *ego* has been likened to a ripple raised by wind upon water, displaying in visible form the motion and influence of the operating breath, without being permanently differentiated from the vast whole, of which each ripple is a temporarily individualised portion: individualised, yet not isolated from others, but connected with them by the ocean, of whose immensity it may be supposed for poetic purposes gradually to become aware:

But that one ripple on the boundless deep
Feels that the deep is boundless, and itself
One with the boundless motion of the deep
For ever changing form, but evermore'.[40]

Another consequence was explored by Kurt Gödel, who described a 'rotating universe'—matter rotating in 'a vast cosmic whirlpool'[41] , which causes '... space-time projectories that loop back on themselves, returning to places they've already been. It follows from this that time is not a straight linear sequence of events, but something that bends around the universe in a curving line. ... By making a round trip on a rocket ship in a wide curve, it is possible in these worlds to travel into any region of past, present, and future, and back again'.[42] Gödel's 'cosmic whirlpool' has parallels with my recall of a 'before-birth experience' that I had when I was only a few years old, and which I describe in chapter 8.

To get our feet on solid ground again—but also to remain very aware of the illusionary thinking that we know so much of the 'well-known horizontal' domain of physics—the following remark made by the physicist Henry Morgenau is very appropriate here: 'I would be tempted to say that the ratio of what we know scientifically to what we do not understand in scientific terms has been, is and will forever be zero. This is the reason why I believe that science will never do away with politics, poetry and religion'.[43] I can only say a heartfelt Amen to his remark, and will just mention here a few remarks by other scientists that all point to the importance of what I have called the vertical dimension.

Fritjof Capra's trail-blazing *The Tao of Physics* has already become a classic, and his approach has been followed by many others. For instance, Paul Davies states in the preface to one of his books: 'It may seem bizarre, but in my opinion science offers a surer path to God than religion' and confirming that statement at the end.[44] This sentiment finds support in Einstein's writings as well: 'A contemporary has said, not unjustly, that in this age of ours the serious scientific workers are the only profoundly religious people'.[45]

How far indeed is all this removed from Gladstone's remark: 'Let the scientific men stick to their science, and leave philosophy and religion to poets, philosophers and theologians'.[46] And as an illustration of scientists being able to convert others to the acceptance of the reality of the vertical dimension, take the travel writer Bill Bryson, who—after having researched science and written the book *A Short History of Nearly Everything* about it—answered the question whether the writing of this book had changed any of his beliefs: 'I would have said that I'm a completely unreligious person. I have no dimension of spirituality to me at all. But I'm a lot more inclined that way now than I was. I mean, I would be more susceptible to spirituality now than before I started out on this, and I would have expected exactly the opposite to happen'.[47]

On the other hand it could be very harming to your career prospects, when as a scientist you seem to take the study of paranormal (vertical) phenomena serious. John Hasted and Sue Blackmore come to mind, initially showing an interest in, and publishing on paranormal phenomena, but later recanting. Both have left these fields of research declaring their commitment to 'psi equals zero'.[48]

Again we can learn here so much from an Eastern tradition; long ago Kaibara Ekken (1613-1714) wrote: 'the aim of learning is not merely to widen knowledge, but to form character. Its object is to make us true men, rather than learned men'.[49]

Trying to protect their 'learnedness' some scientists go to such extremes as vigorously attacking everything that even smacks of some vertical contamination. The psychologist Jan Ehrenwald makes a very interesting observation about this: 'The fact is that to the scientifically less sophisticated observer all manifestations of psi are equally disturbing and intellectually repugnant. They are all incompatible with common sense; they run counter to his everyday experience and provoke well-nigh automatic resistances against them'.[50]

I will give the final say to one of my favourites, Albert Einstein, who was called by George Bernard Shaw '... the foremost natural philosopher of the last 300 years'.[51] Einstein said, referring to the vertical origin of his theories: '... there is no logical path to these ... laws. They can only be reached by intuition, based on intellectual love of the object of experience'.[52]

So I do think that we can safely conclude from the examples I have given, that although the 'church' of science is firmly embedded in the horizontal dimension, its 'prophets' tell a very different tale. And this is very much leading to the conclusion that real, paradigm shifting, progress in science originates in the unpredictable intuitive vertical, rather than in the intellectually safe horizontal dimension. The following profound saying in, of all places the *Wall Street Journal*, comes to mind:

If a little science takes one away from God, a great deal of science brings one back to God.[53]

5.2 BIOLOGY

… I cannot anyhow be contented to view this wonderful universe, and especially the nature of man, and to conclude that everything is the result of brute force.[54]

Charles Darwin

It is one of the great paradoxes of our age that people claiming the proud title of 'scientists' dare to offer such undisciplined and reckless speculations [of evolutionism] as contributions to scientific knowledge—and that they get away with it![55]

E. F. Schumacher

Of course such a [horizontal] view of cosmogenesis is crazy. And I do not at all mean crazy in the sense of slangy invective but rather in the technical meaning of psychotic. Indeed such a view has much in common with certain aspects of schizophrenic thinking.[56]

Karl Stern

We are not human beings having a spiritual experience. We are spiritual beings having a human experience.

Pierre Teilhard de Chardin

We are not just highly evolved animals with biological computers embedded inside our skulls; we are also fields of consciousness without limits, transcending time, space, matter, and linear causality.[57]

Stanislav Grof

Much more so than physics, most of academic biology is still firmly embedded in the horizontal dimension, and when we listen to a number of present day biologists, Charles Darwin is the clear victor in the battle between his (and A. R. Wallace's) ideas of evolution and those of Jean-Baptiste de Lamarck, who advocated the possibility of the inheritance of acquired characteristics.[58] However, recent developments seem to make Lamarckism more acceptable, such as studies of how 'nutrition and smoking in early life can be passed down the male line to influence the health of sons and grandsons'; and this is now being accepted as evidence, because 'the gene centred approach does not have enough explanatory power to account for the variety and complexity of organisms'.[59]

Richard Dawkins, one of the neo-Darwinian cheerleaders, is a very powerful advocate of the 'psi is zero' school; cultivating the belief that all living beings we see all around us, have come about by random mutations over a very long period of time. Inherited characteristics can only be transferred to future generations by means of genes. You can even replay the process of random evolution on your personal computer.[60]

But in effect these neo-Darwinians are more Darwinian than Darwin himself, who not only wrote in *The Origin of Species* that expecting that the eye could be the product of random natural selection was "absurd", but in his later years he even expressed his recognition of '... the impossibility of conceiving of this immense and wonderful universe, including man ... as the result of blind chance or necessity. When thus reflecting I feel compelled to look for a First Cause having an intelligent mind in some degree analogous to that of man and I deserve to be called a Theist'.[61]

The biochemist John Peacocke writes: 'Confidence in the centrality of the neo-Darwinian explanation of the evolutionary process in principle is entirely consistent with acknowledging ignorance about how particular transformations came about in the inaccessible past'.[62] And if we move a moment from science to theology, we could underline this insight with what Paul Tillich wrote: 'As the power of life, spirit is not identical with the inorganic substratum which is animated by it; rather spirit is the power of animation itself and not a part added to the organic system'.[63] From this, Tillich concludes that this 'power of animation' culminates in man as 'that organism in which the dimension of spirit is dominant'; or along the lines expressed in the previous chapter, and in line with the Teilhard de Chardin quotation at the beginning of this section, Kevin Bean expressed this concisely as, 'We are not bodies with souls, we are souls with bodies.'

Although today they may be using sedatives to lighten the suffering of the animals they are experimenting on, biologists are often still behaving as if Descartes' claim—that animals had no souls and hence were just mechanisms and could not feel pain—is true. Often they consider animals just as pieces of laboratory equipment that happen to be alive, so that we can subject them to all kind of interesting experiments.

For instance, take Karl Lasley cutting out more and more areas of rat brains to discover where the memory to negotiate a maze was located. To his amazement he found no specific area, but it seemed very much as if the memory was stored holographically, which fits in very well with our image of memories being stored below the ocean's surface and the brain just being the interface between the mind and the body. And what should we think of Paul Pietsch removing and chopping up salamander brains coming to the same conclusion?[64] Or take the 'scientist' dipping living animals' tails in boiling water to measure their reaction to pain?[65] And another, cutting off the tails of nearly a hundred generations of house mice to prove that they continue to be born with long ones? All these disgusting experiments were undertaken by highly intelligent people to enable them to dismiss Lamarck's claim of the possibility of inheritance of characteristics beyond the horizontal pathway of the genes.

Lamarck certainly taught that newly acquired characteristics could be passed on to the next generation, but as there is no horizontal mechanism for that information transfer, his ideas have been branded as heretical. Fortunately, the days of literally burning heretics are over, but at least we can condemn their books to be burned, which is exactly what the editor of *Nature* in his fervour to keep the horizontal teachings pure, advised his readers to do with Sheldrake's book.[66]

Although Rupert Sheldrake called his courageous book *A New Science of Life,* [67] he returned to the ancient Platonic idea of the Ideas/Forms influencing what happens at the surface level of biological evolution. Socrates had already argued that all that is known is stored somewhere: '... there is no such thing as teaching, only recollection'. And in the *Meno* he illustrates that fact by demonstrating that an uneducated slave boy could solve intricate geometrical problems, and hence that he knew things which he could only have obtained from that other realm.[68] In our model, that other realm is of course in the vertical dimension, below the ocean's surface.

Sheldrake calls the process of tuning in to that information bank 'morphic resonance', and I agree totally with him that that is the process by which the Lamarckian propagation of acquired characteristics proceeds.[69] In his books, Sheldrake illustrates these ideas in many fields ranging from crystals to people. One of his later books dealing with vertical interconnectedness is called *Dogs that know when their Owners are coming Home*, in which he declares poignantly that he is 'more interested in dogs than dogmas'.[70]

He illustrates the scientific attitude of applying impressive labels, such as 'inherited spatiotemporal vector-navigation program' to the mysterious knowledge of migrating animals about where they have to go, rather than explaining the phenomenon.[71] And I completely agree with him that the only sensible explanation for the many examples he describes in his books can be given by inferring a guiding 'transmission' emanating from the vertical dimension, into which many living beings have the capability to tune into.

In figure 5.2 I have reproduced one example of the many Sheldrake uses to illustrate that lessons learned can indeed be passed on to future generations. This graph is based on research done by W. M. McDougall and depicts the average number of errors rats make in crossing a maze as a function of the number of previous generations that have been familiar with this particular maze.[72] We see that the acquired experience is indeed stored somewhere outside the realm of horizontal biology, which, as mentioned before, accepts transmission via the chromosomes only.

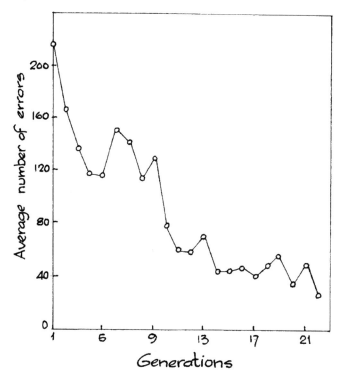

Figure 5.2 Rats learning to master a maze (R. Sheldrake)

An even more drastic demonstration of the vertical guidance exerted by the Forms, is given by Eric Butterworth (and I sincerely hope that worms are less sensitive to pain than the animals used in the biological experiments I condemned earlier): 'If you cut one of the Planaria [worms] in half, you find that each part, each half, develops into a whole worm. The front part acquires a new body, and the back part organizes itself a new head, complete with brain. Let us reflect on this astounding statement, "the back organizes itself a new head." What is this "self" which creates a new brain—a brain that must guide the regenerated organism as a whole? How can it create a brain without a brain to guide the process?'[73] And even if you ponder the possibility that the genome could contain the brain's building plans, Gerald Edelman dismisses this possibility for humans, writing 'Indeed a simple calculation shows that the genome of a human being (the entire collection of an individual's genes) is insufficient to specify explicitly the synaptic structure of the developing brain'.[74]

Because the Forms/Ideas/archetypes are stored in the unconscious, i.e. outside of spacetime, in a sense the whole of future development is already available in that timeless realm. Wolfgang Pauli, who knew Jung well, 'expected that the idea of the unconscious would spread beyond the "narrow frame of therapeutic use" and would influence all natural sciences that deal with general life phenomena'.[75] Hence, all this points to the conclusion that evolution is the direct result of 'tuning in' to the pre-existing end products of this process, which can take a very long time indeed in the time restricted horizontal dimension.

I repeat that—because time does not exist outside the surface layer of our spacetime prison—these templates are already present, even from before time began. So the process of evolution is being 'pulled' along a preordained direction rather than blundering along via the process of random mutations. The archetypes are involved in an act of *'creatio continua'* (What Jung calls synchronistic events are in fact something like "acts of creation in time".)[76]

That this wisdom is very ancient indeed, is witnessed by Plato calling the universe very appropriately 'a moving image of eternity'. Max Planck expressed this same idea concisely as: 'I regard consciousness as fundamental. I regard matter as a derivate of consciousness.' And to Frithjof Schuon's quotation, which I mentioned in the previous chapter, he added the following footnote, which is very relevant here: 'It may be pointed out here that the evolutionist error has its roots in this prejudice [denial of the existence of the vertical dimension]. Instead of conceiving that creatures are archetypes "incarnated" in matter, starting from the Divine Intellect and passing through a subtle or animic plane, they restrict all causality to the material world, deliberately ignoring the flagrant contradictions implied by this conceptual "planimetry"' [limited to the horizontal realm only].[77]

Although I have pointed out already that most new ideas have been resisted vigorously; one of Darwin's contemporaries, St George J. Mivart, challenged the random selection process thoroughly. To illustrate again the point I am making, I will just mention here one of the many cases he presents in his book.[78] He uses the baleen whale as an example of a development, which could not possibly have proceeded, in the random way of a random (neo-) Darwinian evolution process. A baleen whale has supposedly evolved from precursors with teeth, but possesses more or less horn on the palate. For its survival it depends critically on the presence of an efficient filter, made out of baleen, to filter out the enormous quantities of small organisms from seawater it needs to stay alive. As this baleen curtain will perform its filtering function only when it is fully developed, an 'accidental' outgrowth on its horny palate would have offered no survival value and hence not increase its fitness to thrive and propagate at all.

Danah Zohar gives an example at the other end of the mass scale: recent experiments with bacteria have demonstrated that when their survival is threatened by manipulating their environment, 'adaptive mutation' can make bacteria adapt much faster to this environment than predicted by classical Darwinian mutation rates. She describes this miracle as follows: 'If all their genes had mutated at this alarming rate, the bacteria would have been destroyed—unless natural selection itself had operated 100 million times faster than normal to choose only those mutations that would lead to survival. On the basis of conventional evolutionary principles, this is impossible'.[79]

Having kept bees for many years, I am still amazed how identical eggs either develop into a worker or a queen, seemingly only depending on the size and food conditions of the cell in which it is laid. But they are very different animals indeed (shape, legs, egg depositor, etc.), definitely not just a matter of a queen being a bigger bee. Is it a process of switching on different genes by the presence of more food, or rather more likely of tuning in to a different Form? And don't the so very differently looking caterpillar, pupa and butterfly have exactly the same genome?

I think that genes are the recipes for the building blocks of an organism, while its final shape results from morphic resonance with its Form template stored below our ocean's surface. I find confirmation for this view in the opening lines Robin Orwant wrote in a recent article in *New Scientist*: 'The bubble burst sometime in February 2001. Before then geneticists expected humans to have about 100,000 genes, reflecting how big and clever we are. Now we know better. The result of the human genome project suggest the figure is closer to 30,000—only five times as many as your average bacterium and roughly the same as mice. To add insult to injury, most of our genes are virtually identical to those of chimps'.[80]

Some 95% of our genes are now considered as 'Junk DNA', so if not in our genes, where are the building plans stored? With the same building materials you can indeed choose to build either a palace or a hovel; it depends completely on the architectural drawings (Forms stored below the ocean's surface). Darwin himself seems to support that view when he wrote in a letter to Asa Gray: 'I am inclined to look at everything as resulting from designed laws [Forms], with the details, whether good or bad, left to the working out of what we may call chance'.[81]

Michael Newton published some interesting reports obtained during sessions of regressive hypnotherapy of souls who, between incarnations are actively engaged in helping evolution proceed into a desired direction; he also mentions that this corresponds to an old belief of the Jains.[82] Because of all of this, I prefer to call the manner in which life unfolds 'guided evolution' rather than 'intelligent design'. This viewpoint, taking into account the influence exerted by entities stored in the depths of the ocean of the One, can also explain many other life phenomena, which I will deal with in some more detail in the next section.

Above all we need to be open-minded. Stephen Jay Gould in his book *Rocks of Ages* points out that 'The enemy is not religion but dogmatism and intolerance...'[83] And where dogmatic adherence to the neo-Darwinian gospel can lead to is illustrated further on in his book when he quotes Vernon Kellog, who was posted at the German headquarters at the beginning of the First World War. Kellog was appalled to witness the discussions stating German supremacy based on evolutionary dogmas: 'The creed of the *Allmacht* ["all might," or omnipotence] of a natural selection based on violent and competitive struggle is the gospel of the German intellectuals; all else is illusion and anathema'.[84] And we have seen how this idea of the Übermensch, practised by a powerful political system, has led directly to so much suffering and the horrors of Auschwitz and the many other torture and death factories.

The same warning comes from a book *Shattering the Myths of Darwinism*, in which Richard Milton has collected a large amount of evidence undermining the horizontal foundations of neo-Darwinism thoroughly. Again he should consider it very much as a compliment that, according to a review by Richard Dawkins, the book is "loony", "stupid", "drivel" and its author a "harmless fruitcake" who needs "psychiatric help". Milton's comments to these remarks are worth mentioning here: 'Dawkins is employed at one of Britain's most distinguished universities and is responsible for the education of future generations of students. Yet this is not the language of a responsible scientist and teacher. It is the language of a religious fundamentalist whose faith has been profaned'.[85]

Many years earlier Aldous Huxley warned in a similar vein: 'Literary or scientific, liberal or specialist, all our education is predominantly verbal and therefore fails to accomplish what it is supposed to do. Instead of transforming children into fully developed adults, it turns out students of the natural sciences who are completely unaware of Nature as the primary fact of experience, it inflicts upon the world students of the humanities who know nothing of humanity, their own or anyone else's'.[86]

I can wrap up these outcries of what is wrong with our system of education with a student's voice from the floor: 'Sitting around, I see that I'm not the only one who's unhappy. Hell, most of this campus is unhappy. And those that aren't unhappy are either too stupid or don't give a shit'.[87] Victor Frankl puts this unhappiness more delicately and in figures: 'A statistical survey recently revealed that among my European students, 25 percent showed a more-or-less marked degree of existential vacuum. Among my American students it was not 25 but 60 percent'.[88] And this observation is further confirmed by Joseph Campbell, writing: 'The sense of threat [contemporary youth experiences] from every quarter of what is known as the establishment—which is to say, of modern civilization—is not altogether a put-on or an act for many of these young folk, but an actual condition of soul'.[89]

Following the field of biology (admittedly only superficially by reading *New Scientist*), I regularly come across phenomena that, with the best of intentions, cannot be fitted into a strict horizontal neo-Darwinian mould. Take, for example, this one about the fertility-reducing effects of pesticides on the offspring of those exposed to them: '... if it did turn out to have a genetic basis, it would have to involve mutation of a kind with which we are not yet familiar'.[90]

Or about the organisational capabilities of slime moulds: '... where these enigmatic creatures get their computing power from is still very much a mystery'.[91]

Instead of going on and on with similar remarks, I will round this section off with a statement from the book by Paul Davies and John Gribbin that I quoted from earlier, which seems very appropriate here: 'Materialism dominates biology. ... Many people have rejected scientific values because they regard materialism as a sterile and bleak philosophy, which reduces human beings to automata and leaves no room for free will or creativity. These people can take heart: materialism is dead'.[92]

This might be a good point to wrap up this section with the wise words of the French statesman François Guizot who, when he was asked by academicians to ban homeopathy, replied: 'If homeopathy is a chimera or a valueless method, it will collapse. If, on the contrary, it represents an advance, it will spread whatever we do to stop it; and the Academy should desire this above all—as her mission is to stimulate scientific advances and encourage discoveries'.[93] And this wise statement leads directly to our next section, dealing with the goings-on in the field of medicine.

5.3 MEDICINE

We would be a better doctor if we could produce correction at the etheric level, because then the cure would last longer. However, it will not be permanent because we have not altered the basic hologram at the mind and spiritual levels.[94]

William A. Tiller

... only fifteen percent of medical interventions are supported by solid scientific evidence.[95]

Dennis Mc Callum

Whenever doctors go on strike the number of people dying falls.[96]

Vernon Coleman

What once was called pseudoscience occasionally turns into real science.[97]

Henry H. Bauer

Most people suffer not from physical illness but from spiritual aimlessness. They have lost their aim. They have lost sight of who they really are and what is really valuable.

Carl G. Jung

I can die without the help of doctors.[98]

Albert Einstein

Medicine tries to be taken seriously by the scientific establishment and with double blind trials of new medicines; everything should be under firm horizontal control. Unfortunately for that scientific approach, human bodies are not just complicated machines that can be made to perform better when the right additives are added to their fuel. Paul Davies and John Gribbin end their book *The Matter Myth*, with the very relevant remark: 'Ryle was right to dismiss the notion of the ghost in the machine—not because there is no ghost, but because there is no machine'.[99]

That doesn't imply that additives cannot make a difference, you only have to think of the many, mainly herbal, concoctions that are used in a country like China.

Of course China is now following firmly the Western horizontal materialist tradition resulting in its successes in atom bomb and space technology. That young Chinese are often not aware anymore of their very rich vertical heritage was illustrated by the fact that, when I tried to discuss the wisdom of Lao-tzu with one of my Chinese colleagues—who often invited me for a cup of green tea in his office—he seemed to have no idea of the ancient wisdom of his own tradition.

Just to illustrate the extreme Western obsession with limiting even the mind to the horizontal dimension, I will quote the psychiatrist Henri Maudsley, who declared in the nineteenth century in his book *Body and Will* that: 'Mind and all its products are a function of matter, an outcome of interacting atomic forces not essentially different in kind from the effervescence that follows a chemical combination or the explosion of a fulminate'.[100]

A long time ago in the Netherlands I was involved in a computer user group and remember that we once visited a university hospital where we were proudly shown a tangle of wires connected to computerised electronic equipment measuring nerve reaction times. Seemingly as an afterthought, there was among all that fascinating electronic equipment, a bed for a patient who was to be wired in, so that we could see the results of his nerve reactions to electrical stimulation on a screen next door. This is not the art of healing, but engineers like me—very much riding a horizontal scientific hobbyhorse—having sometimes found (I do not deny it) a useful medical application.

Someone who has admirably researched what is happening in the medical field is Lynne McTaggart. Her book *What Doctors don't tell You* is a veritable treasure trove if you want to do more than just follow orders and swallow your pills. She illustrates that you have to be a very strong medical doctor indeed to resist the overwhelming pressure exerted by the pharmaceutical zillion-euro/dollar/pound industry.[101] And of course, only medicines that have been patented are promoted and sold, often at exorbitant prices; leading to the fact that countries such as India, trying to play their own game, are being subjected to the full wrath of the IMF (International Monetary Fund) for not playing that game assiduously.

If I am allowed to be a bit cynical, it is of course obvious that from a purely commercial point of view, the best thing that can happen to the pharmaceutical industry is the proliferation of disease, and the last thing they really want is to cure people of their afflictions.[102] For them, and their shareholders, the best prospect is that all of us are on expensive medication for the rest of our lives. And that doubts about the motives of the 'pill sellers' is nothing new is testified by this comment from Oliver Wendell Holmes in 1883, 'If the whole *Materia medica* as used, could be sunk in the bottom of the sea, it would be all the better for mankind and all the worse for the fishes'.[103] If you are in any doubts whether this observation—now over a century old—is still relevant today, there is plenty of information on recent drug trial disasters that can be found on the Internet. Take for instance the reported suicides linked to prescribing the drug Seroxat for teenage depression.

Experiences of this kind led David Healy to state: 'During the course of the last five years, the pharmaceuticals industry has gone from being highly regarded to looking little better than the tobacco industry'.[104] Vernon Coleman, focussing on the dangers of testing new drugs on animals and extrapolating its results to humans, predicted this kind of thing happening in a book written in 1991: '... doctors who have studied the subject now believe that by testing new products and procedures on animals research scientists are endangering human lives'.[105] Much more related information can be found in the many other books he wrote.

When my mother died not long ago, I was shocked by the amount of pills that she was still expected to swallow during her final days. When I protested about it, the visiting doctor tried to explain to me, which pills were actually for treating symptoms, while others were for combating the undesired side effects of the first lot. Although fortunately in Europe we do not (yet?) suffer from the American 'suing at the drop of a hat' and 'taking to court for negligence' culture, it seems that prescribing medicines and even operating is often considered the acceptable 'playing it safe' option. On the other side of the balance is the fact that my mother would never have made it to ninety-six without modern medicine; immediately followed by the question, would it not have been better if she had been allowed to die earlier, because the quality of life during her last years, sitting in her wheelchair, brought her sometimes to despair?

Therefore I fully agree with something Joan Grant wrote which I came across a few months after my mother's death: '... we should all be prepared to accept full responsibility for expediting our own death when our body is no longer a useful vehicle through which to transmit our personality. ... Therefore few people are able to die by the simple act of deciding that the time is ripe to do so. Even when this intention has been clearly formulated there is now the risk that it will prove ineffective, because the efforts of the supra-physical to shed its physical particles may be foiled by complicated medical techniques with which it is entirely unfamiliar'.[106] And her statement is supported by the experience of her friend Ray dying of cancer: 'To start with I must get out of hospital, for there are too many interruptions—nannies popping in and out with cups of tea and the thermometers—to have a chance even to sleep—much less practise dying'.[107]

Joop van Montfoort

Elisabeth Kübler-Ross makes the same point I made earlier, observing that 'our professionals have learned to become experts in the management of technological instruments and tools' and summarises her concern pithily: 'We must shift from procedure-oriented patient care to patient-oriented procedures'.[108] And elsewhere she elaborates further: 'We shouldn't nail the dying between two states of consciousness. We shouldn't prolong their lives with medication, injections and life support machines. We should let them go. They're not going into nothingness. They're entering another state of being. We must let our dead go into that world'.[109]

I would like to conclude these reflections with the thoughtful words of Vernon Coleman, writing under the heading 'The final dignity': 'When life is artificially prolonged, pain and distress are only too common. People who die natural deaths, however, do not usually suffer any considerable pain or discomfort as death approaches. When medical intervention is kept to a minimum the body usually ensures that the final hours and days are as peaceful as possible. Pain-relieving endorphins are secreted automatically and the individual drifts slowly, almost contentedly, into an unconscious state'.[110]

In the current climate of a patient dying being considered as a failure, it is understandable that doctors try to escape from the pressures they are under, often via alcohol and drugs. A recent BMA[111] investigation revealed that one in five doctors are addicted to either of these.[112] Indeed, what we urgently need is a complete change of orientation, not only when the patient is dying, but also in medical care in general. We should accept that there are often very simple remedies such as change of diet or using herbs growing in the back of your garden. Or take for instance a pet; Sheldrake—referring to a book dealing with the human-cat relationship—writes that: 'The cats also had a favourable effect in reducing blood pressure in people with hypertension, and in reducing the need for medication'. And further down on the same page: '... pet owners who had been hospitalized with heart

108

disease, including heart attacks, showed an improved survival rate a year later than a control group of non-pet owners.'[113] All this confirms the conclusion that a change in attitude is urgently required: from being preoccupied with symptoms and their treatment, to concentrating instead on the cause of the problem. Again I can illustrate this remark with a personal experience:

Some years ago I had difficulty closing my right hand, and when I forced it, some fingers locked in a closed position, and all knuckle joints were painful when squeezed. At first I thought that it might have to with the large amount of physical work in and around our house that I was then involved in. But as it did not improve after taking things a bit easier, I went to my GP, who referred me to an orthopaedic surgeon here in the UK (private clinic to jump the NHS queue). He wanted to solve the problem by slitting the carpal tunnels surgically under full anaesthetic.

His arguments convinced me that it was sensible to undergo that operation, but fortunately when Emmy returned from visiting friends on the Continent, she stopped me at the last moment from going ahead. Instead, she made an appointment for me with an orthopaedic surgeon in Germany (via one of her friends who worked in his practice). Before going there, a few months later, the same symptoms manifested themselves in my left hand, so that hand would have to have undergone the same operation here in the UK.

The first thing the German specialist asked was whether a blood test had been taken and when I had to reply in the negative, he expressed his amazement, because that was, he said, the first thing you did for my condition. He also would do anything to avoid an operation (he mumbled something that 'we stopped operating for this condition thirty years ago').[114] The test results revealed that the uric acid level in my blood was too high, and he explained that my symptoms were caused by the accumulation of uric acid crystals in my joints, a condition known as *gout*. He added that this could possibly be cured with a simple change of diet. He gave me a diet sheet to enable me to avoid food with high uric acid levels (the top scorers being: lentils, cow's liver, grilled chicken with skin and herring with skin). He also advised me to take vitamin E and drink a lot, especially nettle tea, which I have been doing every morning since.[115] If the diet did not have the desired effect, the next step would have been an injection. But after about six weeks following his advice, the swellings and painfulness disappeared completely and have not returned since. Thank you, Germany!

Maybe the German doctor knew his classics and followed the advice Socrates had given Charmides a very long time ago: 'Perhaps you have yourself heard good doctors say to a patient who comes to them for eye-trouble, that they cannot heal the eyes alone but that it is necessary to treat the whole head before they can effect a cure, and further that they believe it is sheer ignorance to treat the head by itself apart from the rest of the body. Hence they turn their attention to diet for the whole body and attempt to cure the part along with the whole'.[116]

My story is also a beautiful confirmation of what Philip James told Andy Coghlan: 'The greatest killers are diet-related...' [117] James went on to describe the successful attitude of the Finnish government denying heart 'patients drugs ... until they had tried a healthier diet'.

In this context, what is much more insidious is the global pollution we are causing by our irresponsible activities. Everyone on earth has now some measurable outfall from atom bomb tests in their bodies, and the widespread chemical pollution is now blamed for what some describe as an epidemic of major proportions, mentioning allergies, asthma, immunodeficiencies, eczema, etc. Our generation vividly remembers what the result was from *Softenon/Thalomide* being prescribed to pregnant women; but at least that disaster resulted from a deliberate decision to prescribe that medicine.[118] What is much more treacherous is the chemical pollution we are completely unaware of because it is hidden in everything we eat and drink, and in the very air we breathe. Full details on metal toxicity can, for instance, be found in Pat Thomas', well-referenced book, *Living Dangerously*. In an article he writes: 'Compelling evidence now links exposure to a wide range of environmental toxins with a number of emotional and behavioural problems in children and adults, including violence, addiction, learning disabilities, hyperactivity, intolerance, lowered intelligence and dementia. These problems can cause tremendous difficulties within families, communities and even on an international scale'.[119] This last point is very much accentuated by a claim, made during a recent BBC documentary programme, asserting that the Suez Canal war was started, practically on his own, by Prime Minister Anthony Eden while he was on a high dose of amphetamines.[120] As I have illustrated, several of my personal experiences confirm that some medical problems can indeed be solved at little cost without resorting to expensive surgical or pharmaceutical treatment with their potential risk of side effects causing unwanted complications.[121] I think that the possible beneficial effects of a change of attitude *from curative to preventive medicine* could save our society an enormous amount of money. Back in 1998, I sent a letter describing my gout experience to the UK Health Secretary for his consideration; I didn't even receive an acknowledgment.

Note that here in the UK we have not only a 'Health Secretary' but also a similarly named 'National Health Service', which one would expect to be involved in *health* rather than *medication*. It is fortunate that ideas are now changing, which is testified by what Matthew Fox wrote: "... a Canadian physicist who is a member of the Ministry of the Environment in Ontario told me: 'Here in Ontario there is a serious effort going on at the government level to achieve a *healthier* society as opposed to a *more medicated* society ... We have had a medical system and not a health system'".[122] To stress the point that there is nothing new in this respect and although I have quoted Socrates already, here is a fitting comment by Plato: 'This is the great error of our day in the treatment of the human body that physicians separate the soul [vertical] from the body [horizontal]'.[123]

The same lesson comes to us from the ancient Chinese civilisation. Acupuncture has recently become respectable after Western doctors were invited to a Chinese hospital to witness major operations, such as the removal of a cancerous lung, being done on fully conscious patients; indeed, completely without anaesthetics, but just with the insertion of a few acupuncture needles. And, of course, acupuncture is very much cause oriented rather than concentrating on symptoms. Worsley confirms this, writing the following on the aims of acupuncture:

To treat the patient as a whole, This means that the practitioner considers the physical body, the mind and the spirit together as a whole; as a unity...

To seek the cause of the disease. It is most important that the manifest complaint itself should not be considered the prime concern. The complaint is only a distress signal (or symptom) of the disease.[124] On the next page he cautions us to be 'aware of the dangers of symptomatic acupuncture', while I can only endorse his concluding diagnosis: 'This ignoring of the spirit is why we are not winning the fight against disease. We are abandoning and neglecting the most essential part of man. And, if the spirit within us is denied, then we will not keep in harmony and balance. Thus we will be more susceptible to disease'.[125]

Here again we could learn from ancient China, where the doctor was paid only as long as his client was healthy; so he had every incentive to cure him/her as soon as possible. Our present system *rewards illness* instead. Doctors generate their income from sickness and the remuneration stops as soon as the patient is cured, and I repeat that it is extremely unlikely for the pharmaceutical industry to promote medicines that really will cure all ills.

Fortunately, perhaps as a result of the above mentioned recent demonstrations of the analgesic effects of acupuncture during major operations shown on our television screens, there seems to be more open mindedness. A very good survey of more holistic methods of healing than our Western horizontal approach is Richard Grossman's *The Other Medicines*, in which he explores Far Eastern and Western holistic approaches and gives many practical applications. That we should get out of our ivory towers because knowledge can be derived form many sources, he illustrates with a quote from Paracelsus: 'I went not only to the doctors, but also to the barbers, bathkeepers, learned physicians, women, and magicians who pursue the art of healing; I went to alchemists, monasteries, to nobles and the common folk, to the experts and the simple'.[126]

My own exploration of the medical scene can be condensed in a—perhaps too cynical—quote from the Canadian Institute for Advanced Research: 'Medical services have little if any effect on national health levels'.[127] And after our exploration of the effects of restricting ourselves to what are supposedly disciplines limited to the horizontal dimension only, in the next chapter we will investigate activities that are supposed to be dedicated to exploring the vertical one.

6 VERTICAL PURSUITS

6.1 PHILOSOPHY

I look in your inmost self and see the universe not yet created.[1]

Rumi

Transpersonal consciousness is infinite, rather than finite, stretching beyond the limits of time and space. To grasp the full dimensions of the transpersonal realm is perhaps as much a challenge for our everyday minds as lying out under the stars on a clear night and attempting to grasp the breadth and width of the vast unfathomable space where the heavenly bodies reside. ... And what is true for the outer space of astronomers is equally applicable to the inner space of the psyche.[2]

Stanislav Grof

We feel that even if *all possible* scientific questions be answered, the problems of life have still not been touched at all.[3]

Ludwig Wittgenstein

... the greatest of all the accomplishments of twentieth century science has been the discovery of human ignorance.[4]

Thomas Lewis

It is difficult to distinguish the proposals of prophets of those of charlatans.[5]

James Van Allen

We don't see things as they are, we see things as we are.[6]

Anaïs Nin

In the previous chapter I have tried to illustrate that what are usually considered to be disciplines well entrenched in the horizontal dimension (and subject only to the power of the intellect) are intrinsically linked with intuitive ideas welling up from the depths of the vertical dimension. In this chapter I will concentrate on disciplines that are supposedly exploring primarily that vertical domain.

Philosophy translates as 'love of wisdom', and wisdom can be defined as intellect/mind guided by the heart/soul. So its basic guidance should be oriented vertically, but again we can see the process of its exponents desperately wanting to be taken seriously by the scientific establishment; reducing philosophy to a purely intellectual pursuit, leading directly to its degeneration. This fact is illustrated by, for instance, concentrating on the investigation of the meaning of words as a valid subject for philosophical studies. John Sanford expresses this tendency very appropriately: 'The soul today is an orphan. ... Philosophy, her father ... turned himself away from the pursuit of wisdom and became confined to the narrow realm of semantics and semiotics'.[7] The ancient Greek philosophers had their differences but most of them agreed on one important fact, viz. that 'philosophy was a therapeutic art, not just an idle pastime for people who were too clever by half'.[8]

Anthony Gottlieb points clearly to the vertical dimension when describing that in the third century *CE*, Plotinus '... knew that he was trying to describe the indescribable. The goal of his philosophy was union with a God-like One, which he claimed to have experienced himself now and then. ... He held that the One was beyond rational comprehension. ... The One (or whatever) could not even be called a being, because it was 'beyond being' to use a phrase of Plato'.[9] Meister Eckhart made this last point in a way that was for him characteristically direct: 'It is God who has the treasure and the bride in him, the Godhead is as void as though it were not'.[10]

Early philosophy may be hidden in the mists of prehistory, but we are so fortunate that we can still return to its expression blossoming in ancient Greece. One of my favourites is Socrates who, living nearly 2,500 years ago, used the stirring tale of prisoners in a cave to convey the message that the exploration of the vertical dimension in the sunlit splendours of the outside world is far superior to being trapped inside the darkness of a cave, representing our horizontal spacetime prison.[11] Plato wrote it down for us as a dialogue between Socrates and Glaucon in *The Republic*.[12] As it illustrates my previous remark that the message of the importance of the vertical dimension is so ancient, I will summarise the simile of the cave using several of Socrates' (translated) original lines.

Socrates sets the scene as follows: 'Imagine an underground chamber like a cave, with a long entrance open to the daylight and as wide as the cave. In this chamber are men who have been prisoners there since they were children, their legs chained and their necks being so fastened to the wall behind their backs that they can only look straight ahead of them, so that they are unable to turn their heads.

Some way off, behind and higher up, a fire is burning, and between the fire and the prisoners ... a curtain-wall has been built, like a screen at puppet shows between the operators and their audience, above which they show their puppets'. Men carry figures of men and animals along this curtain-wall casting shadows on the cave wall in front of the prisoners, and as they have had no other experiences ever, they are convinced that this shadow world is the whole of reality. Their situation is sketched in figure 6.1. Of course this view is only possible thanks to our modern night vision camera, because the cave is very deep and in its complete darkness only the shadows on the wall in front of them will be visible to the prisoners.

Figure 6.1 Plato's Cave

Socrates continues: 'Then think what would naturally happen to them if they were released from their bonds and cured of their delusions. Suppose one of them were let loose, and suddenly compelled to stand up and turn his head and look and walk towards the fire; all these actions would be painful and he would be too dazzled to see properly the objects of which he used to see the shadows. What do you think he would say if he was told that what he used to see was so much empty nonsense and that he was now nearer reality and seeing more correctly, because he was turned towards objects that were more real, and if on top of that he were compelled to say what each of the passing objects was when it was pointed out to him?' The answer is that he would be at a complete loss to identify the objects and still considered their shadows, he had grown up with, as his only reality: 'And if he were made to look directly at the light of the fire, it would hurt his eyes and he would turn back and retreat to the things which he could see properly, which he would think really clearer than the things being shown him'.

Subsequently Socrates describes that if he were to be forcibly taken outside, his suffering would be even greater, and it would take a very long time before his eyes would be able to distinguish anything at all. After this adaptation, he would slowly start to appreciate what the 'real' world was like; with the sun producing the seasons and the years, and he would come to the insight that this sun 'is in a sense responsible for everything that he and his fellow-prisoners used to see'.

Now he fully realises that what passed for wisdom amongst the prisoners, and even the 'prizes for keen sightedness for those best able to remember the order of sequence among the passing shadows and so be best able to divine their future appearances'— all this was absolutely nothing compared to the reality outside their cave. And 'if he went back to sit in his old seat in the cave', he would 'be blinded by the darkness, because he had come in suddenly out of the sunlight'. He had lost the prisoner's prized faculties of seeing the faintest details in their shadow world and he would 'be likely to make a fool of himself. And they would say that his visit to the upper world had ruined his sight, and that the ascent was not worth even attempting. Also, that 'if anyone tried to release them and lead them up, they would kill him if they could lay hands on him'.

That outcome is, of course, not only exactly what happened to Socrates himself—who was condemned to death by having to drink a poison filled beaker—but to several other messengers of the Light; telling mankind about what the reality outside our cave, our four-dimensional horizontal prison, is like.[13]

A bit earlier in *The Republic* Socrates elucidates the advancement from the visible realm of shadows and images via their physical presence to their forms in the intelligible realm, as progressing along a line.[14] This could give the false impression that they are on a kindred level (i.e. in the same dimension), which mistake is avoided by introducing our ninety degree angle between the two realms. This has been sketched in figure 6.2. in which the 'Forms' in the 'Intelligible Realm' are guiding the 'Physical things' in the 'Visible Realm'.

Physical things, Shadows ← Visible Realm

↑ Forms   ↑ Intelligible Realm

Figure 6.2 Socrates' line elaborated

After this vivid illustration, taken from the philosophy of Europe's earliest civilisation—of stressing the foremost importance of what I have called the vertical dimension—we now turn to more recent developments in the field of helping people to cope with their suffering, i.e. psychology. The importance of its purported aim of helping others was already pointed out by Epicurus, another ancient Greek sage, who wrote:

Empty are the words of that philosopher who offers no therapy for human suffering.[15]

6.2 PSYCHOLOGY

I, of course, have tried to cure my own loneliness and helplessness by becoming a psychotherapist.[16]

Sheldon Kopp

A dream not considered, is like a letter from God left unopened.

Gnostic Proverb

Unconscious mental processes are in themselves timeless. In the id there is nothing corresponding to the idea of time.[17]

Sigmund Freud

Psychoanalysis in particular and "depth psychology" in general seem to me to be increasingly out of touch with all that has been going on in the sciences of human behavior during the last thirty years, and many of us are wondering seriously how long it will be possible for psychology, the study of an alleged psyche, to remain a department of science.[18]

Alan Watts

An appealing analogy, but no more than an analogy, is to regard the body and brain as a superb computer built by genetic coding, which has been created by the wonderful process of biological evolution ... the Soul or Self is the programmer of the computer.[19]

John Eccles

In our ocean model, the ego is found at the top of the wave, while the soul, self or psyche is the part of our 'wave' underneath the ocean's surface. Often this is called spirit as well, which is confusing because, as we will see below, *spirit* should be reserved for the vertical energy flow ultimately coming from the One. Psychology is the study of that deeper realm, while psychotherapy treats problems or diseases manifesting themselves at the surface, but originating in the depths of the vertical dimension. Sigmund Freud, the founding father of psychoanalysis, was so keen on being taken seriously by the scientific establishment of his day that he ignored anything that could not be fitted into a horizontal framework. For instance, Anthony Storr writes that 'In Freud's view, religion should and could be replaced by science'.[20] Freud's opinion of human motivations was so grim that he argued that 'Christ's injunction to love thy neighbour as thyself is a psychological impossibility'.[21] He realised, however, that there was a hidden realm below the ego, which he described as the 'subconscious'.

Although psychology in our context implies the very exploration of the vertical dimension; the 'psi equals zero' school has its disciples here too. Take for instance Peter Watson writing in a recent article: 'But introspection is like imagination, only more so: it is an ancient practice out of kilter with a scientific world.

In my recent book *Ideas: A history from fire to Freud*, I explored the many times humans have turned "inward" to find "the truth": from the prophets in ancient Israel, the Buddha and the writers of the Upanishads in India, Confucius in China and the Athenian Plato, who famously thought that the ideal realm of the forms could be apprehended only by looking in, to the introspections of St Augustine, Savonarola, Luther, Descartes, Vico, Kant and the Romantics, it is a dominant theme in the history of ideas. Freud's tripartite structure of our inner world (id, ego, superego) is the latest tuning-in. But my conclusion after this tour was that this approach hasn't worked. Looking in we have found nothing,

nothing stable anyway, nothing we can agree upon, nothing conclusive, because there is nothing to find'.[22]

But again, all this says nothing about reality, but rather a lot about Watson; personal experience is critical for accepting the reality of the vertical dimension. Take for instance Carl Gustav Jung, Freud's disciple and earmarked successor, who—guided by his own personal experiences—was unable to follow Freud in his fervent denial of the reality of the vertical dimension. This resulted in him breaking away from Freud's group, and founding his own school of 'analytical psychology'. According to Jung it was only after 'some years' that Freud came around and 'recognised the seriousness of parapsychology and acknowledged the factuality of "occult" phenomena'.[23] Jung's many books, firmly based on what he encountered in his medical practice, are a gold mine of information on paranormal phenomena. Because he was too honest to deny them, but incorporated them in his understanding of psychology, he earned the wrath of many of his scientific contemporaries. A contemporary psychologist, Lee Lawson, was sufficiently honest to write after four decades of clinical practice and enquiries: 'It was in those enquiries that I first realized empirically that self-reported external and internal psychic experiences of the populace were far more extensive, far more common, than classical psychology had ever catalogued'.[24]

If, however, someone like Anthony Storr tries to fit Jung's message inside a horizontal framework, it is difficult to avoid Storr's conclusion that 'Jung himself was exceedingly bad at putting his ideas across'.[25] But for me, because of the similarity between the experiences reported by Jung[26] and my Lac Noir 'dream'[27] (chapter 3) and other similar events; his ideas on our basic interconnectedness—the effect of which he labelled 'Synchronicity'—make perfectly sense for me.

Again that giant of twentieth century physics comes to the fore, Jung writing: 'It was Einstein who first started me off thinking about a possible relativity of time as well as space, and their psychic synchronicity'.[28] But for Storr, who obviously lacks that so essential personal (vertical) experience, it can be understood very well that '[Jung's] writings upon synchronicity seem to be both confused and of little practical value'. And on the next page he quotes Jung, complaining, 'Nobody reads my books,' and, 'I have such a hell of a trouble to make people see what I mean'.[29] This remark vividly underlines again that nothing in the world is a valid substitute for personal experience, and already as a teenager discussing religion with his father, when his father advised him: 'One ought not to think but believe', Jung thought, 'No, one must experience and know'.[30]

Several examples of Jung's personal experiences of the reality of the vertical dimension can be found in his own books and in the many written about him. As an artist Jung designed mandalas, which for him were very symbolic of the process of opening up the vertical dimension: 'When I began drawing the mandalas, however, I saw that everything, all the paths I had been following ... were leading back to a single point—namely, to the midpoint. ... It is the path to the centre, to individuation'.[31]

Jung's personal experiences, and those he came across treating his patients, led him to propose an island model, as described for instance in this quotation from Victor White's book: "[Jung] compares the sphere of consciousness—the domain which is in view of the conscious ego on its peak—with an island in the midst of an ocean. The ocean is the unconscious. Directly below the surface of this ocean, and nearest to consciousness, is what he calls the 'personal unconscious'. It consists of 'what has been forgotten or repressed, and of subliminary perceptions, thoughts or feelings of every sort'".[32]

Including others as islands in this model as well, leads to an archipelago model (figure 6.3) in which each island is resting on the bottom of the ocean representing the collective unconscious. Although this unconscious domain has been given many different names, the basic idea remains the same.[33]

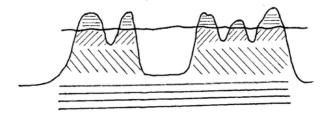

≡ Personal Conscious Mind.

/// Personal Unconscious.

\\\ Collective Unconscious of a Race.

≣ Collective Unconsciousness of Humanity.

Figure 6.3 Jung's archipelago model

This representation corresponds very much with our ocean model, and indeed if you do not like the lack of a boundary between 'your' wave and the others', you can make them more identifiable and solid by imagining them as little icebergs floating in the ocean of the collective unconscious. Ian Parrot has no need for any separation, he writes: 'The mind of man is surely not a container like a bucket, ... It has no bottom, nor is it confined to the individual like a personal possession. More likely, we are "plugged in" to the source of life, as a bulb is to the electric light supply'.[34] And as the ocean's depths are beyond the spacetime prison at its surface, this is the way predictive dreams come about; the dreamer, by leaving the spacetime surface and being "plugged in" to the collective experiences stored underneath the surface of our ocean, can return from his/her vertical dive in the ocean of the unconscious with information about events that have not yet happened.

Many of such instances have been published, ranging from predicting the sinking of the *Titanic* to the mine disaster at Abergavenny. Emmy had several of these predictive insights, such as 'seeing' Halsecombe in repetitive dreams before we had ever been there (chapter 10). And another occasion was during a gale when she 'saw' a large tree near the house being blown over. She told me that that tree had to be made safe right now, so during the gale we took down several of its larger branches. Later when we cut down its trunk, we found that it was completely rotten inside, and that in its exposed position, could very well have blown over. In this case the vision obviously did not reflect a 'reality' that did actually happen, but was about a potential 'reality'.[35]

One of the many ways in which Jung illustrated the reality of the collective unconscious was by relating the story of how one of his patients (a local farmer) told him about a dream he had, which corresponded in detail with what Jung had recently read in an obscure mediaeval Latin manuscript. The only sensible explanation is that there was an interconnection between them in the vertical realm.[36]

Again I can illustrate this with something similar in my own experience. When I left in 1963 for a job in Italy, I cancelled my Dutch postal giro account. On returning after nearly five years, I again applied for an account, asking if I could have my old number back. I was told that that was impossible because it had been issued to someone else. Years later I moved to England and went to the local post office to apply for a UK postal giro account, and to my amazement the number I was issued with contained the same sequence of six numbers of my original Dutch account. On top of this event, years later I was issued by different firms with two identical identification numbers which were very easy to remember because for me they referred to the same significant date. Of course I know that the chance of the occurrence of these events is not beyond the limits of probability, but for me they add to the evidence that there is more to life than just the horizontal dimension.

As a result of his explorations Jung acknowledged that he was merely rediscovering facts that had been part of a much older Eastern wisdom: '... when I began my life-work in the practice of psychiatry and psychotherapy, I was completely ignorant of Chinese philosophy, and only later did my professional experience show me that in my technique I had been unconsciously led along that secret way which has been the preoccupation of the best minds in the East for centuries'.[37] But in our twentieth century arrogant ignorance, 'horizontal' psychologists such as Watson and Skinner even went as far as '... rejecting "mind" on the ground it had no basis in physical science...'[38] Indeed, even if we allow for another (subjective) realm, it is to be subjected to the rigours of the horizontal one: 'It is the objective world in which we live and to which the subjective world must pay deference'.[39]

In psychology, the vertical energy flow is often called the 'libido', manifesting itself as the complementary 'anima' and 'animus'. This reminds me of the Hindu chronicle that Brahman (the One) manifests itself e.g. as both Shiva (male) and Shakti (female): 'Shakti is forever seeking Shiva and the union (*coniunctio*) between them is their mutual fulfilment. This fulfilment is represented by the lotus with a thousand petals adorning man's brow, an image which, seen from above, appears as a mandala, the symbol of wholeness and completion'.[40] In Greek philosophy there is a similar story, in which man was originally whole, symbolised by a sphere. The sphere split into two halves, which are born as female and male, and each half is desperately searching for its complementary half.[41]

By being so courageous as to venture beyond the boundaries of the prison of science, Jung attracted a sizeable following, but was also (as could be expected) scorned by a large part of the scientific community. One of his followers is Roberto Assagioli, and he introduces a seemingly different model of our personality.

However, his model fits our wave model as well if we realise that Assagioli gave a plan view, i.e. our wave seen from above which can be transformed into a side view, as depicted in figure 6.4.[42]

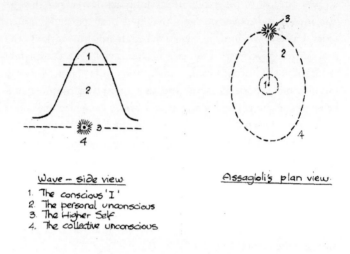

Wave – side view
1. The conscious 'I'
2. The personal unconscious
3. The Higher Self
4. The collective unconscious

Assagioli's plan view.

Figure 6.4 Assagioli's model, my side and his plan view

The numbers corresponding to:
1: The Conscious 'I'
2: The Personal Unconscious
3: The Higher Self
4: The Collective Unconscious

Again, to illustrate that the same message has been repeated over and over, I will quote some of Assagioli's writing: 'There is another dimension in man. Though many are unaware of it and may even deny its existence, there is another type of awareness, to the reality of which the direct experience of a number of individuals has testified throughout history. The dimension along which this awareness functions can be termed "vertical." In the past it was generally considered the domain of religious or spiritual experience, but it is now gaining increasing recognition as a valid field of scientific investigation.

This is the specific domain of transpersonal psychology, which deals with what Maslow, a pioneer in the field, has called the "higher needs."[43]

Jung also considered a vertical orientation indispensable for curing his patients: 'During the past thirty years, people from all the civilised countries of the earth have consulted me. I have treated many hundreds of patients, the larger number being Protestants, a small number of Jews and not more than five or six believing Catholics. Among all my patients in the second half of life—that is to say, over thirty-five—there has not been one whose problem in the last resort was not that of finding a religious outlook on life. It is safe to say that every one of them fell ill because he had lost that which the living religions of every age have given to their followers, and none of them has been really healed who did not regain his religious outlook.'[44] He added that 'This, of course, has nothing to do with a particular creed or membership of a church'.[45]

Although Jung saw himself very much as a scientist, which he expressed as: 'I pursue science, not apologetics or philosophy. I have neither the competence nor the inclination to found a religion...;'[46] psychology is intrinsically a vertical discipline, and if you want to limit yourself to the horizontal/scientific dimension only, you have to limit your outlook to deliberate tunnel vision, as e.g. Freud did. According to Victor White: 'It is said that Freud withheld for ten years the considerable body of so-called paranormal material he had accidentally collected in the course of his psycho-analytic work, "for fear," as he put it, "of our scientific world-view being menaced by it"'.[47]

Then, Erich Fromm is right indeed, when he pointed out so deftly: 'Psychology became a science lacking its main subject matter'.[48] And here again we can learn so much from ancient masters: Jung writing in his foreword to *The I Ching* 'The thoughts of the old masters are of greater value to me than the philosophical prejudices of the Western mind'.[49] Appropriately I would like to conclude this section with a part of the Rock Edicts that Ashoka Maurya had inscribed on pillars all over his Indian empire:

Do not perform sacrifices or do anything else that might hurt animals...
Be generous to your friends...
Do not get involved in quarrels and arguments...
Try to be pure of heart, humble and faithful...
Do not think only of your good points; remember also your faults as well and try to put them right...[50]

My heartfelt reaction to such ancient wisdom from the third century *BCE* is a heartfelt *Amen*.

6.3 ART

And the fire and the rose are one.[51]

T. S. Eliot

'Good art' is the work of the Imagination and 'bad art' of the mind of the ratio.

William Blake

Poetry redeems from decay the visitations of divinity in man.[52]

Percy Bysshe Shelley

Who is man, the artist?
He is the unspoiled core of everyman, before he is choked by schooling, training, conditioning until the artist-within shrivels up and is forgotten.[53]

Frederick Franck

Art without spirituality is cynical, manipulative, commercial and consumer oriented, pessimistic, ego centered, competitive, tired, afraid to die because it has not lived, fame seeking, exclusive, elitist, expensive, anthropocentric, and self serving—just like politics without spirituality, health care without spirituality, or religion without spirituality.[54]

Matthew Fox

Art is the expression of the vertical dimension in the horizontal one, and as such often tries to express the basic oneness of the all. Take for instance the line from Eliot that I opened this section with: 'And the fire and the rose are one.' Perhaps I should have said 'true art', because much of what passes for art is not a spontaneous upwelling from within, but can be a means by which to register a protest or just simply to earn a living. Frederick Frank saw the real vocation of art, when he wrote, 'True art is not an indulgence of the little self, but a manifestation of the Self'.[55] This implies that art cannot be analysed intellectually, but should be experienced on the heart level. Renoir too saw this clearly when he stated: 'What goes on inside my head doesn't interest me ... When I think I might have been born in a family of intellectuals! It would have taken me years to get rid of all their ideas and see things as they are'.[56]

So the artist has to get the ego—bound up with the horizontal dimension—out of the way, so that the vertical upwellings find their expression in whatever medium the particular artist is versed in (music, paint, textile, etc.). Then the artist can come to the realisation—often to her/his own surprise—so concisely expressed by Eliot: 'There is much more to art than the artist himself realises'.

But as we all know, there can be big money in art, especially in painting, and so the horizontal organisers will try to take over. Especially in the Victorian era, we have seen that as soon as art is institutionalised, it is killed. The ego has taken over in the race for recognition, funding, titles and medals. Most of the winners of all those medals that were awarded during that era have been forgotten, while outsiders like Vincent van Gogh are now world famous.[57] Even the artist himself might think that his art is coming from horizontal interaction. For instance towards the end of the eighteenth century Joshua Reynolds wrote in his 'Discourse VI': 'The mind is but a barren soil; a soil which is soon exhausted, and will produce no crop, or only one, unless it be continually fertilized and enriched with foreign matter ... The greatest natural genius cannot subsist on its own stock: he who resolves never to ransack any mind but his own, will soon be reduced, from mere barrenness, to the poorest of all imitations; he will be obliged to imitate himself, and to repeat what he has often before repeated'.

Perhaps William Blake was a bit unfair when he wrote in the margin of his copy of Reynolds' book: 'The Mind that could have produced this Sentence must have been a Pitiful, a Pitiable Imbecility. I always thought the Human Mind was the most Prolific of all Things & Inexhaustible, I certainly do thank God that I am not like Reynolds'.[58] But for me Blake expresses, in a rather uncouth way, the basic issue that art is very much a vertical rather than a horizontal activity, and that it wells up from an infinite source (remember my psi is infinite argument in chapter 4). And indeed, when we limit our approach to art to an intellectual exercise only, the result is what Athena Leoussi writes: 'The decline of art is part of the decline of wisdom'.[59] This leads directly to the conclusion Paul Klee reached, writing in his *Diary* during the horrors of the first World War in 1915, that: 'The more horrifying this world becomes (as it is in these days) the more art becomes abstract; while a world at peace produces realistic art'.[60]

Next we will take a brief glance at the art of play writing, starting with the English giant Shakespeare. In chapter 4, I listed his *A Midsummer Night's Dream* in table 4.1, with *Athens* and the *wood* as his names for the horizontal and vertical dimensions respectively. I did that because for me this play is such a beautiful example of the message that the problems created in (horizontal) Athens can only be solved in the (vertical) wood, the realm of fairies, elves and fauns. A modern example, expounding the same lesson is e.g. Peter Wolf in his radio play *City of the Mind* with his 'fifth dimension of love'.[61]

Indeed, art cannot be organised horizontally, as is clearly explained in this Chinese text: 'Yet as the splash of ink descends upon the paper, guided by the artist's spirit, it comes out in myriad forms entirely beyond the original plan ... If the artist insists on doing what he did yesterday, he cannot do it. Why? Because when an artist insists on something, he is already obstructing the free flow of the spirit'.[62]

Shelley also saw this very clearly when he testified: 'True art is not subject to the power of the will'. And he pointed to its vertical (divine) origin: 'Poetry thus makes immortal all that is best and most beautiful in the world ... Poetry redeems from decay the visitations of divinity in man'.

If we now turn to classical music, we see the same process repeated that Klee identified for the visual arts. Completely at odds with the situation in the technical domain, and to the amazement of some academics, we have entered a phase in which most of the music performed in our concert halls was composed hundreds of years ago.[63] And this is very much a recent phenomenon, because until a few hundred years ago this was never the case. The music performed then was from living composers, and they would hardly be heard after they had died and a new generation had taken over.

What this phenomenon illustrates is that classical music lost its soul a few hundred years ago. With a few notable exceptions, there is hardly anything in modern classical music that can replace the mysticism of Pachelbel's Canon, the magic of Bach's toccatas, the majesty of Beethoven's symphonies or the moving intensity of 'Pie Jesu' from Fauré's late nineteenth century Requiem. For me, their music is in the same category as experiencing a beautiful sunrise, a silent spring, a landscape with early rising mist in the woods, a thundering waterfall or with man made temples or cathedrals. Its roots lie in the vertical dimension, as e.g. the composer Puccini realised when he declared that the music for *Madame Butterfly* 'was dictated to me by God; I was merely instrumental in putting it on paper'.[64]

Of course, as in the visual arts, there is an abundance of classical music expressing suffering. In particular the Passion of Christ has been the motif of many compositions. Some choral music is better sung in Latin than in a translation because the text in graphically describing suffering often distracts from the beautiful music. For me, a modern exposition of suffering expressed in a haunting way is Henryk Górecki's *Symphony of Sorrowful Songs,* which he composed in 1976 about the suffering of the Polish people during World War II. One of the songs is based on a prayer scratched by a girl in her Gestapo prison cell wall.[65]

On the other hand, so-called modern classical compositions, played by people with serious faces and in grand concert halls under a famous conductor, to my ears are often absurdly dissonant and repulsive. For me, the ancient Chinese tale of the 'emperor's new clothes' seems so relevant here. They are in the same 'art' category as high-rise apartment buildings, multi-storey car parks, motorways and airports: it's noise all right, but not of the soul. The poet Philip Larkin expressed my feelings about so much of modern art succinctly as follows: 'All that's left for us is concrete and tyres'.

But again if one spring dries up, another one takes over, and now we can often turn to modern non-classical music for inspiration. In contemporary music there is magic for me now in, for instance, John Lennon's 'Imagine', the musical spectrum of Eva Cassidy and the message of the brotherhood of man in Melanie's songs.

The already quoted graphical artist, Frederick Franck, wrote: 'It must be because of this [vertical] mode of seeing that I have become incapable of doing "illustrations", of drawings as a command performance, whether it is I who issues the command or another. It just does not work anymore'.[66] While Socrates expressed his wish to restrict artistic freedom to what is in his view its task, viz. expressing the message of the 'Good': 'It is not only to the poets therefore that we must issue orders requiring them to portray good character in their poems or not to write at all; we must issue similar orders to all artists and craftsmen, and prevent them portraying bad character, ill-discipline, meanness, or ugliness in pictures of living things, in sculpture, architecture, or any work of art, and if they are unable to comply they must be forbidden to practise their art among us'.[67] Of course, although I do see art as a message from the 'Good', I do not agree with Socrates' press-ganging of artists by ordering them to comply with what he considers a positive message, which should rather be expressed spontaneously.

I have personally been blessed in that my electronic design work, that I was engaged in most of my working life, was not a 'must do', but a 'delight to do', and I do see that as a form of artistic expression. Indeed over the ages, many sages have proclaimed the message that it is not important what you do, but how you do it; unfortunately their warnings have been mostly ignored by our horizontal society. Blame me as well, because after all it took me half a lifetime to get an inkling of what the many sages were talking about. Now I realise that Coleridge was referring to people like me, who have: '... dearly purchased a few brilliant inventions at the loss of all communion with life and the spirit of nature'.[68] He himself expressed his experience of oneness as:

All self-annihilated it shall make
God its identity: God in all!
We and our Father one![69]

Thomas Carlyle too was scathing about our engineering skills: 'Men have grown mechanical in head and heart, as well as in hand'.[70] Fortunately there is definitely hope for people like me, otherwise I wouldn't be writing this book, would I? And surely there is great assurance in what Richard Bach wrote: 'You teach best what you need to learn most'.[71]

Here again we can learn from the East; Joseph Campbell writing: 'Art in the ancient East was the art of life. In the words of Dr. A.K. Coomaraswamy, who for some thirty years was a curator of the Boston museum of fine arts: "The artist, in the ancient world, was not a special kind of man, but every man a special kind of artist."'[72]

Some artists have spontaneous upwellings, others have given it a helping hand by the use of stimulating drugs. In the very village where we lived for many years, Coleridge was staying at one of the farms and had taken some opium, which triggered him into the writing of 'Kubla Khan'. Unfortunately, before he had finished it, 'a man from Porlock' turned up, bringing him back to the horizontal dimension; as a result of which he was never able to complete that poem. So although drugs might be one way for some people to open up to the vertical dimension, they are notoriously unpredictable and can be very dangerous, so we will explore much safer ways in the next chapter.

Campbell compares the difference between the mystic's exploration of 'the same deep inward sea' to that of the druggie as between 'a diver who can swim and one who cannot'.[73] And further on he expands this line of reasoning: 'In short, ... what I find that I am saying is that our schizophrenic patient is actually experiencing inadvertently that same beatific ocean deep which the yogi and saint are ever striving to enjoy: except that, whereas they are swimming in it, he is drowning'.[74] But before we explore what it takes to learn to swim, let us now turn from art to religion, which should have been a major way of opening up the vertical dimension. Perhaps we will then be able to answer Daito's question:

Is Art one of the Ways to solve the riddle only to be solved by un-knowing?[75]

6.4 RELIGION

The lamps are different, the light is the same.

Mediaeval Sufi

The gods are one nature but many names.[76]

Maximus of Tyre

Any religion which is not a cause of love and unity is no religion ... All the manifestations of God and His Prophets have taught the same truths and given the same spiritual law. They all teach the one code of morality. There is no division in the truth.[77]

Abdu'l-Baha

It is precisely among the heretics of every age that we find men, who were filled with the highest kind of religious feeling, and were in many cases regarded by their contemporaries as Atheists.[78]

Albert Einstein

As all men are alike (though infinitely various), so all Religions, as all similars, have one source.[79]

William Blake

When you smash the jugs, the water is One.

Rumi

The word 'religion' expresses so beautifully what should have been its primary goal; deriving from the Latin *re ligare*, 'tie again' or 're-connect'.[80] Indeed the wave experiencing that it is part of the ocean has been described in many traditions, resulting in different names for that experience: enlightenment, satori, samadhi, etc. Irrespective of the tradition, there have always been people who had their vertical channel spontaneously open, vividly experiencing their being at one with the rest of creation.

The beautifully concise Sufi statement that I opened this section with, has been expressed by Joseph Campbell's 'old professor ... in Comparative Religions' as: 'In its subjective [vertical] sense the religion of all mankind is one and the same. In its objective [horizontal] sense, however, there are differing forms'.[81] In our own days the Dalai Lama expressed the same sentiment: 'Despite the differences in the names and forms used by the various religions, the ultimate truth to which they point is the same'. And a bit more light-heartedly: 'Religion is a food for the mind, and as we have different tastes, we must take that what is most suitable for us'.[82] With an engineer's thoroughness, Roland Peterson has—in his book *Everyone is Right*—collected and systematically tabulated writings from a wide range of religious pursuits, thus demonstrating that the same (vertical) message, often using very similar imagery, has been proclaimed over and over again across the whole width of planet earth.[83]

When we hear the word enlightenment and the associated experience of oneness, we automatically think of Eastern religions and sayings such as: 'They call it Indra, Mitra, Varuna, Agni, and it is the heavenly bird that flies. The wise speak of what is one in many ways'.[84] But that this experience is very much universal is something we can see, for instance, in a poem originating from the Celtic tradition of Ireland, expressing this same oneness so beautifully. It is attributed to Amergin, who lived around 100 *BCE*:

I am the wind which breathes upon the sea,
I am the wave of the ocean,
I am the murmur of the billows,
I am the ox of the seven combats,
I am the vulture upon the rocks,
I am a beam of the sun,
I am the fairest of plants,
I am the wild boar in valour,
I am a salmon in water,
I am a lake in the plain,
I am a word of knowledge,
I am the point of the lance in battle,
I am the God who created the fire in the head.[85]

Indeed, one of the worst things that happened to Christianity in the West was that at the Synod of Whitby (664 *CE*), the Celtic, much more vertically oriented, form of Christianity was suppressed by the much better (horizontally) organised Roman version. Ivan Selman makes the valid point that this change in orientation could well be at the root of the ongoing emptying of our churches: 'The Celtic way may speak to those disillusioned by an over-institutionalised and over-intellectualised Christianity in our time'.[86] And the RC priest Victor White is so honest—when writing (with Vatican Imprimatur) about a Gnostic revival— as to state: 'The passionate interest in these movements arises undoubtedly from psychic energy which can no longer be invested in obsolete forms of religion...'[87]

Obviously some people have the awareness that they are part of a greater whole spontaneously, and because their remarks resonated with some of the people around them, they often became the founders of the various religions. Like Muhammad: 'He who knows himself, knows his Lord,' and Jesus realising: 'I and the Father are One'.[88] When Jesus was attacked about this statement, he referred to the Old Testamental Psalm 82: 'I have said ye are gods; and all of you are children of the most High'.[89]

Or take the Sufi mystic Mansur al-Hallaj, darting out of his house and shouting, 'I am Allah!' and like Jesus, being rewarded for this profound insight by being tortured and executed. Meister Eckhart escaped a similar fate by dying just in time before the 'Holy' Inquisition could lay its bloody hands on him. One of his sins was to express his experience of oneness as 'God is the same One that I am'—and on a wider scale: 'Everything that is in the Godhead is one, and is not to be spoken of'. He also claimed that God is not good 'for what is good can grow better, what can grow better can grow best'. Therefore he rather used the expression 'Godhead' instead of 'God' for the ultimate source of all being.[90]

Although ending up incarcerated, George Fox fortunately lived in less drastic times, because when he was asked by the magistrate in Carlisle, 'Are you a son of God?', he replied with a firm 'Yes', and, although imprisoned, he lived to spread his message. A modern saint, Sai Baba made it quite clear that: 'Yes, I am God. And you too are God. The only difference between you and me is that while I am aware of it, you are completely unaware'. And little Anna explained this vertical oneness to the much older Fynn by using a representation from his own electronic engineering hobby.[91] In his lovely little book, *Mister God this is Anna*, Fynn describes how he had been building a radio but when he switched it on it did not work as expected. With Anna looking over his shoulder, he tried to find the fault. First he measured voltages at different points around an electrical circuit and confirmed his suspicion of which component was defective by opening the circuit, and measuring the current inside it. That confirmed his diagnosis and by replacing the defective component, made the radio play happily. But Anna wanted him to put the faulty component back in, and repeat the procedure explaining to her how he had reached his conclusion.

At two o'clock in the morning she woke him up exclaiming that what he had been doing with the radio was just 'like church and Mister God'. But because today hardly anybody repairs radios anymore, I have modified Fynn's radio circuit into a chain of

143

Christmas tree lights. They are of different shapes and colours and are connected in series to the electrical mains socket as sketched in figure 6.5 below.

Figure 6.5 Christmas tree lights

The lights represent the different religions, and as with Fynn's radio, going around the circuit with a voltmeter you read different (horizontal) values. Anna explains that this corresponds with people 'when they go to church, '... measure Mister God from the outside...' adding, 'They don't get inside and measure Mister God'. And Fynn comments 'As a supposed Christian you can stand outside and measure Mister God. The meter doesn't read voltages, it reads 'Loving Kindness, All-powerful, Omnipotent, etc'.

But Anna insists, 'That's like people in church—they keep outside and they ought to go inside'. So now the meter is switched to read current and is put in series with the lights, measuring the current that is going through all of them. Fynn asks, 'So if I get into the circuit and measure Mister God that way, then I'm a real Christian?' Anna waggles her head explaining that he might as well be a Sikh or a Jew, because '... it don't matter, if you measure Mister God from the inside'. Then you discover that: 'you're like a bit of Mister God'.

Although we will never know in Fynn's writings where Anna ends and he begins, Fynn later revealed that this episode had been of great significance to him. By using the language of his radio building hobby, Anna communicated to Fynn the so essential truth that we are all waves on the same transcendental ocean. And that is of course the same message that the mystics of all traditions have been expressing through the ages.

We do indeed know that, irrespective of the many different traditions of mankind, there have always been people expressing this so important message. Krishnamurti is very much on the same wavelength, explaining why he resisted the pressure and did not found a 'church' himself: 'I felt profoundly that there is no fixed programme through which truth can be delivered. Truth is a pathless land. No religion can lead us to spirituality or to freedom. Religions are as much a cause of bondage as anything. They can only offer us a religion of the prison or the cage. To walk free we have to throw away all crutches. Religions are nothing but the vested interests of organised belief, separating and dividing people. Religions are essentially based on fear. When I realised this, as clear as daylight, I said to myself: if this is so, then I cannot lead a religious order myself'.[92]

Or take these words from Matthew Fox stressing the experiential side of our search: 'It is essential to remember that *Spirituality is praxis*, the praxis of religion. So much of religion in overdeveloped countries is in books, buildings, academic institutions, degrees, sermons, and words. While learning is certainly essential to healthy religion, it is no substitute for praxis. *Thinking* about God is no substitute for *tasting* God, and *talking* about God is no substitute for giving people ways of *experiencing* God'.[93]

Translated into our model, all this expresses in different ways that, although we are individual waves, we are very much part of the ocean of the beyond; of which we all are a part and from which we derive our life energy. As mentioned before, the source of that energy is 'located' at the 'bottom' of the ocean. And in many religions we can recognise our basic model of a source (1), radiating an energy flow (2), which expresses itself in our spacetime realm in all that we see around us (3). We should not be confused by the fact that such a widely varying language to express the same basic message is used, and I will illustrate this shared model with the aid of table 6.1 below.

Source	Energy flow	Manifestation	Tradition
sun	solar radiation	warmth/light/nature	physics
Ra	Ka	Thoth/Ma'at	Egypt
Tao	Ch'i/Ki	ten thousand things	China
Brahman	Sarasvati	Shiva/Vishnu	Hindu
Shiva/Vishnu	Parvati/Laksmi	world	Hindu
Sat	Aum	Tat	Hindu [94]
The Mother	Aluna	world	Kogi Indian [95]
Yahweh	Ruach	Shekinah/world	Judaism
Ein Sof	Or Ein Sof	world	Kabbala (Luria)
Buddha	Law	Monk	Buddhism [96]
Father [97]	Holy Spirit [98]	Son	Christianity
Sun	gravity	[world]	Keppler
Pleroma	Abraxas	creation	Gnostics / Jung
Self	ego-Self axis	ego	Edinger
battery	current	voltage	Anna
generator	current	light/power	electrical

Table 6.1 Similar imagery in very different traditions

What I have listed there has to be taken for indication only, as especially in the Hindu tradition there are many variations, for instance depending on whether you consider Shiva, Vishnu, or another deity as the most important one. All over our planet we also encounter a 'sacred impersonal force' going under many different names.[99] It is best known as the Polynesian *mana*, which—when the cradle of mankind is indeed in Africa—might well be predated by the African concepts of *nyama* or *ashé*, the origins of which are hidden in a prehistoric traditional wisdom of tribal Elders.[100] And I can underline this observation with a quotation from Voltaire: 'I do not believe that there is among us a single system which is not to be found among the ancients. The materials of all our modern edifices are taken from the wreck of antiquity'.[101]

It is interesting to note that in the Gnostic tradition, God is described as Father, Mother and Son, alluding to the importance of the feminine in that tradition.[102] And that *Ch'i*, *Ruach*, *Nafs* and *Spirit* all translate as 'breath', underlining the life-giving character of the vertical energy flow.[103] Of course, many other expression could be added to the list, such as the Hindu *Devi*, derived from the Sanskrit for 'to shine', or Shakti personifying 'sacred energy'. Also Schoppenhauer's 'will', Harold Saxon Burr's 'vital field' and Bergson's *élan vital* (life force) are all different expression for the same vertical energy flow.[104]

Holger Kalweit in his interesting book, *Shamans, Healers, and Medicine Men* illustrates our ignorance of tribal wisdom with many examples, and writes: 'Each tribe has its own concept of this universal energy. Pacific peoples call it *mana* ...' He goes on to list well over twenty different names from all over the planet for this vertical energy flow.[105] And Jung describes in one of his visions: 'That the green gold is the living quality which the alchemists saw not only in man but also in organic nature. It is an expression of the life-spirit, the *anima mundi* or *filius macrocosmi*, the Anthropos who animates the whole cosmos'.[106]

While Raymond Hostie points out: 'In a special chapter of his *Contributions to Analytical Psychology*, Jung gives a list of the many different words used by primitive people in different continents—*wakanda* (Dakotas), *oki* (Iroquois), *manitou*, (Alonquins), *wong* (Gold Coast), *chirunga* (North Australia), *mana* (Melanesia), etc.—to signify a force that manifests itself in both living and inanimate objects'.[107]

In figure 6.6 I have illustrated this concept of source, transmission and manifestation with concepts from the ancient Chinese tradition.

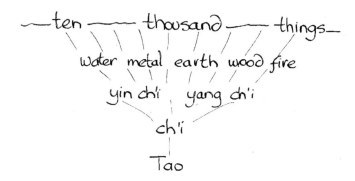

Figure 6.6 Source, transmission and manifestation

For the source, many names can be recognised as well; Teilhard de Chardin's 'Omega', Plato's 'Master-Craftsman', and Hinduism's 'Brahman' come to mind; the latter being the source of the lesser gods such as Indra, Mitra, Varuna, Agni; or Chronos, Zeus, Hera and the rest of the extensive Hindu and Greek pantheons. The Buddha refused to be drawn into describing the One, yet in Buddhism we read of 'the Unborn, Unoriginated, Unconditioned'. Later on in this tradition, we read of 'Adi-Buddha, Dharmakaya, Sunyata, Mind-Only and the Essence of Pure Mind (or No-Mind)'.[108]

But Anne Bancroft when people ask her, 'Are you a Buddhist?', makes the insignificance of surface definitions in her reply very clear: 'And I usually say yes, because in many ways I am a Buddhist, in that I have found the Buddha's teaching immeasurably helpful, understanding, compassionate and wise. But in my heart of hearts I think I remain uncommitted to any 'ism' or religion, because I know that the truth and the splendour transcends them all'.[109] While Alan Watts puts Buddhism's relation to Hinduism very concisely: 'Buddhism is Hinduism stripped for export'.[110]

To see the role of the three persons of the Trinity fitting in so well in the table above makes much more sense than the representation of the Trinity as three bearded men which I once saw on one of the sides of an early Christian sarcophagus.[111] I am convinced that in the *'filioque'* dispute between the Roman and Eastern Orthodox branches of Catholicism, the Orthodox position—rather than the Roman one of adopting ancient pagan ideas to elevate the Son to the level of the Father—is right.[112] And that Isaac Newton was on the same wavelength in this argument can be found in the writings of his biographer John Maynard Keynes: 'He [Newton] was persuaded that the revealed documents gave no support to the Trinitarian doctrines which were due to later falsifications. The revealed God was one God. But this was a dreadful secret which Newton was at desperate pains to conceal all his life'.

Even in the gospels, which have most likely been doctored to fit the doctrines of the early church, Jesus assumes nowhere a position which makes him unique and on a different level to that of his followers.[113] Yes, he is reported to have said, 'I and the Father are one', but the same New Testament also reveals 'We are God's children',[114] or 'I said, you are gods'.[115] And I could give many more similar examples.[116] Apart from the examples of Fox and Sai Baba that I gave a few pages earlier, many others have expressed that same experience of oneness as well; take my sixteenth century countryman Ruysbroeck, for example: 'We can speak no more of Father, Son and Holy Spirit, nor of any creature, but only of one Being, which is the very substance of the Divine Persons. There were we all one before our creation, for this is our super-essence. There the Godhead is in simple essence without activity'.[117]

Just a few more illustrations how the common vertical message is expressed in different traditions: Jesus is reported to have said, 'I am the way, the truth, and the life: no man comes to the Father, but by me', and Sri Krishna, 'I am the goal of the wise man and I am the way', and finally the Buddha: 'You are my children, I am your father; through me you have been released from your sufferings. I myself having reached the other shore, help others to cross the stream; I myself having attained salvation, am a saviour of others...'[118]

And scholars have discovered ancient legends all over the world of 'virgins giving birth to heroes who die and are resurrected. India is chock-full of such tales...'; while even, in the Aztec version of this same legend, 'one of the [Saviors] symbols was a cross'.[119]

We humbly have to accept the validity and wisdom of other paths, and here again we can learn so much from other traditions, even those who we in our arrogant ignorance call 'primitive'. Take for example the American Indian's wisdom so movingly collected by T. C. McLuhan in *Touch the Earth;* or on a much wider planetary scale in her *The Way of the Earth.* Matthew Fox confirms this experience and relates the following moving story: 'Recently I met a young Jesuit priest in Brazil who has been working with the tribes of the Amazon for two years. When I asked him what he had learned from them, he replied without hesitation, "Joy. They experience more joy in a day that we do in a year. And they don't live as long or have as much as we do."'[120] And as far back as 1676 a Red Indian chief, speaking to a group of French captains, expressed a similar fact: 'Learn now, my brother once for all, because I must open to thee my heart: there is no Indian who does not consider himself infinitely more happy and more powerful than the French'.[121]

This fact was not long ago confirmed by Schumacher, who—when sent to Burma to advise the government on economic development in accordance with our Western model—could not help noticing how much more relaxed and happy the people passing his office window were compared to those in a Western city. He wrote to his wife: "Even some of the Americans here say: 'How can we help them, when they are so much happier and nicer than we are ourselves?'"[122] We should indeed learn from them rather than trying to convert them to our Western ways. These kinds of experiences contributed to Schumacher becoming the advocate for 'Small is Beautiful', for which he is known so well. His insights are fully supported by recent research reported on by Michael Wiederman, detailing that: '... the buying power of the average American had tripled since 1950. So were Americans three times happier in 2000 than fifty years earlier? ... Despite being far better off financially than previous generations, we are no happier. In fact, young Americans are more anxious than in the past. ... The average American child in the 1980s reported more anxiety than child psychiatric patients of the 1950s'.[123]

It would indeed have been much better for the state the world is in, if we had been taught in our Western schools the wisdom that is available from other cultures; instead of us forcing our bad habits upon them. There are some revealing crime statistics collected in the nineteenth century in India ('hence before the levelling influence of modern communication media and violent computer games'), which shows that the crime rate of Muslims was three times lower, of Hindus nearly five times and of Buddhists nearly fourteen times lower than that of Europeans.[124] These statistics were reprinted in the leading Roman Catholic organ in Britain, *The Tablet*, with the honest comment: 'The last item is a magnificent tribute to the exalted purity of Buddhism... It appears from these figures that while we effect a very marked deterioration in the natives by converting them to our creed, their natural standard of morality is so high that, however much we Christianize them, we cannot succeed in making them altogether as bad as ourselves'.[125]

Because of my own childhood experience (chapter 2), I very much like Red Jacket's reaction to the missionaries' threats of hell: 'The Great Spirit will not punish us for what we do not know'. And he responded to a missionary who was eager to 'spread the Word' to his American Indian people as follows: 'Brother, you say there is but one way to worship and serve the Great Spirit. If there is but one religion, why do you white people differ so much about it? Why not all agree, as you can all read the book? ... We never quarrel about religion, because it is a matter which concerns each man and the Great Spirit. ... Brother we have been told that you have been preaching to the white people in this place. These people are our neighbors: We are acquainted with them. We will wait a little and see what effect your preaching has upon them. If we find it does them good, makes them honest and less disposed to cheat Indians, we will consider again of what you have said'.[126] After Red Jacket had made this statement, the missionary Cram refused to shake hands with him because 'there was no fellowship between the religion of God and the Devil'. Whereupon Red Jacket 'smiled and retired peacefully'.

Or take Eastern religious teachers, such as Swami Prabhavananda explaining that 'Vedanta ... teaches that all religions are true inasmuch as they lead to one and the same goal—God-realization'.[127] In his turn he quotes Swami Vivekananda who explains: 'Two ways are open to us—the way of the ignorant, who think that there is only one way to truth and that the rest are wrong—and the way of the wise, who admit that, according to our mental constitution or the plane of existence in which we are, duty and morality may vary'.[128] And that these insights are part of ancient Chinese wisdom as well, we can see from this dialogue attributed to Hui Hai:

Question: Do Confucianism, Taoism and Buddhism really amount to one doctrine or three? Answer: Employed by men of great capacity, they are the same. As understood by men of limited intellect, they differ. All of them spring forth from the functioning of the one self-nature.[129]

The ancient Hindu scriptures also underline this theme, that 'there are many faiths but only one religion'. Take this from the Svetasvatara Upanishad, for example:

Thou, Lord God, bestoweth all blessing, ...
Of all religions thou art the source. ...
The source of all scriptures thou art,
And the source of all creeds.[130]

As mentioned earlier, Peterson's book—from which I took this quotation—is a treasure trove of quotations very much in support of the theme of my book. His book is well organised and has many tables illustrating the common message and wisdom of various religions. Reading his book will also correct any misinformation such as I was subjected to during my schooldays about, for instance, Islam; which—when compared with the widespread misunderstanding about its teachings—is in its writings a paragon of tolerance. Take this from the Hadith for example: 'Muhammad was asked to curse the infidels, and He answered: "I was not sent to curse the infidels but to have mercy on mankind."' [131]

As we saw in the Psychology and Art sections above, wisdom seems now to flow from East to West, as already acknowledged by Schopenhauer: 'In India our religions will never take root. The ancient wisdom of the human race will not be displaced by what happened in Galilee. On the contrary, Indian philosophy streams back to Europe, and will produce a fundamental change in our knowledge and thought'.[132] And I am in complete support of Neale Donald Walsch who has God say in his book *The New Revelations*: 'No path is more direct than any other path. No religion is the "one true religion," no people are "the chosen people," and no prophet is "the greatest prophet"'.[133]

But we have to be very clear in our own minds about the fact that—however much we are ourselves convinced of the truth of the vertical message—we cannot push it down people's throats; only when they are ready for it will the message arrive. Swami Brahmananda used to say: 'How many are ready? Yes, many people come to us. We have the treasure to give them. But they only want potatoes, onions and eggplants!'[134]

However, while on our life's search for meaning, we have to realise that we can only try to create the conditions facilitating the experience that we are one already. John Templeton expresses this oneness as: 'The idea that an individual can find God is terribly self-centered. It is like a wave thinking it can find the sea'. And also: 'The question is not is there a God, but is there anything else except God? God is everyone and each of us is a little bit'.[135]

For those who have difficulty with the word 'God', take John Tillich's advice: 'If that word [God] has not much meaning for you, translate it, and speak of the depths of your life, of the source of your being, of your ultimate concern, of what you take seriously without any reservation. Perhaps, in order to do so, you must forget everything traditional that you have learned about God, perhaps even that word itself'.[136]

Indeed, we are all waves on the same ocean and the aim of all religions should be to teach us how to reconnect with the one source of all being, and love the other waves as ourselves. I deliberately wrote 'should' because what we see around us is often a far cry away from that important objective. Deepak Chopra expressed this basic requirement in the same vein: 'Loving another person is not separate from loving God. One is a single wave, the other is the ocean'.[137]

While our local squire, Richard Acland, expressed this common purpose as: 'Allah and Jahweh and Gautama Buddha are all on the same side as Jesus against the brash materialism, the arid intellectualism and the rampant individualism of our day'.[138] And already Meister Eckhart warned: 'He who seeks God under settled forms lays hold of the form while missing the God within'.[139]

Every religious teacher has put up a signpost indicating the direction to follow; but instead of doing that, we are glorifying the signpost itself and building cathedrals, temples and organisations around it. We see over and over again that a spiritual guide opens up a vertical pathway and gets followers; but that as soon as the founder has died, his/her followers start to organise the movement horizontally. They often start to bicker amongst themselves with the predictable result of fracturing the body of followers, and clearly corrupting the original message of oneness. St Bonaventura expressed in his way, that the only path to follow is the inner (vertical) one, rather than staying (horizontally) on the outside: 'Love knocks and enters, but knowledge stands without'.

For me the teachings of Jesus are very simply an admonition to give priority to vertical pursuits; he called the vertical dimension the *kingdom of Heaven,* or *the kingdom of God.* His most important advice is to 'seek ye first the kingdom of God'.[140] Then he explains that this cannot be found in the horizontal dimension because this 'kingdom is not of this world',[141] and finally that 'the kingdom of God is within you'.[142] His saying to his disciples: 'Because it is given unto you to know the mysteries of the kingdom of heaven',[143] can in my view very well be interpreted that he had taught them how to open their vertical channel, so that they 'knew' the reality of the vertical dimension from personal experience. And this personal experience is the only explanation for inciting them to spread the message of the 'good news' so widely in such as short time.

That this 'kingdom is not of the world' implies that we will never find the goal of life in the glitter and glamour of horizontal pursuits such as status, titles and possessions. Stephen Levine mentions a line in a song—'I've not seen one rich man in a thousand with a satisfied mind'.[144] While Deepak Chopra puts the reason for their vain pursuits in sharp focus: 'Although men may trivialize the beauty issue as female vanity, their own huge expenditures on sports cars, designer golf clubs, and power suits is a product of the same insecurity'.[145]

Indeed, the absurdity of shirts with the labels of their expensive makers on the outside, sunglasses or watches costing a fortune, driving around in an expensive car or advertising your material wealth in other ways, should be a matter of embarrassment and shame rather than of misplaced pride. In fact, it only exhibits glaringly one's unhappiness and insecurity, which one is trying in vain to hide behind a glittering exterior. Albert Einstein expresses the same message as follows: 'Possessions, outward success, publicity, luxury—to me these have always been contemptible'. While Veblen Thorstein labelled this behaviour as: 'conspicuous consumption'.[146]

Again, all this is nothing new, take for example this quotation of Celsus, living in Alexandria at the end of the second century *CE*, in his turn quoting Jesus: "It is easier for a camel to go through the eye of a needle than for a rich man to enter the kingdom of God." Yet we know that Plato expressed this very idea in a purer form when he said: "It is impossible for an exceptionally good man to be exceptionally rich."[147] While that great soul Mohandas Gandhi expressed a similar teaching in his candid way: 'Live simply so that others may simply live'.[148]

That all this is not just an interesting theory far removed from real life, was illustrated by a successful business acquaintance telling me that in his field he had done everything to reach the top. But when he finally attained his aim of reaching that goal, he discovered there was, in his words 'no view at the top', and as a consequence had a complete nervous breakdown and had to be nursed back to sanity by his caring wife. I met him after he had sold everything and had settled for a less challenging life.

It would indeed be easy to make a list of rich/unhappy people, and if people trust you sufficiently to tell you their stories, you will often discover that your postman or fireman has deliberately chosen their job after e.g. a glittering but unnerving career in the City. Indeed, the essential message—that inner exploration should have absolute priority above everything else—has through the ages been expounded by every spiritual teacher. Take this saying attributed to Muhammad for example: 'God doesn't look upon your clothes and appearances but upon your heart and thoughts'.

Completely at odds with these teachings and those of Jesus, the church did not only take over so many of the older pagan customs, such as simply renaming the Vestal virgins as 'Brides of Christ' (nuns); but even taking over the glamorous frontage with which many of these ancient faiths impressed the crowds. Take for instance the pomp and circumstance the poor Pope is subjected to, even to the extent of having the title of the ancient Roman pagan high priest 'Pontifex Maximus' added to the collection of titles behind his name, as you can see on many buildings and monuments in and around Rome. This link is pointed out by W. Y. Evans-Wentz writing that there is not only a 'remarkable parallelism ... between the texts of the *New Testament* and the texts of the Buddhist Canon', but he also gives an extended list of 'the survival in modern Christian churches of the symbolism of paganism'.[149]

My God, how far is all this pomp and circumstance removed from the profound but simple teachings of that carpenter's son from Galilee. Although I have no idea how well Sai Baba can handle hammer and chisel, I like what Hazel Courteney reports him saying—that 'hands that work are holier than lips that pray'. She adds, 'He is not decrying prayer—merely saying that in many cases actions speak louder than words'.[150] Also very much to my liking is what the local vicar called himself, signing a card warning people not to throw certain items into the toilet (in a cottage we once rented from him) with: 'John—Loo cleaning executive'.

Emmet Fox is very much on my wavelength as well, writing: 'Perfectly sincere men, for example, have appointed themselves Christian leaders, with the most imposing and pretentious titles, and then clothed themselves in elaborate and gorgeous vestments the better to impress the people, in spite of the fact that their Master, in the plainest language, strictly charged his followers that they must do nothing of the kind. "But be not ye called Rabbi: for one is your Master, even Christ; and all ye are brethren." (Matt. 23: 8)'[151]

Of course it is so much easier to indulge in highly intellectual debates of who is right and who is wrong, which is what so much of theology is committed to, rather than finding ways to open up internally. Raymond Moody writes of people who have had a life changing near-death experience (NDE) that: 'An NDE almost always leads to spiritual curiosity. Many NDEers study and accept the spiritual teachings of the great religious thinkers. However this doesn't mean that they become pillars of the local church. To the contrary, they tend to abandon religious doctrine purely for the sake of doctrine'.[152] And on the following page he quotes one of his NDE cases as saying: 'A lot of people I know are going to be surprised when they find out that the Lord isn't interested in theology'. While further on in his book he concludes: 'People who undergo an NDE come out of it saying that religion concerns your ability to love—not doctrines and denominations'.[153]

Carl Jung describes what he experienced with his father, who was a well-educated minister of the church: 'Once I heard him praying. He struggled desperately to keep his faith. I was shaken and outraged at once, because I saw how hopelessly he was entrapped by the Church and its theological thinking. They had blocked all avenues by which he might have reached God directly, and then faithlessly abandoned him'.[154]

In this respect we can again learn so much about what is really important in life from what not long ago we used to dismiss as 'primitive people'. Take Chief Joseph of the Nez Percés and his reaction to the proposal to have schools for his people:

"Why do you not want schools?" the commissioner asked
"They will teach us to have churches," Joseph answered.
"Do you not want churches?"
"No, we do not want churches."
"Why do you not want churches?"
"They will teach us to quarrel about God," Joseph said. "We do not want to learn that. We may quarrel with men sometimes about things on this earth, but we never quarrel about God. We do not want to learn that."[155]

Apart from teaching the intricacies of dogmas and regulations (see e.g. chapter 9 on the Article 31 controversy in the church of my childhood), one Christian missionary, instead of standing up for the scandalous violation of the Indians' rights, even supported that violation by expressing that 'what the Indians needed is less land and more Christianity', and that is indeed what happened[156]

This fact has been expressed similarly in various traditions, but here I will quote Desmond Tutu, because he being a Christian archbishop amplifies the relevance of his statement: 'When the missionaries came to Africa they had the Bible and we had the land. They said "let us pray," we closed our eyes. When we opened them we had the Bible and they had the land'.[157]

Although we can have some sympathy for Karl Marx's well known (out of context) remark that '[Religion] is the opium of the people,' and that 'The abolition of religion as the illusory happiness of the people is at the same time the demand for their real happiness,' even a committed scientist as T. H. Huxley (Darwin's bulldog), stressed that 'a deep sense of religion' is 'compatible with the entire absence of theology'.[158] And that is the same wisdom that Shankara taught in India many centuries earlier: 'When a man follows the way of the world, or the way of the flesh, or the way of tradition (i.e. when he believes in religious rites and the letter of the scriptures, as though they were intrinsically sacred), knowledge of Reality cannot arise in him'.[159]

Herbert Benson is right to point to the delicate balancing act the churches are involved in: 'Many mainstream religious denominations also walk a kind of narrow theological balancing beam, invoking and enjoying the presence of God while associating passionate or transcendent spiritual experiences with cults, extremists and hippies. Rather than enjoying the idea of a transcendent and relatively unknowable God—a being that defies exact description but nevertheless feels close to us, is good for us and for humanity—we are zealous in our attempts to pin personal, identifiable traits on God'.[160]

Every religion is 'right' but do not judge it intellectually from without and get stuck in its metaphoric aspects; see these as poetry (vertical) rather than prose (horizontal). Remember that the message is to 'seek and you shall find' within. The intellect (head) is fine but it should be guided by love (the heart), or in other words: the horizontal should be subject to the vertical. Yes, I do very much realise that there has to be bread on the table, but we should not make material welfare our prime concern. We expect our governments to deliver continuous economic growth, but a simple calculation will demonstrate that this is an impossible goal. As an economist, Schumacher warned that we live by spending our planet's capital rather than living of its interest, and as everyone knows that can only end in bankruptcy. Especially so, when we realise how high the price of our wealth is for the rest of the planet. Many years ago Gandhi warned us: 'There is enough on this planet for everyone's need, but not for everyone's greed'.

If experiencing the 'oceanic feeling' of the oneness of the vertical dimension was the basic message of the founders of the many religions, and if that message is not obvious anymore, what went wrong? I will explore this issue further in chapter 9, but here are just a few remarks. As already indicated, because the founders themselves radiated this 'experience of oneness', they attracted followers, but when their number became significant, the horizontal organisers and administrators took over. Alan Watts summarises this process concisely: '... the medicine of the discipline becomes a diet, the cure an addiction, and the raft a houseboat. In this manner, a way of liberation turns into just another social institution and dies of respectability'.[161] And later in the same book he writes in a similar vein: 'For when we have Eros dominated by reason instead of Eros expressing itself with reason, we create a culture that is simply against life, in which the human organism has to submit more and more to the needs of mechanical organization ...'[162]

Christmas Humphreys stresses that Buddhism is very much a 'do it yourself' way of life, i.e. you have to explore the path yourself: 'It is a Buddhist commonplace that none can enlighten another, for 'even Buddhas do but point the Way'.[163] And he keeps on hammering home the paramount message that '... the answer lies within, and nowhere else. Here, and only here, in the dismal fog of our private thoughts and feelings, hopes and beliefs, social habits and present set of values, will the truth be found. Not in the mouths of self-proclaimed Swamis, gurus or the textbooks of untested thought, but within, in the deep thoughts, feelings and intuitions of odd moments of the day or in the quiet hour of prayer or meditation'.[164] And he accentuates a very important point: 'Again, the forms of ceremony and methods of meditation become fixed and traditional. What is worse, they acquire for their followers that 'authority' which the Buddha himself, in the *Kalama Sutta* of the Pali Canon, so strongly condemned'.[165]

Indeed, the Buddha kept stressing the message that personal experience is the only way: 'Only when you know for yourselves ... they produce positive benefits and happiness'. What the result is, when we focus on the organisation instead of on the message, is vividly expressed in the *Gospel of Thomas* : 'He said: "Lord there are many around the well, but none in the well"'.

Freud's diagnosis was that 'Religion is comparable to a childhood neurosis' and dismissed it intellectually because '... these ancestors of ours were far more ignorant than we; they believed in things we could not possibly accept to-day; so the possibility occurs that religious doctrines may also be in this category'.[166]

That is the reason why I have deliberately only scraped at the horizontal surface of the religions I mentioned. As my father tried to explain to me a very long time ago, their essence lies in the vertical dimension (see chapter 9). And again someone from the East—Deepak Chopra—puts this in sharp focus: '... spirituality is a domain of awareness where we can experience our universal nature; that if we want to truly understand the divine then we have to go beyond the boundaries set up by traditional religions because religion has generated more conflict, more anguish, more killings, more ethno-centric behaviour, more ethnic-cleansing, more violence than any other institution'.[167]

So I do hope that I have—with these many examples—made the point not to consider your religious faith to be the goal, but rather as a means to a priceless end. The essential message of all religions is to focus on, and how to open up, our inner channel. Some people are obviously born with their vertical channel open, but our society will do its utmost to make them close up and conform to its horizontal dictates. But as we have seen, fortunately there have always been people proclaiming a different message, and when we have found that inner path into the kingdom, there is no need anymore for believing, *because then you know*! In a BBC TV interview in the 1950s, Jung was asked by John Freeman whether he believed in God. His reply was: 'No, I do not believe, [long pause] I *know* that he exists'. And as religion should basically be an experimental pursuit, trying to make it academically respectable is missing the whole point. Peter Spink warns: "The fervent propagation of 'truth' thus becomes the great hindrance and substitution for true learning. Indeed, it makes understanding impossible for it ignores the fundamental requirement of all who would come to a knowledge of the truth, that is the necessity for discovering first of all the 'How of learning'".[168] And further on in the same book from which I took this quotation, we find: "It is from this morass of self-deception where teaching is equated with indoctrination and where learning has become mere intellectual acquisitiveness that modern spiritual man longs to be extricated. Only then can he receive his spiritual heritage and know 'the secrets of the Kingdom of God'".[169]

Indeed, religion instead of desperately trying to become academically respectable should be totally focused on finding that light within. In the *Tibetan Book of the Dead* it is explained that we should be beacons of the 'Radiance of the Clear Light of Pure Reality', while Gabriel Marcel emphasises: '... we all have to radiate this light for the benefit of each other, while remembering that our role consists above all and perhaps exclusively in not presenting any obstacle to its passage *through us*'.[170]

Testimony that that message is indeed a very ancient one can be found in Proverbs 10: 27: 'The spirit of man is the candle of the Lord'. But so often we see no candles anymore, and religion seems to have lost most of its appeal. It is often seen as if it is '... merely an expression of impotence, which man's growing power will overcome. This belief is succinctly expressed in the observation of Bertrand Russell that fishermen with sailboats incline to be religious while those who boast the possession of motorboats divest themselves of religion'.[171]

Religion should be experienced, not studied, or in the words of Happold: 'the only acceptable religion will be a mystical one'.[172] His words find support in Einstein stating, 'The most beautiful and most profound emotion we can experience is the sensation of the mystical'. And also Jung stressed the importance of finding that inner sensation, stating: 'The majority of my patients consisted not of believers but of those who had lost their faith'; and he claimed, that of his patients in the second half of their lives 'every one fell ill because he had lost that which the living religions of every age have given to their followers'.[173]

Pointing to the fact that you can easily lose that essential experience when you organise religion, he also wrote, '[organised] Religion is a defence against a religious experience'.[174] And if religion is blamed for so many of the conflicts and wars that have scourged mankind, remember the words of the American clergyman, Henry Ward Beecher: 'War and intolerance are not the fault of religion. ... They are the fault of those who misuse and distort its truths'.[175] Eric Butterworth underlines this: '... Jesus stressed a spiritual philosophy that is *you* centered. You do not accomplish Jesus' ideal simply by believing things *about* him. You must come to believe about yourself what Jesus believed about himself. [It] is not something to believe ... it is something to do'.[176] And again Jung expressed that same point concisely: 'Belief is no substitute for inner experience'.[177]

The next question is of course what we—who are not so naturally gifted that we know that 'All is One'—should do to gain the experience of that oneness. This will be the theme of the next chapter, but here I would again like to stress as a concise conclusion from the foregoing, that:

Religion is about doing and not about believing!

7 How to open up the 'vertical' dimension

7.1 WHY ARE WE IN NEED OF OPENING UP AT ALL?

The slenderest knowledge that may be obtained of the highest things is more desirable than the most certain knowledge obtained of lesser things.[1]

Thomas Aquinas

There is a fine story about a student who came to a rabbi and said, "In the olden days there were men who saw the face of God. Why don't they any more?" The rabbi replied, "Because nowadays nobody can stoop so low."[2]

Carl G. Jung

Benares is to the East, Mecca to the West; but explore your own heart, for there are both Rama and Allah.[3]

Kabir

In order to understand properly the utterances of the mystic describing his overwhelming mystical experience so, it is said, the scholar must himself have a similar religious experience.[4]

Rudolf Otto

Our society is based on horizontal values and, with a few exceptions[5], our whole education system is geared to deliver products who are well 'adjusted' so that they can function as useful cogs in our so called normal society. As I have mentioned before, in every tradition there have always been people who 'knew' spontaneously that there is another more important pursuit; notably in those populations which we, in our ignorance, often have labelled as primitive and hence in urgent need of our 'civilising' interference. Take, for example this description of seers from the Mayan Popul Vuh, which miraculously escaped the destroying frenzy of Christian priests: '... they saw and instantly they could see far; they succeeded in seeing; they succeeded in knowing all that there is in the world. The things hidden in the distance they saw without first having to move. Great was their wisdom; their sight reached to the forests, the rocks, the lakes, the seas, the mountains and the valleys'.[6] In the language of our model: for these seers it was quite normal to explore beneath the ocean's horizontal surface. Indeed we have to accept that, because of its horizontal outlook, science stands completely helpless in this exploration; which fact Gilbert Wright expressed concisely as: "Science, reasoning, intelligence are but tools that we use to compensate for our lack of 'sight' or 'insight'".[7] And Raynor Johnson expresses the result of this lack of 'sight' or 'insight' thus: 'It will be a misfortune if conservative science remains aloof and indifferent much longer to what can now be regarded as the thoroughly tested and well-established data of para-psychology'.[8]

But before we start searching for people who are spontaneously open to the insights of the vertical dimension, it pays to look at children first. Some of them will convey very wise sayings which they cannot have read or heard about elsewhere but seem to know internally. Jesus is reported to have astounded the scholars of his time when, as a young boy, he discoursed with them in the temple.[9] But even he, who knew that 'I and the Father are one', could be overwhelmed by stressful horizontal events leading to his exclaiming, while hanging on the cross: 'My God why have you abandoned me?'

For me religion is basically feminine, but we can all see around us what happens when the male organisers take over; expressed so pithily by Alfred Loisy as: '... Jesus came preaching the Kingdom of God but what happened was the church'.[10] Therefore, in the previous chapter I have deliberately chosen to mention little Anna in my sampling of the great religious teachers. She is a beautiful illustration of the lesson Jesus taught his disciples when they asked him who the greatest was in the kingdom of Heaven: '... unless you turn around and become like children, you will never enter the kingdom of Heaven'.[11]

Anna was the little battered girl found by the young Fynn in the grimy 1930s Docklands of East London, probably the last place you would expect to find a spiritual teacher. She was the one who helped to open Fynn's eyes, resulting in him writing down her true story for us in *Mister God, this is Anna*.[12] Of course, a girl like Anna ran into serious trouble, not only with her schoolteacher, but with the vicar as well. In a later book Fynn reports on what Anna said to make his 'world stand still': 'Fynn, you have to know much more to be silent than you do to keep talking'.[13] And I am sure she never knew that Ignatius of Antioch had said almost the same thing.[14]

Compare that profound wisdom with the goings on in our world where we are buried under a continuous torrent of so often empty words, and a constant pressure by travel and holiday companies 'to get away from it all'.

There has been a recent upsurge in messages of peace, reportedly coming from psychic children. I am thinking of James Twyman, who as their mouthpiece published the book *Emissary of Love*.[15] Although with Twyman's books it is not clear where fact ends and fiction begins, his message of love is so important that I have mentioned it here.[16] Another possibility for gaining insight is listening to 'wise old people', as I have illustrated above for my own case in chapter 2, and as Fynn experienced with his old schoolteacher John Hodge.

For Fynn, his spending time with Anna was a very helpful and life changing experience indeed. Also his mother was wise, telling him for example: 'Too much learning makes people lose heart'. Important too were the discussions he had with his retired, very rationalistic mathematics teacher John Hodge, who is the "Black Knight' in the title of one of Fynn's later books. Hodge obviously saw something delicately special in the young Fynn, because while Fynn had expected an explosion of anger when he told the atheist Hodge that he intended to go into the Church, to his amazement he did not object.[17] In fact Hodge was so concerned that the young Fynn would loose his openness by studying too much, that Fynn once told me that Hodge forcefully warned him not to go to university, even threatening never to talk to him again if he did.[18]

I was so fortunate to befriend Fynn in his old age. He was a big man with gentle eyes and smile, but was everything but an airy-fairy saintly person. Anna looked straight through his external cover and wrote of him: 'Somtime I think that Fin is an angel. If you want to know the diffrence from a person and an angel I will tell you. An angel is easy to get inside of, and a person is not. Every bit of an angel is inside and every bit of a person is not and most of a person is outside'.[19]

Just to give a little bit of background on the type of man who wrote down Anna's antics, and to stress the point that he was in no way an airy-fairy, gullible character, I will side-track momentarily and spend a paragraph on Fynn.

For outsiders, Fynn was a big, seemingly gruff man, but Emmy told me that he had the eyes of an angel. He liked his fags very much and once told me that I was 'a disgusting man' for not smoking. A recent mishap was that one of his cigarettes had disappeared between his bedding, and the resulting smoke set off the fire alarm system so that the whole care-home—in which he was then living—had to be evacuated. Although he maintained that according to the basic laws of physics, the offending cigarette could never have jumped by itself from his ashtray onto his bed, after this calamity he was not allowed to smoke on his own anymore. The matron also threatened him that he would be frisked to check for contraband cigarettes. With a glint in his eyes he told me that in that case he would cut the pockets out of his trousers, just to see her face when putting her hands into his pockets.

Therefore, when visiting him, my first task always was to get some cigarettes and a lighter from the matron, and I had to promise her that I would stay with him until they were finished. Then we would sit outside, he smoking and me often just being with him. Sometimes we would discuss issues, ranging from radio valves via computers to the fifth dimension, but we hardly ever talked about Anna; I didn't think that was necessary.

After this brief exploration of childlike spontaneous openness to the vertical dimension, for those of us who are not so gifted naturally, I will explore some alternatives below. However, even if you accept the existence of an extra dimension or inner space, you cannot open your inner channel by just talking or reading about it. Although admittedly these preparatory activities could be helpful in finding a recipe, there is no alternative but following that recipe conscientiously.

In the next section I will describe a recipe that has worked for me, but I am fully aware that what worked for me does not necessarily work for you as well; so I repeat that there is really no alternative to experimenting for yourselves. And if that voyage of exploration yields positive results, you will understand the meaning of what William Blake expressed so many years ago:

If the doors of perception were cleansed, everything would be seen as it is, infinite.

7.2 HOW TO OPEN UP

Here is what we will do with man's divinity. We will hide it deep down in man himself, for he will never think to look for it there.[20]

Brahma (in Hindu legend)

Look within; thou art Buddha. [21]

The Voice of Silence

Truth is beyond any limiting concept for it is Infinite - while we may talk about it, we can only comprehend it by living within it. It is to be experienced not discussed.[22]

Baba Dovid Yusuf

Feel your intentions in your heart. Feel not what your mind tells you. Rather than serve the fake gods of your mind, serve your heart, the real God. You will not find God in your intellect. Divine Intelligence is in the heart.[23]

Gary Zukav

Meditation is the royal highway to man's understanding of himself.[24]

W. Y. Evans-Wentz

Meditation should form the basis for action.[25]

The Dalai Lama

In 1976 an article appeared in *Intermediair,* a Dutch tabloid sized cross between *Scientific American* and *New Scientist.*[26]The article dealt with 'Transcendental Meditation' (TM), brought to the West by a middle-aged Indian who looked like an Old Testament prophet and was called Maharishi Mahesh Yogi.[27]The article claimed that by embarking on TM, one could influence one's well being significantly. I found many of the claims very unlikely, but they were backed up by an impressive list of references, several of them in peer reviewed scientific journals.

It also referred to an article in *Scientific American,* which for me had always been a paragon of straight science, and I could simply not imagine it propagating such an (for me) hazy idea like meditation.[28]Wasn't it obvious that you could not change your metabolic rate and other autonomous bodily functions, as the article claimed?[29]At that time I usually read *Scientific American* from cover to cover, but could not remember ever having come across an article about such an airy-fairy subject as meditation (you can only see what you expect to see). So I went to our library searching for the particular issue. The article was indeed there, and reading it made me curious, triggering the desire in me to subject myself to an experiment to see if it really worked. Emmy agreed to go with me, and we booked in for an introductory session after which we decided to go ahead, even if it cost what for a frugal Dutchman seemed like a substantial sum of money.[30]

After initial corrections—because I was such a pusher and had to learn to go with the flow and take things more easily—we became so enthusiastic about its effects that after some time our house became the local TM centre, and I became one of the members of the board of the national TMVV, a TM practitioners support association.[31] Several friends and colleagues (who at that time still took me seriously) followed our example, and for some of them too, it changed their lives very positively.

I can only write about meditation based on my own experiences, so please keep in mind that blind acceptance of what I am writing here won't do you any good whatsoever; and as I have mentioned before, the assignment is to experiment yourself and keep searching until you have found what suits you. Also, the Maharishi's insistence that it is so easy might be true for some, but do not take that as a general truth; we are all very different and have to find our own path. Reginald Ray pointed out that the Buddha fully accepted our differences, and referring to Ringu Tulku, he writes about '... the original teaching of the Buddha that sentient beings have different capacities, propensities, and needs. In response to this situation, the Buddha gave eighty-four thousand different dharmas or types of instruction to address the various situations of beings'.[32]

How much wisdom is expressed in this statement, and how much does it contrast to my own fundamentalist upbringing, where I was indoctrinated that our church was the only one with the correct teachings (see chapters 2 and 9)![33] But the hippy wisdom that 'There are no free rides', applies here as much as anywhere else.[34] So, after having been convinced of the necessity of embarking on a meditation practice yourself, the next question is how to create the conditions beneficial to its routine. The Dalai Lama refers to an ancient sage, Kamalashila, who wrote these very wise words: 'The prerequisites necessary for the development of calm abiding meditation are: to live in a conducive environment, to limit your desires and practice contentment, not being involved in too many activities, maintaining pure moral ethics, and fully eliminating attachment and all other kinds of conceptual thoughts'.[35] And that watching what you eat can also contribute to the process of enlightenment is illustrated by the same sage advising on diet: 'Yogis should at all times avoid fish, meat and so forth, should eat with moderation, and avoid foods that are not conducive to health'.[36]

By practising consistently we may be rewarded with the unforgettable experience of the opening up of a channel to our inner light that will change our outlook on life completely. Ramakrishna was told by his guru: 'You will then find the world of name and form vanishing into nothing, and the puny ego merging into the cosmic consciousness. You will realize your identity with Brahman'.[37]

This identity is concisely expressed in Hinduism as 'Atman is Brahman' which we can translate as: 'The (little) self is the (great) Self', or referring to our ocean model, that the wave is at one with the ocean. Meister Eckhart expressed this same experience in a few more lines: 'As the Godhead is nameless, and all naming is alien to Him, so also the soul is nameless; for it is here the same as God'.[38]

The advice of accepting the importance of personal exploration, which I keep stressing, is also emphasised by the Buddhist Suzuki: 'Personal experience is ... the foundation of Buddhist philosophy. In this sense Buddhism is radical empiricism or experientialism, whatever dialectic later developed to probe the meaning of enlightenment-experience'.[39] And that same message we find in Chinese wisdom as well: 'This truth is to be lived, it is not to be merely pronounced with the mouth...'[40] Or to use the image of the light of the inner 'sun'; the Samaritan Marqah is quoted as saying: 'Respond to the light within you, and it will develop until it is one with the Light'.[41]

The Japanese Masahisa Goi also uses this same 'light' image: 'This caused people's karmic causes to deepen even further, reaching the state where human beings could no longer be awakened to their original divinity unless divine light were radiated through the spaces between their karmic causes'.[42] A similar light representation we encounter in the Middle-Eastern Sufi tradition where the spiritual master—after having made the disciple aware of his state of being and 'Using the sun as a symbol for God, and likening the heart to a mirror'—distinguishes the developmental stages of 'the realisation that the heart is a mirror that does not reflect the sun' via cleaning the mirror of the 'rust of forgetfulness' to the 'acknowledgement that in reality only the sun exists'.[43]

A modern Western exponent of this same wisdom, expressed differently, is Dean Inge, describing the meditation experience as follows: 'Rightly or wrongly (genuine mystics) are convinced that they have been in contact with objective reality, with the supreme spiritual Power behind the world of our surface consciousness. If they are right, this intuition must be a factor in what we believe about reality, it means that reality is spiritual.[44] If such a view is to be expected from the Dean of St Paul's in London, what about the same message coming from a young woman from the other side of our planet, who describes herself as a practical minded 'Aussie Sheila'? She claims: 'The biggest joke of all is the Western world-view that spirituality is a luxury, not a necessity'.[45]

A true spiritual life is immeasurably practical, you don't have to be a staunch churchgoer or an airy-fairy flower power generation hippy to experience its life-changing breakthrough. Read for instance how John Coleman, an espionage agent of the CIA stationed in Bangkok, experienced a supernatural incident, and the effects it had on him when he sought the coolness and quiet of a Buddhist temple. He writes about meditation: 'The fruits of meditation, when it is truly achieved, give one a new lease on life, redouble the individual's capacity for vigorous and creative action by eliminating all obsession with the pursuit of pleasure or the evasion of pain, and indeed *promote* the full enjoyment of life with all its good and bad, its beauty and ugliness. It permits one to act instead of constantly reacting. It frees the mind from the eternal conflict of opposites. Even more, it enhances one's feelings of compassion so that this freedom cannot be used to the detriment of others - and that alone is no small virtue in today's environment'.[46] And to underline what I have stated before, he quotes Krishnamurti, whom he met by chance, and as Krishnamurti was then completely unknown to him, he described him as an 'elderly man' who introduced himself by saying 'I am a sort of philosopher': 'The spoken or written word is not the truth. Truth can only be experienced directly at the moment it happens. Any thought or intellectual projection of the truth is a step away from the truth, sir. ...

No organisation, however old or however recent, can lead a man to truth. It is a hindrance, it can only impede. ... The truth comes from within, by seeing for yourself. ... Then you understand. ... A man is his own salvation and it is only through himself that he will find the truth, not through religions, thoughts or theories, and certainly not through following a leader. Leaders and followers exploit each other and I will have nothing to do with such activities. ... All organised religions are forms of escape, sir. They offer comfort, tell you what to do. If you behave properly you will be rewarded. It is childish. It is a block to understanding'.[47]

But Krishnamurti also cautions us to keep very much in mind that: 'Meditation in which any form of effort is involved ceases to be meditation. It is not an achievement, a thing that is practised daily according to any system or method to gain a desired end'.[48] Further on in Coleman's book, he refers to a book written by Mary Lutyens, in which Krishnamurti dismisses mantra-repeating meditation techniques: 'There are systems of meditation, which give you a word and tell you that if you go on repeating it you will have some extraordinary transcendental experience. This is sheer nonsense. It is a form of self-hypnosis'.[49]But Joel Goldsmith explains more subtly how mantra meditation can be helpful: 'That mind can be attained only in silence, not with words or thoughts, although words and thoughts may be used as a preliminary step in what we know as meditation, which plays a vitally important part in the development of our spiritual life'.[50]

Based on my own experience, I support his view and do think that Krishnamurti, in dismissing from his lofty heights churches, leaders and mantra meditation techniques, is judging far too harshly. Transcendental Meditation (TM) has certainly been of great benefit to me and several others I know of; so therefore I consider it very unfortunate that disenchanted TM teachers (who all committed themselves to confidentiality) have published the entire range of TM 'secrets' on the Internet, where you can indeed find all the mantras and details of other procedures.

Apart from the point of view of academic interest, this does not serve any useful purpose, such as teaching people to meditate. Those who have 'unmasked' TM have completely overlooked the importance of the mystical atmosphere, with its chanting, candles, incense, offerings, etc., deliberately cultivated when one is initiated, using a centuries old 'secret' procedure. All these 'embellishments', and the payment of a substantial sum, contribute greatly to the success of taking the following of a certain pathway for opening up the vertical dimension seriously.[51]And if you want to explore further what is available, an extensive survey of meditation techniques can be found in David Fontana's *Meditator's Handbook*.[52]

Also, the social aspects of choosing a certain pathway should not be overlooked: participating in community activities, whether via a church, temple or mosque, etc., can be experienced as a very helpful supporting environment, especially when going through a rough patch. Furthermore following a leader can make all the difference between being in despair and seeing drugs as the only escape, and being kept on the straight and narrow. To underline that the 'way' can be found in different traditions, Coleman points out that: "The seal of respectability was placed on the Maharishi's mission by no less a figure than the Archbishop of Canterbury, Dr Michael Ramsey. Speaking at Bede Theological College in the North of England, he declared there was a genuine analogy between the Christian forms of prayers and the Oriental meditations 'recently adopted by the Beatles'".[53]

As mentioned already, not only for me, but several others I know personally, a mantra meditation technique can cause enormously beneficial changes in one's life.[54]And these beneficial changes have been reported on in many books as well. Just take for instance the case of Deepak Chopra who—as a modern Indian medical doctor educated along Western lines—came to the insight that 'Modern people in India may regret, and regret very deeply, that the tradition of enlightenment no longer appeals to us'. He learned TM, and not only did it change his stress level significantly, but it also was detrimental for the turnover of his local cigarettes and Scotch whisky traders. He shares with us that 'These few improvements in my life made a dramatic difference out of proportion to the way they sound on paper. I began once again to feel extraordinarily well'.[55]

Therefore—repeating that we are all very different—I have deliberately refrained from giving advice on which method for opening up the vertical channel to follow. And, as mentioned above, according to Krishnamurti I have done everything completely wrong because his advise is not to read books and stay far away from Transcendental Meditation.[56]

Fortunately there are other traditions—accepting that there are people like me—such as Tibetan Buddhism, of which Reginald Ray writes: 'Within Tibetan buddhism there are two major ways in which any individual can follow the Buddhist path: the way of study and the way of meditation'. He then quotes Chökyi Nyima Rinpoche: 'A strong fascination with critical questioning and analyzing prevents one from following the approach of a simple meditator and from gaining an immediate certainty about the profound nature of emptiness, the basic wakefulness that is at the very heart of all the buddhas. Due to these reasons some people find much greater benefit from the analytical approach of a scholar through which doubts and lack of understanding can be gradually cleared away. ... This is one type of approach and it is excellent'.[57]

Thanks, Tibet, for accepting that there is indeed hope for people like me!

For a general survey of meditation techniques, an excellent and well researched book on the effects of meditation is *Timeless Healing* by Herbert Benson—who was told by his colleagues at Harvard that he was risking his career by doing research on the facets of such an unscientific subject as meditation. But whatever we do, he also stresses that 'we should experience life directly instead of blindly following teachings based on the second-hand experiences of others'.[58]And to accentuate again this very important point of personal experience from other traditions, take this quote from the Japanese Suzuki: 'The essentials of Zen doctrine can never be accurately and fully described because they are an experience and not a set of ideas'.

Further on in his book, from which I took this quotation, Reginald Ray quotes from a completely different tradition: 'To us Quakers, creeds, rituals, sacred books, sacramentals, priesthood and religious institutions are nothing without the inner experience of the presence of God'.[59]

To underline that this inner experience is no new idea at all, we find the same message in an ancient text from the *Apocryphon of James* :

> So it is possible
> For you to receive the kingdom of heaven;
> Unless you receive it through direct knowledge
> You will never be able to discover it.[60]

In the same vein Raymond Hostie writes about Carl Jung, quoting a very significant statement from Jung's *Psychology and Alchemy*: 'There is a certain impatience in Jung's retort to the critics who accuse him of being a religious innovator: "With a truly tragic delusion these theologians fail to see that it is not a matter of proving the existence of light, but of blind people who do not know that their eyes could see. It is high time we realized that it is pointless to praise the light and preach it if nobody can see it. It is much more needful to teach people the art of seeing. ... How this is to be done without psychology, that is, without making contact with the psyche, is frankly beyond my comprehension."[61] Hostie explains that Jung regarded dogma only as 'a useful, in fact indispensable, by-product for people who were not in a fit condition to have a direct experience of the numinous'.[62]

To honour again the Far-Eastern tradition, from which we can indeed learn so much, I will quote Swami Vivekananda, making the same point that we are all so different: 'Two ways are left open to us—the way of the ignorant, who think that there is only one way to truth and that all the rest are wrong—and the way of the wise, who admit that, according to our mental constitution or the plane of existence in which we are, duty and morality may vary. The important thing is to know that there are gradations of duty and morality, that the duty of one state of life, in one set of circumstances, will not and cannot be that of another'.[63] And to round this off with a modern herald of the same essential message that knowledge rather than faith is the aim of all spiritual endeavour: when Sathya Sai Baba was asked by someone in his audience whether he was God, he replied, 'The only difference between us is that I know that I am God'.[64]

But like TM, which has come to us from a Far-Eastern Hindu tradition, there have been many other teachers from that same tradition coming to the West. It is easy to drop a few names like: Yogananda, Krishnamurti, Maharishi, Sathya Sai Baba and Bhagwan Shree Rajneesh (Osho).[65] Why don't we seem to have anything comparable rooted nearer to home? A partial answer to that question was given during one of the TM retreats by padre Luchesius Smits, who was then teaching theology at a Roman Catholic university in the South of the Netherlands.

He had become a Capuchin monk when he was eighteen years old, and told us that one of their practices was sitting barefoot in a circle on a wooden floor around a burning candle at three o'clock in the morning. The monks would recite an ancient Latin Psalter, which he knew by heart after a few weeks. Then he told us how during this reciting he had experienced a blissful feeling of oneness, first with his fellow monks and later with all of humanity.

But some years later, someone in Rome decided that the Latin grammar of that ancient Psalter was not up to scratch, and they had to learn a sanitised version, which in its turn was replaced by a Dutch translation, and in the end the whole practice was abandoned. He shared with us that, after learning TM not long ago, he had experienced that same feeling of oneness again, and ended his discourse with the conclusion that various meditation techniques had been very much part of the Christian tradition, but that they had in ignorance been thrown overboard.[66]

Practices such as saying the rosary as a meditation technique come to mind, and in fact its beneficial effect on cardiovascular rhythms has been demonstrated in a recent comparative study.[67]

The English priest, Peter Spink, quoting the editor of *Alternative London*, confirms the above conclusion and also that this throwing overboard in the West, often results in the fact that so many people now search for enlightenment in the East. He writes: 'Many people have glimpsed something beyond, a sort of knowledge that cannot be described in words but is the essence of religion. Somehow Christianity has lost this essence, probably through adapting itself to be acceptable to materialistic trends, but it is still present in Eastern religions, so that is where many seekers are now turning'.[68] All these stories highlight the fact that so many of the participants in the TM retreats I was involved in, were Christians, mostly Roman Catholics, of whom several were ex-priests. Perhaps unconsciously, they were looking for something that they missed in their own tradition after the rationalisations of recent times.

Fortunately these errors are now being corrected by several people. One is the above mentioned Peter Spink, another Dom Bede Griffiths, a Benedictine monk who lived in an Indian ashram wearing the orange dress of a sanyasin;[69] while John Main, another RC monk, initiated a major Christian meditation movement in the West.[70] In one of his many books he defines meditation as: 'Meditation is simply a way of coming to basic healthiness of spirit. It is a state wherein our spirit has room to breathe because it is not assailed and weighed down by trivia or by what is merely material. In this healthy state we are open to ultimate truth and ultimate love. We are summoned beyond many trivia to live our lives, not out of the shallows but at the source of the river of life where the life-stream springs up with power in crystal clarity. The ultimate frontier we are called upon to cross is the frontier of our own identity, the frontier of our own limitation, in order to be one with the All'.[71]

The scientist Rupert Sheldrake, I mentioned earlier, wrote most of his influential book *A New Science of Life* (see chapter 5) in Griffiths' Indian ashram. Another Christian monk, John Teasdale—who wrote *The Mystic Heart*—was not only influenced by Rabbi Gelberman (see chapter 10), but spent time in Bede Griffiths' ashram as well. Within the Christian tradition, the above mentioned John Main has truly initiated an important breakthrough by setting up many meditation centres all over the world, and I will quote in full the answer he gave to the question 'What is the *immediate* objective of saying the mantra?': 'I think the immediate objective is to bring you to silence. This is what most people will experience when they begin to meditate for the first time. Most people find, not everyone, that very early on they come to a most extraordinary silence and peacefulness. But then as they proceed this gives way to a very distracted state of being, and they begin to think during this stage, well, that it is hard, perhaps meditation is not for me. I have no talent for it, all I seem to get now when I meditate is more and more distractions. But I think that is the crucial moment to persevere. The *ultimate* aim of meditation is what motivates you then, and that aim is to bring you to *total* silence. As I've probably said to you before, it has to be a silence that is entirely unself-conscious and so as soon as you realize, consciously, that you are in this silence and that it is very marvellous, you must begin to say your mantra again immediately. That trains you in the generosity of not trying to possess the fruit of your meditation. It is very difficult for people today to accept this teaching of the mantra because most people in our society go into something so that they can experience the experience. Meditation is different from that. It is an entry into pure experience. ... And don't try to make that silence happen ... We must just meditate and say the mantra and when you realize you are not saying it, say it again'.[72] Elsewhere John Main quotes *The Cloud of Unknowing* calling meditation 'the process of one-ing, becoming one'.[73] And I completely agree with him that he keeps on stressing the point that 'The core of the Christian way is experiential not speculative, interior not objective'.[74]

Another exponent of his Benedictine meditation movement is Laurence Freeman, who in his book *Light Within* explains their background and meditation technique.[75] He answers the question 'Why should we meditate *together*?', with: 'The negative answer is clear enough whenever one meets with a religious community in the Church that has stopped praying together. As a spiritual community it has fallen apart, and the isolated, lonely lives of its individual members hold together with one another merely through social or professional bonds'. On the next page he clearly distances himself from the numbers game: 'Such [meditation] communities exert an influence in their social environment far beyond their numerical size. Most meditation groups meeting in parishes, colleges, hospitals, or private homes are healthily small. They become centres of Presence and bring into being the new form of missionary endeavour that Western society now needs: a contemplative mission of Presence'.[76] And to the questions 'How long and how fast?', he replies: '... these are questions we may ask of all journeys except meditation, because they are [horizontal] questions of time and space. Meditation is a [vertical] journey into God...'[77]

Many research programmes have confirmed the benefits of meditation; a recent one was described in *New Scientist* in an article headed, 'If meditation is good, God makes it better'.[78] Reading all these articles and excellent books is fine, but as you must have realised by now that the only way to 'enlightenment' is personal experience; so unless you are born enlightened, there is simply no other way but to perform the meditation experiment yourself, typically mornings and evenings for some twenty to thirty minutes. Freeman states that '... the *practice* of meditation is much more important than the *theory*'.[79] And he stresses that indeed 'Nothing stands between us and our real selves'.[80]

But also do keep very much in mind this gem from the Buddhist tradition: 'Long hours of meditation have their value, but in themselves will no more lead to enlightenment than polishing a tile will turn it into a mirror'.[81] Francis Younghusband reaches the same conclusion in his book, *Modern Mystics*: 'For this experience of the fundamental realities of existence gained in meditation is life itself—not merely the means to it, as is that part of life concerned with bread-winning and the ordinary social amenities. It is of the very essence of life. And for that reason, on an early morning or an evening, on walks or amongst crowds, or during a holiday—whenever or wherever leisure may be found or made—the modern mystic would be wise to resort to meditation'.[82]

The next quote, coming from the Buddhist tradition, appeals to me very much, because it uses an ocean image: 'Thou shalt not separate thy being from BEING, and the rest, but merge the Ocean in the drop, the drop within the Ocean'.[83]

This might be the right moment to concentrate on some practical advice. If you think it cannot possibly work for you, I repeat: just persist for a significant time, don't hop around trying out one method after another without giving each of them a real chance. Here is John Main again: 'But it really is because 'nothing happens' that you are on the right path, the path of simplicity, of poverty, of an empowering surrender'.[84]If you are still worried that 'nothing happens', keep also very much in mind what the author of *The Cloud of Unknowing* said about nothing: 'Who is it that calls it nothing? Surely it is our outer man and not our inner man. Our inner man calls it All'.[85]

Rooted in the Christian tradition, but ignoring all its dogmas and creeds, is the extensive survey of ideas for meditation practices listed by Andrew Harvey in his book *Son of Man*. [86]However, what worked best for many people (including me) is going on a longish (say at least two to three weeks) retreat, preferably in a quiet, beautiful location where you can distance yourself from the daily chores and upsets; so for heaven's sake don't take your mobile phone, iPod or laptop computer with you!

But also be very much aware that meditation can lead to an explosion of 'distressing' from the hidden depths of the unconscious. I remember that a reliable friend told me once that one of the people who was initiated in a TM centre in her town ended up by smashing the place to smithereens. Therefore I will copy the very sensible warning John Snelling (quoting in his turn Ken Wilber) gives at the end of *The Buddhist Handbook* "... only those with a 'more-or-less intact ego' should undertake full Buddhist training, for applying methods like intensive meditation to subjects lacking the necessary ego strength can be disastrous: '... meditation, far from being a cure-all, can be *extremely detrimental* to borderline and narcissistic disorders (simply because the person is desperately attempting to create a strong and viable ego structure, and intensive meditation tends to dissolve what little structure the borderline has)'".

Clearly, meditation should be approached with a certain amount of caution and with proper guidance,[87] but whatever you do, keep very much in mind this wise saying from the Zen tradition that: 'enlightenment is a divine accident, but meditation makes you more accident-prone'. Reginald Ray clarifies: 'Meditation is definitely not healthy for the ego. It is not possible to meditate unless you are more interested in finding out what is going on than in maintaining a particular idea of who you are'.[88]

Just to give a brief survey of different techniques, I will list a few here: attention on breathing; counting breaths; repeating a mantra, varying from the monosyllable ones promulgated by the author of *The Cloud of Unknowing* such as 'God' or 'Love', the two syllable ones often associated with Hindu meditation techniques, to longer ones such as John Main's *'Maranatha'* or the Eastern *'Om mani padme hum'*, etc. *A Comprehensive Guide to Eastern & Western Meditation Techniques* is the subtitle of David Fontana's *The Meditators Handbook*,[96] while Aryeh Kaplan's book *Meditation and Kabbalah*,[90] treats this subject coming from the Jewish tradition. I could easily have listed many more books here, but because I am so very much a 'doer' myself, I have full understanding of the fact that the last word in Chris Griscom's book on our subject is: 'Begin!'[91]

But we also have to keep very much in mind that, although we can create the conditions to facilitate the opening up of the vertical dimension, its actual coming about is beyond our control. Therefore I want to close this section with the profound insight the young woman Miranda MacPherson (Holden) received while meditating in Raman's cave:

Be nothing, do nothing, get nothing, become nothing, seek for nothing, relinquish nothing, be as you are, rest in God.[92]

7.3 MIRACLES ARE POSSIBLE

Before enlightenment, chop wood and carry water,
After enlightenment, chop wood and carry water.

Buddhist saying

The world is large, but in us it is deep as the sea.

Rilke

I can write no more, for everything that I have written seems like straw, by comparison with the things which I have now *seen*, and which have been *revealed* to me.[93]

Thomas Aquinas

The happy man is not he whom the crowd deems happy, namely into whose coffers mighty sums have flowed, but he whose possessions are all in his soul.[94]

Seneca

Calvin had declared that supernatural events happened daily.[95]

Keith Thomas

Why are we not enlightened to start with and do we need to meditate at all, when we are so obviously all children of the One? The simple reason is that, because we are so imprisoned in the bumpy surface layer of the ocean of the beyond, the light of the One can hardly reach us through that frenzy and the thick layer of 'seaweed' below us. On top of this, as the soldier Er explained in Plato's *Republic*: before we incarnate, we have to drink from the 'river of forgetfulness' (see chapter 8). Hence we have forgotten our heritage and the purpose of enlightenment is, as Joel Goldsmith explained '… to be the transparency through which the Light—not we, but the Light—performs Its mighty works, to be the instrument through which the Divine can manifest and express Itself on earth as It does in heaven. We are never the doer; we are never the actor: We are always the vacuum through which Spirit flows. Let us never for a moment believe that by our spiritual endowments we will ever attain personal or spiritual power. There is no room in spiritual living for egotism or for the exercise of personal power'.[96]

A rather drastic way of awakening is the one that has been reported on by many people who have been revived after having been clinically dead, the so-called near-death experience (NDE). Although I will deal with this subject more fully in chapter 8, but because it can also be a means of opening up the vertical dimension, I will give a brief survey here. Raymond Moody's pioneering studies of this phenomenon have been followed up and confirmed by several others.[97] For example: 'Peter Fenwick … showed that no fewer than 86 percent felt that their experience had made them more religious. Following an NDE, most people claim to be less materialistic, more grateful for life and more concerned with the welfare of others'.[98] I just mention here the fact that reading Moody's descriptions, triggered the resurgence of my own very early childhood recollection of the experience of going in the other direction, and this subject will also be further elaborated upon in chapter 8.

Although there are many variations of the NDE, Moody was able to describe a series of common themes, which with few exceptions, all boil down to experiencing feelings of bliss when going from the darkness through a 'tunnel' towards the light. In the language of our ocean model: diving through the surface layer to the light at greater depths. St Augustine describes this experience in his *Confessions*: 'I will pass even beyond this power of mine which is called memory; yea I will pass beyond it, that I may approach unto Thee, O sweet Light'. And as we can see from their lives, for many of those having had this transcendental experience, it has indeed changed their lives completely. They now know that there is a deeper meaning to life; that death is not the end and they often have lost all fear of dying completely.

As there is no clear separation between the subject covered in the previous section and this one, there will be some overlap and I will be referring to the meditative path as well, illustrating that fortunately there are less drastic ways of opening up our inner channel than having an NDE. And as I mentioned earlier, for several of my friends and acquaintances, TM has been a blessing, but for others definitely not. As I briefly pointed out as well, many religions have experienced a revival of interest in their mystical/contemplative traditions and so there are many different meditation techniques to experiment with.

In several of these traditions there are detailed descriptions of the different layers we can possibly encounter during our descent from our surface awareness to the light of the One in the ocean's depths. Take for instance Deepak Chopra's several different descriptions of the seven levels he identifies in his book *How to Know God*, which he subtitled *The Soul's Journey into the Mystery of Mysteries*.[99]Here I will describe what happened to me and how it had a profound effect on my understanding, so that I could recognise what other explorers had been describing using an often completely different terminology.

Like any good marketing manager does, follow-up programmes were devised by Maharishi and we joined the very first *Sidha* course for couples in the Netherlands.[100] Now things really took off. The programme is based on Patanjali's *Yoga Sutras,* culminating in the 'flying sutra'. This is no secret anymore as during election campaigns here in the UK, the TM sponsored 'Natural Law' party showed Sidhas hopping across the television screens on national television.

The *sidhi* sutras are 'thought' after the mind has been stilled by a previous period of meditation. My own experience was that during the 'thinking' of the sutras, a spontaneous pulse of energy surged through me which—when I did the 'flying sutra'—resulted in a hop. This physical result 'happened' to me, rather than that I 'did' it consciously—or in other words—I was 'being hopped' rather than 'hopping'.[101]

In our group, Emmy was the first to hop, and I was looking at her exploits when she did something that was absolutely impossible. She hopped towards a couple sitting in the middle of our room-sized mat, and instead of bumping into them; in mid-air at the top of her hop, she just turned around 180 degrees. No swinging out of arms, legs or her long hair, just cleanly rotating in mid-air.[102]Right there in front of my eyes she clearly violated the 'Law of Conservation of Angular Momentum'. That provoked in me a severe crisis. Was nothing sacred anymore, not even such a basic law of physics? [103]

Much later I discovered that I could have found comfort in the wise words of Thomas Aquinas: 'Nothing is contrary to the laws of nature, only to what we understand about the laws of nature'. Or what George Gurdjieff wrote much later: 'No miracle (by which he meant psychokinesis, telepathy and so forth) occurs as a result of the violation of these [horizontal] laws; a miracle can only be a manifestation of the laws and forces of a higher world'.[104]But at that time I was completely unaware of this profound wisdom.

During a subsequent meditation I suddenly experienced what I can only describe as a vision, and found myself sheltering inside a foxhole on the frontline of a warzone.[105]Cowering in my hole, I was told to peer over the edge, and when I did that, I saw running soldiers and tanks and all kind of military hardware coming towards me. Even the sky was obscured, because above the silhouettes of the approaching army on the ground, I could hardly see the sky, as it was simply filled with fighters and bombers; I have tried to express that experience in the bottom picture of figure 7.1.

Figure 7.1 The front-line and walking towards the light

Next I was told to get out of my shelter and walk towards the solid front of the oncoming army. I clambered out and noticed that as I walked into the approaching mass of soldiers, tanks etc., their hard outlines mellowed and they became smaller so that I could see more of the sky in the distance, and I could slip forwards between them.[106]I went on and as I progressed they became still smaller and 'softer' until I could see the place where they originated, which experience I have tried to express in the middle picture of figure 7.1.

They originated as tiny puffs of smoke and I realised that I had full power over them and could just snuff them out as soon as they appeared. I understood that when I let one escape, it would grow into a full-blown aeroplane, tank, cannon, soldier or whatever. I also understood that these images represented my thoughts, and that the meditation technique was taking me to their source, where I had the power to replace them with thoughts of my own choice, in this case the seed thoughts (sutras) selected by Maharishi from Patanjali's *Yoga Sutras*.

Where I was now, the view of the sky in front of me was completely unobstructed; it was blazingly aglow, just like before a beautiful golden sunrise on a clear day. I have tried to express this experience in the top picture of figure 7.1, but of course this sunrise picture is only a vague shadow of this breathtaking moment.[107]

This profound experience made me understand how the sidhis worked: Normal life is like cowering in our private foxhole, feeling desperately alone. Often you are overwhelmed by thoughts, you simply have no power over them, they just roll over you, one after the other. These thoughts are represented by the tanks, aeroplanes, etc. Most of the time you do not think, it seems more like that you are being thought. Preparatory meditation was like getting out of your foxhole and walking towards the horizon, into the silence and towards the light. Having arrived there, you could think a thought, in this case one selected from the Hindu tradition, and in the Sidha practice you were in control of it and could snuff it out again.

Once I'd left the foxhole—representing our spacetime prison (Plato's cave) where the laws of physics rule supreme—everything, including miracles flouting these laws (remember what I quoted about the 'vacuum' in chapter 5), is possible. At this 'place' you understand what Jesus meant when he said that '... the kingdom of God comes with power'; and its location is made clear in the ancient psalm: 'Be still and know that I am God'; as well as in the words of a modern saint Ramana Maharshi: 'All that is required to realize the Self is to *Be Still* '.[108]

For me it is very significant that in the collection of essays: *Why I am Still an Anglican*, Caroline Chartres described her profound spiritual experience occurring during ... a Latin Mass, celebrated by a French priest with a speech impediment, which was almost entirely incomprehensible but one of the most profoundly worshipful experiences I have ever had.[109] Indeed when the head has to give up by being still, we may *know* with the heart.

But how far have we moved away from that ancient and profound wisdom in our wired-up, TV, radio, mobile phone, iPod, etc. society, making silence all but impossible. Although in my case experiencing these paranormal Siddhi phenomena has led to greater understanding, generally spiritual teachers are often very loath to give them any attention. The ancient Buddhist saying comes to mind: 'Before enlightenment, chop wood and carry water. After enlightenment, chop wood and carry water', so keep it simple. And in the same vein Aldous Huxley warns: 'The Sufis regard miracles as 'veils' intervening between the soul and God. The masters of Hindu spirituality urge their disciples to pay no attention to the *Siddhis*, or psychic powers, which may come to them unsought, as a by product of one-pointed contemplation. The cultivation of these powers, they warn, distracts the soul from Reality and sets up insurmountable obstacles in the way of enlightenment and deliverance'.[110] Consequently, after the message had arrived and the programme fulfilled its purpose, I stopped doing the Sidha programme a very long time ago.[111]

When in my 'frontline' experience, you rotate the ground-plane stretching out in front of you, ninety degrees down, so that the horizon is below rather than in the distance, then its representation corresponds closely with the model used by Maharishi and others in the Hindu tradition, see figure 7.2 below.

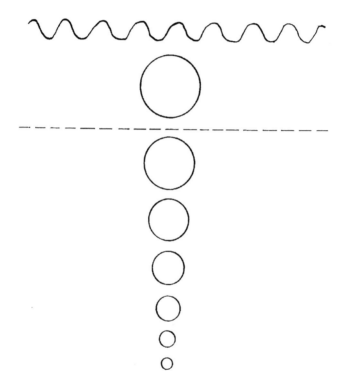

Figure 7.2 The rising 'thought' bubble

A tiny air bubble representing a thought originates at the bottom of an ocean and expands as it rises to the surface (materialising in my soldiers, tanks, etc.).[112]The rising thought becomes conscious just below the surface of the ocean; we have indeed lost all power over it. In this model the process of meditation can then be compared to diving into the ocean, thus following the bubbles back to their origin. And the meditation technique should be considered just as an aid, similar to the heavy girdle with lead weights to enable you to descend into the deep as, as every scuba diver can tell you.

In a similar way, our possessions and worries often prevent us from diving into the depths of the vertical dimension; they are like corks keeping us firmly at the surface. And only by letting go of these 'corks'—so that we can dive beyond the ocean's surface—do we experience the oneness of all being, and only then does Mother Teresa's message suddenly make sense: 'The more we have, the less we can give'.[113]

Not only during the series of sidhi introduction courses, but also during several longer duration retreats, I witnessed some amazing phenomena. People often came to me, telling me about their experiences because I had become 'known' for sometimes doing simultaneous translation of the instructions from English— which came over the phone from the TM European Headquarters in Seelisberg, Switzerland—into Dutch.

Many of these phenomena would (in TM jargon) often be classed as 'stress release'. I remember one ex-priest demonstrating to me how he could suddenly read small text without his reading glasses, and another very short-sighted young lady who could now read the time on her small watch from a distance.

Another notable experience of one of the participants was leaving his body. After one of our session, a man in our group shared with us how he had floated out of his body, looking down on the roof of the large villa in which we were having our retreat, so that he could tell us exactly out of which of the many chimneys the central heating fumes emerged.[114] In my own case, not only did I experience a tearful release of an old remorse, but also an explosion of blissful feelings, which were so overwhelming that I wanted to share them with Emmy by rolling across the floor with her. Many years later I encountered one of the other participants of our Sidha course, and she told me that, like me, she would be unable to forget what happened during that course for the rest of her life.

We in the West have to be especially aware that we cannot 'force' the process of enlightenment. It is not something that you set out to 'do'; meditation only creates the conditions for it to 'happen'. Herbert Benson stresses this point: 'The passive attitude is perhaps the most important point in eliciting the Relaxation Response. Distractive thoughts will occur. Do not worry about them'.[115] In a similar vein, John Main quotes the ancient wisdom: '...the monk who knows that he is praying, is not praying. The monk who does not know he is praying, is praying'.[116]And the same advice comes via the Dalai Lama from a completely different tradition: 'I tell my Western friends that wanting to practice the most profound and quickest path is a clear sign that you will achieve no result'.[117]

Also any profound experience is simply impossible to convey in words, as the Kabbalist Abraham Abulafia explains: 'One who reached the highest level cannot reveal it to anyone. All he can do is give over the keys, so that the enlightened individual can open the gates which are sealed to exclude the unworthy'.[118] He also taught that ... when an individual is on the highest meditative levels, he can actually alter the laws of nature through sheer spiritual force.[119]So this voice from a completely different tradition confirmed what I had concluded from my Sidha programme experiences described above. Abulafia also supports my decision not to continue with this programme after its message had arrived. Aryeh Kaplan (from whose book I have taken these quotations), writing that: 'In a number of places [Abulafia] graphically describes the magical techniques of the practical Kabalah, denouncing them in no uncertain terms. The best time for the deepest levels of meditation is in old age, when the intellect is well developed and the pull of the body is weak. ... This reflects the Talmudic teaching that such mysteries should not be taught to an individual unless he is "halfway through his years".[120]

So the Kabbalistic tradition is in clear support of passing wisdom on from older generations to younger ones, a tradition clearly abandoned in our 'enlightened' Western civilisation. Apart from Abulafia's, there is in the Jewish tradition a choice of other meditation techniques, such as the one focussing on *Ain Sof* (Infinite Light).

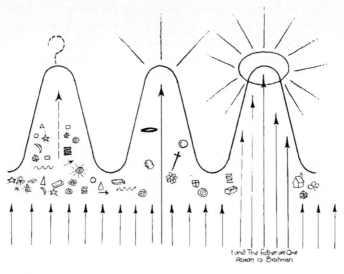

Figure 7.3 The process of enlightenment

Opening up our inner channel is called the process of enlightenment and I have tried to illustrate that process with the aid of figure 7.3. On the left is the condition described by Ron Laing as 'our appalling state of alienation called normality'.[121] In this 'normal' condition we will still receive some energy seeping through the thick layer of 'foam and seaweed', because otherwise we simply wouldn't be alive. The more we open up a channel to the light within, the more we will start to radiate that outwards. That is the reality behind the symbolism of auras and rays of light emanating from the heads of saints in paintings and on statues.

That it can be experienced in reality as well, is reported when Swami Premananda went into ecstasy: 'His face flushed, and then a light started to emanate from his whole body'.[122]

The very purpose of incarnating in a human body is that we all have the possibility to become enlightened. But as we are all waves on the same turbulent ocean, you can never be fully enlightened on your own, because interconnectedness implies that you cannot separate yourself from the suffering and ignorance around you. In our ocean image, the 'seaweed' will be closing in all the time—remember that even Jesus on the cross complained, 'Why hast thou abandoned me?' Enlightenment can never be an egotistical pursuit; it is simply impossible to be fully enlightened on one's own.

One of the effects of being on the right (vertical) path, can be that we lose the highly damaging urge to travel all over the planet in our vain quest to find the 'happiness' that always seems to be just over the horizon. This was powerfully expressed by a recluse—living in a Himalayan cave near a meditation retreat centre where he sometimes came in for a meal—when he refused a fully paid-for excursion to England by one of the participants, with the concise reply: 'I am England'.

Let me now conclude by briefly returning to what I covered in the previous section. If you really do not know where to start, just go to your local library and look around on the 'Spirituality' or similar shelves. Alternatively type 'meditation' into an Internet search engine and it will come up with millions of sites. A very concise survey is given on the Wikipedia site, with links to all the reviewed methods.

Therefore I have deliberately refrained from listing possible contacts at the end of this book, as nowadays the most up to date ones can be found best via the Internet. We also have to get accustomed to the fact that the same process has been given many different names, and therefore I will just end this chapter by quoting some of the words attributed to various seers extolling the importance of exploring the vertical dimension:

Buddha: 'Awakening from the sleep of ignorance.'

Jesus: '... seek ye first the kingdom of God...'

Masanobu Fukuoka: '... the road of true man is an inner road.'[123]

Sobin Yamada: 'In Zen we don't look outside for God or Buddha. They are within us.'[124]

The goal is to create the conditions allowing that 'aha' experience to take place, an experience described by Bede Griffiths as: 'Suddenly we know that we belong to another world, that there is another dimension to existence. ... We are freed from the flux of time and see something of the eternal order that underlies it. We are no longer isolated individuals in conflict with our surroundings; we are parts of a whole, elements in a universal harmony'.[125] And as must be very clear by now, I completely agree with Neale Donald Walsch, who has God say this to him: 'No path to God is more direct than any other path. No religion is the "one true religion," no people are "the chosen people," and no prophet is "the greatest prophet".'[126]

What I cannot stress enough, however, is that whatever path you choose, the most important message is to keep on trying, to make finding that 'kingdom within' your highest priority! Make this search a regular feature of your daily life. Andrew Harvey cautions: 'It is in this stage of the journey that it is essential to acquire as soon and as sincerely as possible a stable and disciplined spiritual practice of prayer, meditation, and contemplation: if this is not acquired, the awakening into divine origin will fade ...'[127]

In the beautiful Sermon on the Mount, Jesus stresses the same point of having your priorities in the right order:

So do not worry, saying, 'What shall we eat?' or, 'What shall we drink?' or, 'What shall we wear?'

For the pagans run after all these things, and your heavenly Father knows that you need them.

But seek first his kingdom and his righteousness; and all these things will be given to you as well.[128]

While Andrew Harvey also mentions that: 'Modern scholars point out that Jesus consciously identified himself with the "feminine" aspect of Jewish tradition and identified himself on several crucial occasions with "Hochma," divine wisdom (feminine in Hebrew and translated by the feminine noun "Sophia" in Greek)'.[129] Indeed, as I have pointed out in chapter 4, the kingdom of God is very much associated with the vertical (feminine) dimension, and Diane Essler makes the same point: 'Jesus teachings elevate "feminine" virtues from a secondary or supportive to a primary and central position'.[130] If all this has whetted your appetite and you want to revel in an extensive survey of the divine feminine in many traditions across the earth, read the section named 'Five Approaches to Mary's Mystic Motherhood' in Andrew Harvey's book, *Son of Man*.[131]

The recurrent theme of experiencing, rather than studying the vertical dimension, is expressed in all religions. I have stressed this point already several times but I cannot resist quoting the Hindu sage Lahiri Mahasaya, who expressed this essential message as: 'He only is wise who devotes himself to realizing, not reading only, the ancient revelations'.[132]

But while we are opening up our vertical channel, it is vitally important to keep our two feet firmly on the ground, as is so concisely expressed in the Buddhist saying: 'First enlightenment, then the laundry'. Doing the laundry is then not experienced anymore as a chore, and to quote Kahlil Gibran again on our attitude to work: 'Work is love made visible'.[133] We have finally come home and then we understand fully what William Blake intended with his words, 'If the doors of perception were cleansed every thing would appear to man as it is, infinite'. And to conclude with a feminine touch, Dorothy Rowe expresses the experience of homecoming beautifully:

All is all, and everything is everything, and we are part of it all, and we belong.[134]

8 RECAPITULATION AND APPLICATIONS

8.1 RECAPITULATION

I regard consciousness as fundamental.
I regard matter as a derivate of consciousness.

Max Planck

It is our fervent hope that future research will enable us to
establish definitely that some of the people who call themselves
mediums are neither frauds nor freaks but may actually be among
humankind's greatest friends by providing confirmed evidence of
the existence of a larger spiritual family.[1]

Gary E. Schwartz

From What-is all the world of things was born
But What-is sprang from What-is-not.

Lao Tzu, *Tao Te Ching*

...our universe seems "just right" for life. It looks, to use astronomer
Fred Hoyle's dramatic description, as if "a super intellect has been
monkeying with physics".[2]

Paul Davies

Then assuredly the world was made, not in time, but simultaneous
with time.

St Augustine

You are the waves. I am the Ocean.[3]

Sathya Sai Baba

Joop van Montfoort

While I was presenting the ocean model in chapter 4, and using it in the following chapters, I illustrated what I was doing by often diverting onto sidetracks, which might have been confusing. So here I will just give a condensed recapitulation of the basic model to illustrate that it can be fitted in a few pages, and then apply it in order to demystify a number of problems not fitting into what I now consider to be a limited horizontal framework.

Before the beginning was the One, who said, 'Let there be Light'. This initiated the creation of the universe emerging from the vertical dimension, by which time and space came into being. Let us imagine our four-dimensional domain of spacetime as the two-dimensional surface of an ocean. After a very long time the conditions on its surface became suitable for elementary particles—and later, by these clumping together—for stars, planets etc. to form. And finally for living beings to manifest themselves, here on planet earth.

We know from relativity theory that the presence of matter will distort the surface of this thin spacetime surface membrane, so with a liberal amount of artistic freedom we can represent all matter, including our bodies, as waves on the ocean's surface— from large waves representing galaxies, to tiny ones representing bacteria. Their evolution from undefined beginnings was not a random event, but was gently guided by the Forms/Ideas/ Archetypes that are present in the ocean's depths, outside the spacetime prison of its surface.[4] As they are outside time and space, they were present from 'before' the very beginning, and although that goes completely against our ideas of free will, all that will happen in the future is there potentially present as well.

Horizontally—on the surface of the ocean—the laws of physics rule supreme, and there are many people who maintain that that is all there is. But there is another, (vertical) dimension, orthogonal to that surface, extending 'down' into the 'depths' of the ocean. At the 'bottom' of our ocean is the source of all life, and that source has been given many names in different traditions. Although it is beyond naming, I have used one of them,

206

which, I think, expresses its uniqueness very well, i.e. 'the One'. While descending into the vertical depths of the ocean, spacetime peters out quickly, keeping in mind that expressions like 'quickly', 'depth' or 'height' are to be taken symbolically, as outside the spacetime surface realm they have really lost their meaning.

If the horizontal dimension is the realm of our bodies, the vertical one is the domain of our psyche, soul, self, etc. The very top of the wave represents our ego, *jiva*, etc., while deeper down our mind operates. All our memories etc. are stored there, part of them conscious, the remainder 'sleeping' in our personal unconscious lower down in our wave. Going down further, the waves blend into the ocean's depths, which contains the collective unconscious. Superficial memories are still accessible, but when we want to drag up things from greater depths, it gets increasingly difficult, and with a few exceptions, memories stored in the collective unconscious are not subject to the power of the will.

They can, however, well up spontaneously, for instance in dreams, hypnosis or near-death experiences. Everything that has ever happened, or will ever happen—or thought—is stored there, and all this forms a barrier which can be represented in our ocean image by a layer of seaweed, nearly blocking out the flow of life giving energy from the One at the ocean's bottom. Again, that energy flow has been described in many traditions under many different names such as: Chi (Ki), Prana, Holy Spirit, Light, etc.[5]

Although I intended not to be sidetracked, I am simply unable to resist mentioning here how it always amazes me how ancient this knowledge is. Take for instance this quotation from the Chinese *Nei Ching*, or *The Yellow Emperor's Classic of Internal Medicine,* reputedly dating from the reign of emperor Huang-Ti (2697-2596 *BCE*): 'The root of the way of life, of birth and change, is ch'i (energy); the myriad things of heaven and earth all obey this law. Thus, ch'i in the periphery envelops heaven and earth, ch'i in the interior activates them. The source wherefrom the sun, moon and stars derive their light; the thunder, rain, wind and clouds their being; the four seasons and the myriad things their birth, growth, gathering and storing: all this is brought about by ch'i. Man's possession of life is completely dependent upon this ch'i'.[6]

Apart from a few notable exceptions of people who experienced spontaneously that oneness with the source of all being—for instance in different traditions, al-Hallaj exclaiming, 'I am Allah', or Jesus saying, 'I and the Father are one', to Shankara, 'I am all things'—for the rest of us, meditation techniques (see previous chapter) can dissolve some of our seaweed. Then we have a chance to 'see the light' and experience that we are not alone, but are one—not only with all other beings—but with the One as well (satori). 'Seek and you shall find'[7] is a very important advice, never give up, so if one technique doesn't work for you, try another one. The most important message is to keep seeking!

Indeed, whatever I write, and regardless of how many examples and quotations I give, the experience of oneness cannot be attained without immersing oneself fully. Also this is nothing new, as was made crystal clear by Plato in his *Seventh Letter*: 'No treatise by me concerning it exists or ever will exist. It is not something that can be put into words like other branches of learning; only after a long partnership in a common life devoted to this very thing does truth flash upon the soul, like a flame kindled by a leaping spark, and once it is born there it nourishes itself thereafter. ... If I thought that any adequate spoken or written account could be given to the world at large, what more glorious life-work could I have undertaken than to put into writing what could be of great benefit to mankind and to bring the nature of reality to light for all to see?'[8] Yet I have tried to put my experiences in words, and I sincerely hope that my effort towards making the vertical dimension at least acceptable will trigger some recognition and will hence not have been in vain.

As an electronics engineer I also cannot resist drawing a parallel with recent developments such as those involving the World Wide

Web and the interconnectedness via the collective unconscious. Similar to the exploration of meditation practices, we need to use a technique—in the case of the Internet a computer with an Internet Explorer type of software installed—to open up the Internet realm and make all that hidden knowledge—available from all over the earth—accessible. In a similar way, whether it is predictive dreaming, *deja-vu* or any other so called paranormal phenomenon, we can discover that we are one with all of creation and that all our horizontal values, such as money, status, possessions etc. are completely irrelevant for our happiness and fulfilment.[9] And that, of course, is exactly the message that all religious teachers throughout the ages have been extolling over and over, again and again!

Indeed, the only way to solve our problems—and those of the world—is to finally listen to them and to start building a completely different type of community based on spiritual values. And that implies not only ending the exploitation of other human beings, but of animals and the whole of our incredibly beautiful planet as well.

According to a horizontal world view, miracles are simply not possible and hence do not exists, but as I described in the previous chapter, having seen one happening in front of my own eyes, I have become much more open minded and there is a host of books on the subject. Definitely some of the 'miracles' described therein will be chaff, but we should be careful not to throw the genuine ones out with it.

For me the horizontal/vertical model has been a real eye opener and made many of the pieces of life's puzzle fall in their proper place. To illustrate this, in the following sections I have just listed a few of life's problems and how these puzzling phenomena can be understood by applying this simple horizontal/vertical model to them. Some of the problems will be covered extensively because of their importance, or their being part of my personal experiences; other items will be covered only fleetingly. Also, because I have already used several items to highlight points in the foregoing chapters, I ask for understanding for some unavoidable repetition.

8.2 Applications

Nowadays [1891!] we have so few mysteries left to us that we cannot afford to part with one of them.[10]

Oscar Wilde

We do not see things as they are.
We see them as we are.

Talmud

Men are disturbed not by things that happen,
But by their opinions of the things that happen.

Epictetus

So convincing is the evidence in favor of past life influences that one can only conclude that those who refuse to consider this an area worthy of serious study must be either uninformed or excessively narrow-minded.[11]

Stanislav Grof

One definition of heresy is 'an opinion contrary to generally accepted beliefs' - and scientific enquiry cannot survive without such things.[12]

Philip Ball

You feel yourself no longer a wavelet of life, but as the Ocean itself.[13]

Paramahansa Yogananda

- If God is good and all-powerful, why does he allow all this suffering to happen?

How can the existence of evil be reconciled with the concept of a perfect, all-powerful God of love? [14]

Harold K Schilling

Schilling's question is one of the first questions that immediately pop up when the existence of an all-loving, all-powerful god is proclaimed by the leaders of any religious denomination. This very point was recently (end 2006) highlighted in a series of radio programmes in which John Humphrys asked Christian, Muslim and Jewish scholars a similar question.[15]

Likewise after the disastrous tsunami at Christmas-time 2004 in South-East Asia, the Archbishop of Canterbury, Rowan Williams, wrote an article in a British newspaper titled: 'Of course this makes us doubt God's existence'. In that article he repeats the persistent question, 'How can you believe in a God who permits suffering on this scale?' And similar to the results of Humphrys' questioning—he failed to give an acceptable answer.[16] And that this is not a recent quandary at all, I will illustrate with an ancient tale from European antiquity, as retold by Homer in the *Iliad*. There we read that: 'Zeus the Thunderer has two jars standing on the floor of his Palace, in which he keeps his gifts, the evils in one and the blessings in the other. People who receive from him a mixture of the two have varying fortunes, sometimes good and sometimes bad ...'[17] So it seems that we are just puppets and are left to the whims of Zeus. However, that fatalistic conclusion Zeus himself demolishes in Homer's later *Odyssey*, where he says: 'What a lamentable thing it is that men should blame the gods and regard *us* as the source of their troubles, when it is their own wickedness that brings them sufferings worse than any which destiny allots them.'[18]

Later Plato illustrates that same message in Book X of *The Republic*, where he tells the interesting story of Er, son of

Armenius—the soldier who after a battle was discovered still alive on the funeral pyre—and whose near-death experience probably was one of the first recorded ones. Er reports that after having been judged, the souls have to spend a thousand years either in the delights of heaven or in the sorrows and tears of the earth below. After having paid off their karmic debts, before being reincarnated, the souls have to make their choice of the life to come, and the fate Lachesis warns them: 'This is the word of Lachesis, maiden daughter of Necessity. Souls of a day, here you must begin another round of mortal life whose end is death. No Guardian Spirit will be allotted to you; you shall choose your own. And he on whom the lot falls first shall be the first to choose the life which then shall of necessity be his. Excellence knows no master; a man shall have more or less of her according to the value he sets on her. The fault lies not with God, but with the soul that makes the choice.'[19]

Those coming from heaven were often careless in their choice and regretted it deeply, while those who had paid for their errors by suffering were much more careful, resulting in 'a general change of good for evil and evil for good'. Er explained that we do not remember our choice because before being born, we have to drink from the 'River of Forgetfulness'.

Much later, the Roman statesman Seneca tried to explain suffering as someone having been selected by God to be purified as a 'worthy instrument': 'Why is it that God afflicts the best men with ill health, or sorrow, or some other misfortune? For the same reason that in the army the bravest men are assigned to the hazardous tasks. In like manner, all those who are called to suffer what would make cowards and poltroons weep may say, 'God has deemed us worthy instruments of his purpose to discover how much human nature can endure' ... And so, in the case of good men the gods follow the same rule that teachers follow with their pupils; they require most effort from those of whom they have the surest hopes'.[20] And Meister Eckhart thus expressed a similar sentiment in the Middle Ages: 'God has burdened with sin those he most loved'.[21]

Probably as a reaction to people being subjected to the whims of the Greek gods and their Roman equivalents, the Christian God was presented as a loving and caring father, who was declared to be good, omnipotent and omniscient. However, this definition leads directly to the question I opened this section with, and libraries have been filled with theological treatises trying to square the circle of how an all-powerful, loving, good God can allow all the suffering in this 'vale of tears' to happen at all.

The problem arises because we attribute 'human' qualities to God, which for Meister Eckhart implies pulling 'him' down to our level. In one of his sermons he said: '... God is nameless because none can say or understand anything about Him. If I now say God is good, it is not true; rather, I am good, God is not good. I will go further and say I am better than God: for what is good can become better, and what can become better can become best of all. Now God is not good, therefore he cannot become better. And since He cannot become better, therefore He cannot become best; for these three, good, better and best, are remote from God, since He is above them all. Thus too if I say God is wise, it is not true. I am wiser than He. So too if I say God is a being, that is not true. He is a transcendental being, and a superessential nothingness. St Dionysus says the finest thing one can say about God is to be silent from the wisdom of inner riches. So be silent and do not chatter about God, because by chattering you are lying and so committing a sin. ... Nor should you (seek to) understand anything about God, for God is above all understanding'.[22]

That same understanding we could have learned from the much older Chinese civilisation as well; Lao Tzu opens his *Tao Te Ching* with: 'The Tao that can be told of is not the eternal Tao. The name that can be given is not the eternal Name'.[23] And to illustrate the impossibility of defining the Tao (the One),

Lao Tzu writes further on: 'Since before time and space were, the Tao is. It is beyond *is* and *is not*...' To make sure that you do not ever think to have all the answers, he cautions: 'The more you know [horizontally], the less you understand'.

Carl Jung uses the same argumentation in his *Seven Sermons to the Dead*: 'Nothing is the same as fullness' and, 'The Nothing, or fullness, is called by us the PLEROMA [that which fills]'. And this leads directly to: 'What you should never forget is that the Pleroma has no qualities. We are the ones who create these qualities through our thinking'.[24]

Michael Newton obtained interesting answers from his hypnotherapeutic regression cases when he asked his subjects the same question: 'When I ask my subjects how a loving God could permit suffering, surprisingly there are very few variations in their responses. My cases report our souls are born of a creator, which places a totally peaceful state deliberately out of reach so we will strive harder.

We learn from wrongdoing. The absence of good traits exposes the ultimate flaws in our nature. That which is not good is testing us, otherwise we would have no motivation to better the world through ourselves, and no way to measure advancement'.[25] Likewise, Hugh Montefiore supports the viewpoint that suffering may be for our ultimate benefit when—after discussing the suffering of the Jews under the Nazis—he concludes: 'They have emerged from these persecutions, sufferings and murders, with what seems renewed vitality. Is it mere coincidence that post-Enlightenment Jews, out of all proportion to their numbers, have today become leaders in so many fields of life; industry, commerce, medicine, philosophy, sociology, art, music, politics and so on? Persecution, far from blotting them out, seems to have given them new energy and inner resources.'[26]

A cynic might argue that this is just an interesting demonstration of evolution in action; that the softies have been weeded out while the strong have survived. But all of the above leads for me to the conclusion that if you say that God is either good or wrathful, it doesn't say anything about God at all, only about you—and about what you have personally experienced! I have given all these examples and quotations because I wanted to illustrate that there really is nothing new to our problem, and that it has been discussed for ages. And I am convinced that only our horizontal/vertical ocean model—with the One as the source of being, well beyond the categories of good and evil at its spacetime surface—offers a satisfactory explanation.

But I have already 'talked' far too much, so let me repeat Lao Tzu's wise counsel: 'Those who know don't talk. Those who talk don't know'. And to underline that statement let me give the last word to the Buddha:

> Believe nothing because a so-called wise man said it.
> Believe nothing because a belief is generally held.
> Believe nothing because it is written in ancient books.
> Believe nothing because it is said to be of divine origin.
> Believe nothing because someone else believes it.
> Believe only what you yourself judge to be true.[27]

- Major problems in physics

Black holes' are merely the most exotic example of the general principle that the universe registers and processes information.[28]

Seth Lloyd and Y Jack Ng

It now turns out that ninety to ninety-nine per cent of matter in the Universe is utterly unknown to us. It's as if physics has discovered the cosmic unconscious. Dark matter determines the structure and fate of the Universe, and yet we haven't a clue about what it is.[29]

Rupert Sheldrake

Why [vacuum energy] exists is one of the biggest mysteries in physics.[30]

Mason Inman

We have made enormous progress in explaining how the universe could have arisen from nothing, but if you limit your field of view to the horizontal dimension only, this can easily lead to the exclamation of Steven Weinberg: 'The more the universe seems comprehensible, the more it also seems pointless'.[31] An initial quantum variation exploded into the Big Bang and the laws of physics seem to rule supreme from a minute instant after that event. Also the combination of nature's basic constants seem to have been 'chosen' with staggering precision, enabling us to exist at all. The usual explanation of why we are here—based on randomness—leads to the absurd proposal that there are zillions of universes (called the multiverse) and as many big bangs, and that we exist in the one that just happened to have all its basic constants of exactly the right value.[32] An amazing conclusion from detailed studies of the expansion of the universe, summarised by John Barrow in his book *The Origin of the Universe*, requires that '... the universe's launch speed to have been "chosen" to differ from the critical one by no more than one part in ten followed by thirty-five zeros. Why?!'[33] And further on he writes: 'The universe is still in a highly ordered state, despite having expanded in an entropy-increasing manner for fifteen billion years. This is a puzzle. ... and perhaps governed by some grand principle ...'[34]

Amir Aczel comments on this fact with this very far reaching conclusion: 'Since points along various directions in space could not "see" each other once they were at distances beyond their mutual horizons, there was no possible exchange of information among them to effect the homogeneity. To explain these effects, Guth proposed the inflationary theory ...'[35]

Let's return to a much more down to earth problem, such as the mystery of how each of the six branches of a snowflake 'know' what the other branches are 'doing', resulting in a beautiful six fold symmetry, for which no explanation has been found in the horizontal dimension, see figure 8.1.

Figure 8.1 Snowflakes (D. Wollaver)

Philip Ball's comments regarding this are noteworthy: 'A continuing mystery about dendritic snowflakes is why all six of their branches seem to be more or less identical'.[36]

Indeed there is a long list of major problems that cannot be fitted inside the framework of our present understanding of the laws of physics. A concise survey of recent 'impossible' discoveries, some of which caused an uproar in the scientific community and are often resulting in the hounding of the discoverers by the scientific inquisition, can be found in Philip Balls very interesting book *H₂O: A Biography of Water*. He lists the cases of 'polywater', supposedly a new form of water; Fleischman and Pons' announcement of 'cold' nuclear fusion in a glass beaker, which caused a real pandemonium; and the publication by Jacques Benviste's team in *Nature* of effects observed when the active element was diluted to such an extent in water that nothing was present anymore. *Nature's* editor John Maddox commented on these findings: 'There is no objective explanation of their observations' and explained that 'Benviste's observations ... are startling not merely because they point to a new phenomenon, but because they strike at the roots of two centuries of observation and rationalization of physical phenomena'.[37]

Philip Ball comments that Benviste's result '... makes no sense whatsoever in terms of conventional science'. And because Benviste's publication was eagerly used as proving the reality of the effect of homeopathic remedies, he discusses that subject extensively and clarifies that: 'Hahnemann [the initiator of homeopathy] explained his observations on the basis that the body contains a 'vital force' that maintains the body's health. In sickness the vital force is depressed or out of balance. Homeopathic remedies somehow re-energize this extraordinary sensitive life-giving agency. ... Yet I think there are very good reasons to suppose that Hahnemann had in mind something more: a kind of animating spirit of non-corporeal origin'.[38] And that last line fits in very well indeed with the ideas I have presented in this book. Also, the fact that the vertical dimension is associated with feminine intuition is underlined by a very interesting and revealing remark made by Maddox et al., namely that 'in [Elisabeth Davenas'] hands the experiment most often "works"'; indeed also in this Benviste affair it would be advisable to "chercher la femme".[39]

There is indeed no horizontal explanation for these findings (such as the relevant memory being stored in molecules or atoms), but what about the explanation of Elisabeth Davenas being a sensitive woman, hence able to tune into the (Akashic) memory or 'Idea' stored under our ocean's spacetime surface of that particular sample, and 'seeing' that under her microscope?

Conveniently for me, Michael Brooks lists in his cover story in *New Scientist*: '13 things that don't make sense'.[40] I will just indicate how a few of these can be well understood in the context of our model by taking the reality of the vertical dimension into account. He reports on the 'Belfast homeopathy' results, quoting Madeleine Ennis, the pharmacologist in charge: "we are unable to explain our findings" and commenting '... the implications are profound: we may have to rewrite physics and chemistry'. I have already dealt with homeopathy (chapter 5 and above) and I do not see any reason to 'rewrite physics and chemistry'; we only need to accept that these are strictly limited to the horizontal dimension, and that there is obviously much more than that.

In the light of the effects found by Benviste and his team, the placebo effect mentioned by Brooks can be explained via this vertical interconnectedness as well.[41] But, of course, you can counter that all this—which has to do with health—can be explained as a case of human suggestibility; so let us rather consider some 'hard physics' problems, listed by Brooks. 'The 'horizon problem' deals with the disturbing fact of the uniformity of the cosmic background radiation's temperature in whatever direction we measure it. And that uniformity should not be possible because the extremes of the universe are 28 billion light years apart, being the result of the expansion of the universe over 14 billion years. In Brooks' words: 'In scientific terms, the uniform temperature of the background radiation remains an anomaly'. Apart from some explanations such as introducing 'inflation', again this fact can only be explained if we accept that the obvious interconnectedness is not limited by the speed of light—dictated by 'horizontal' science—but operates under the ocean's surface outside our spacetime universe'.[42] Brooks' next problem is 'Ultra-energetic cosmic rays', and again if we consider that our four dimensional universe is just like a thin film on an ocean of infinite seething energy, then everything is indeed possible.

I will end this brief overview with the 'embarrassing hole in our understanding' of 'Dark matter' ('the mysterious, unseen stuff thought to make up nearly 90 per cent of galaxies' mass')[43] and that indeed '... one of the most embarrassing problems in physics' is 'Dark energy' and the 'Not-so-constant constants'. Because of this lack of understanding the quoted figures are rather variable; it seems that according to the latest insights on the composition of the universe, 'just over 4 per cent of its content is ordinary matter, 23 per cent is mysterious dark matter[44] and 73 per cent the even more mysterious dark energy'.[45] Although it is of little help to someone who has been hit with a hammer on the head, matter is in fact emptier than interstellar space as I pointed out in chapter 5 already. Arthur Eddington describes vividly what stepping onto a plank is really like: 'The plank has no solidity of substance. To step on it is like stepping on a swarm of flies. Shall I not slip through? No, if I make the venture one of the flies hits me and gives a boost up again; I fall again and am knocked upwards by another fly; and so on ...'[46]

On top of the few mysteries that I have mentioned here, Aczel reports about a meeting of leading scientists at Fermilab: 'These scientists were facing an almost unavoidable conclusion: there was something very weird going on in the universe—something that no scientist could understand. Nature had a fifth force in its arsenal, one that had never been directly observed.'[47] Indeed, all this is very true if we limit our field of view to the horizontal dimension only, but when we take the vertical dimension's interconnectedness into account and consider our spacetime universe just as the surface epiphenomenon of an ocean containing all the required information and preserving it, and also containing an infinite amount of (dark) energy (the origin of the fifth force), do the mysteries dissolve.[48]

- EVOLUTION

Spirit sleeps in the stone, breathes in the plant, moves in the animal, and wakes up to consciousness in man.[49]

F. W. J. von Schelling

... examples have been reported that break the [10-million-year] time limit, suggesting that maybe silent genes are not the whole story.[50]

Michael Le Page

Starting on the mineral level, it is very interesting to note that Rupert Sheldrake reports on the fact that saturated solutions will crystallise much easier after they have formed crystals before, than if they have to do that from scratch.[51] Although the Form of this 'new' crystal has always been present in the depths of our ocean, it needed effort on the ocean's surface to open up a gap from the surface through the layer of seaweed to that particular Form. Once that route has been opened up, future crystallisation becomes easier as time progresses.[52]

As revealed in the following quotation, plants too seem to have developed means of communication: 'David Rhoades of the University of Washington suggested that when tent caterpillars eat the leaves of willow trees, the insects induce an increase of resistance not only in the affected plants but also in neighbouring trees more than three metres away, which were protected in advance from any attack. Rhoades speculated that plants had evolved means of communicating in some way to defeat herbivores.[53] And unless a horizontal (chemical) explanation can be found, interconnectedness via our ocean again seems the best bet.

Going still higher on the evolutionary ladder, biologists limiting themselves to the horizontal dimension only, have no idea—not only of how a single cell develops into the well-organised billions of cells of a living being—but also of how young animals such as birds, fish, sand eels and Monarch butterflies know how to find their way when migrating sometimes thousands of kilometres across our planet—without ever having been shown the way by their elders. Is there a roadmap stored in their chromosomes?

Or take the mystery of the mass emergence once every seventeen years of the nymphs of periodical cicadas to become adults starting a new cycle again. Are they each capable of counting to seventeen and remembering which year it was?[54] Richard Milton lists under 'The Facts of Life' a number of similar facts, leading him to the exclamation: 'There is a program being executed. How is it coded? Where are the instructions? ... The question is where does this program reside and how is it invoked and executed?'[55] Only by accepting the reality of a vast database 'underneath' the spacetime surface of our ocean of the beyond can these instinctive, as well as many other behaviouristic problems, be explained.

But as we have seen, this acceptance of the reality of our vertical dimension is certainly not yet the mainstream belief of 'hard' evolutionary biologists. They still insist that—given enough time—everything we see is 'just' the result of completely random mutations that have proven to be beneficial. This horizontal slit vision is part of a long tradition as well. Take David Hume for example, who described vertical phenomena as 'violations of the laws of nature' which 'helped to make miracles seem immoral and irrational'.[56] Biologists, like Richard Dawkins, are in a very similar situation as physicists were in a hundred years ago. To open up their minds to the possibility of another dimension, biology needs phenomena of a similar impact as not only the ultraviolet crisis and the Mercury orbital anomaly (solved by quantum mechanics and relativity theory, respectively), but also the effect experimental verification of paranormal phenomena had on physics (chapter 5).

Also note that biology is in no way free of other question marks, because there are indeed many unanswered problems around in that discipline. Take this paragraph from a recent article by Mark Buchanan for example: 'But when it comes to explaining the origin of our altruism, matters get a whole lot more contentious. In evolutionary terms it is a puzzle because any organism that helps others at its own expense stands at an evolutionary disadvantage. So if many people really are true altruists, as it seems, why haven't greedier, self-seeking competitors wiped them out?'[57]

In the same period, *New Scientist* carried an article by Andy Coglan, headlined 'Mendel will be turning in his grave' and subtitled 'Some plants appear to be inheriting genes that their parents did not possess. That should be impossible'.[58] The article describes an experiment with weedy cress in which some 10% of third generation plants of parents, both having abnormal genes, revert to the normal genes of their grandparents. And a similar 'miracle' of eyeless fruitflies spontaneously regaining eyes in later generations has been reported.

Another major problem is the reported reappearance of hind limbs in whales, dolphins and snakes, or webbed feet and more than five fingers or toes or even tails in humans. These traits have supposedly been lost many millions of years ago, but still reappear occasionally.[59] Perhaps these facts are the shocks that will contribute to awakening mainstream biology to the need of becoming more open minded, and to stop vilifying courageous biologists like Rupert Sheldrake.

- PARANORMAL PHENOMENA

Miracles do not happen in contradiction to nature, but only in contradiction to that which is known to us of nature.

St Augustine

No miracle (by which he meant psychokinesis, telepathy and so forth) occurs as a result of the violation of these [mechanical] laws; a miracle can only be a manifestation of the laws and forces of a higher world.[60]

George Gurdjieff

The problem is that these [ESP] events do occur. "Paranormal' is the common word for them.[61]

Lawrence LeShan

As we have seen, the scientific establishment has derided many new discoveries and developments because they could not be fitted into the laws of the reigning paradigm. And unless you yourself witness paranormal phenomena, it is much safer to look in another direction. Robert Oppenheimer was honest enough to acknowledge this attitude as: 'We can't find anything wrong with it so we will just have to ignore it'.

In this section I will just list a number of cases that, as far as I know, have not found a horizontal (scientific) explanation. You are free to add to the previous sentence the word 'yet', and I wholeheartedly support science's efforts to find, whenever possible, a horizontal explanation. After all, that can be tested and reproduced, while the acceptance of vertical explanations can—when not based on personal experience—only be based on faith. We can be very grateful, not only that science has been instrumental in breaking the stranglehold of the Church, but that its methodology is also extremely useful to separate the wheat from the chaff; because there are, unfortunately enough people around who can be exploited because they will believe anything. But I stress again that I am definitely not one of them.

Not only are there now whole sections in libraries and bookshops dedicated to books covering the paranormal, but also there are even specialised bookshops dedicated mainly to this field.[62] During the presentation of my case in the previous pages, I have quoted from a number of sources to illustrate that I am supported by a wide range of authors ranging over a very long period of time indeed. An excellent review of the field is the book

I have already mentioned by Brian Inglis: *The Unknown Guest*, in which he refers to many other sources as well. Indeed, I could go on and on quoting from many others, but I will limit myself to referring to a few more books I have come across.

A recent very readable summary can be found in Anthony North's book *The Paranormal*. He stays with his two feet firmly on the ground—starting out as an agnostic, but like me he was 'converted' by the reality of something beyond the horizontal by a number of personal experiences. Throughout the book he maintains a healthy sceptical attitude when describing personal and reported paranormal phenomena in fifty-two very wide ranging, but brief, sections. Discussing the CSICOP (Committee for the Scientific Investigation of Claims of the Paranormal) having as its stated intention to '... investigate *carefully* the extraordinary claims of true believers and charlatans of the paranormal world', his appropriate comment is worth quoting in full: "Scepticism is a valid approach to the paranormal. I am sceptical of areas of it myself. But scepticism must never be allowed totally to suppress wonder or open-mindedness.

Logical analysis of the paranormal is possible, but not in terms acceptable to CSICOP. But what, above all else, fuels CSICOP's hatred of all things paranormal? As a 1985 fund-raising document made clear: 'Belief in the paranormal is still growing, and the dangers to our society are real ...'"[63] If you, like the CSICOP, still insist on maintaining the 'psi is zero' belief, you will indeed have to dismiss an enormous quantity of contrary evidence described throughout the ages in hundreds of books and articles, and you can do that by adopting the attitude of allowing an extremely limited 'horizontal slit vision' only. Some of these books will indeed have been written 'just to make money', but ignoring these, there still remains a vast quantity of evidence that simply cannot be rubbished so easily. Take for instance events reported today, such as the materialisations described regularly by many of Sai Baba's followers, crediting him with materialising not only of 'holy ash', but gems as well.[64]

There are several books describing a large number of people seemingly defying the laws of gravity by levitating, not only saints, such as Teresa of Avila or Joseph of Cupertino, but also more recently, Daniel Dunglas Home who, in London in 1868, reputedly floated out of one open third-storey window and floated back in via another.[65] I would have dismissed reports of these cases as really beyond the pale, had I not witnessed the antics of a couple of TM Sidhas at close range.

Obviously, human beings are capable of violating the laws of physics, acceptance of which has been very much part of Eastern spiritual traditions for a very long time. Take Milarepa, for instance, who states: 'Thenceforth, I persevered in my devotions in a most joyous mood, until, finally, I actually could fly'.[66]

Also, I was definitely not the first one who was forced to accept that miracles are indeed possible. Commenting on the attitude of those who deny the possibility of paranormal phenomena by stating that '... there is only the material world, and nothing can be real that doesn't obey physical laws', Deepak Chopra, who labels that attitude the 'secular view, and [notes that] even religious people accept it for everyday use', writes: 'Yet total belief in materialism, as we have seen, has become unacceptable for a host of reasons. It cannot explain credible, witnessed miracles, near-death experiences, out-of-body experiences, the testimony of millions of people who have had answered prayers, and most convincing of all, the discovery of the quantum world, which doesn't obey any ordinary physical laws'.[67]

Just as I have described it, David Bohm describes 'our realm of space-time as the flimsy surface on an ocean bristling with infinite energy', and this energy can be made to work in that surface domain when you possess the power to subject it to your purpose.[68] And as I discussed earlier, not only does the availability of that vertical energy flow solve many of the basic questions scientists are confronted with, such as what powered the Big Bang, why the expansion of the universe is seemingly accelerating and why is there so much 'dark matter/energy' about, but it also explains many other mysteries.

Interestingly, it very much seems a fact that this unlimited 'vacuum' energy has been used in ancient times to construct major buildings far beyond the 'horizontal' engineering capabilities of the particular period. The exploits of several enlightened beings have come down to us as those of the gods in traditions as widely dispersed as, for instance, Egypt, South America and Tibet. And solid evidence of their amazing powers is still visible in many corners of our planet today. Michael Hayes lists many of their feats in his book *High Priests, Quantum Genes*. And just to give you a taste of a few very significant ones, I will list some of the many examples described by him:

- Shaping and putting in place of a 1200 ton stone megalith and three other blocks, of some 600 tons each, in the temple of Baalbek in the Lebanon.
- Moving large stone blocks 250 metres up a cliff face seemingly using only music and the energy released by some 240 meditating monks ...[69]
- The evidence still present in Egypt such as the positioning of 200 ton stone blocks at the Sphinx and the amazing speed of building and accuracy of the Giza pyramids, as well as the precision carving of the granite sarcophagus in the King's Chamber.[70]

It is very interesting that Jill Purce—who studied overtone chanting in the Himalayas and teaches that regularly in the UK—alleges that these heavy blocks would have been put in place by 'the chanting of the workforce', and claims that this explains hitherto impossible-seeming feats of prehistoric engineering.[71]

Another writer dealing with the gigantic structures left by ancient civilisations, many of which defy any logical (horizontal) explanation, is Graham Hancock. He has collected many of these 'anomalies' in a book very appropriately called *Fingerprints of the Gods*, from which I will just quote one legend of the Mayas, describing how the ancients moved the gigantic blocks into place: 'Construction was easy for them, all they had to do was whistle and heavy rocks would move into place'.[72] Another baffling fact that Hancock describes is how it was at all possible for the ancients to hollow out stone vessels made of several different hard natural rock materials.[73]

Apart from the few examples I mentioned in this section, for an extensive survey of paranormal phenomena—supporting my statement that miracles are indeed possible—see e.g. Brian Inglis' book *Natural and Supernatural.*, covering reports from the earliest communities to modern times.[74]

– EXTRASENSORY PERCEPTION

The scientific community has been put on notice 'that there is something worthy of their attention and scrutiny' in the possibilities of extrasensory perception.[75]

New York Times editorial

We all begin our lives as psychic children, intimately aware of our spiritual existence. Yet, even the most psychic of us tends to "lose" our connection to our inner being, at least for a while.[76]

James Twyman

In chapter 5, I mentioned the example of the accumulative learning behaviour of rats, described by Sheldrake in his first book.[77] After that book, he wrote several others, all convincingly illustrating the interconnectedness that lies at the root of all the reported cases.[78] He notes that 'I have collected over 1,500 accounts of seemingly telepathic or psychic influences of owners on their pets, and 73 cases where the influence seems to flow the other way'.[79]

If you still have any doubts about the validity of unconscious communication, not only between insects and animals but people as well, I can give you no better advice than to read J. Allen Boone's moving book about his communication with animals, such as the German shepherd dog *Strongheart*, who became a movie star around the 1950s. Very appropriately he concludes from his experiences that: 'Neither Strongheart nor I was doing any communicating as of ourselves. Neither of us was expressing himself as an original thinker or an independent source. On the contrary, we were being *communicated through* by the Mind of the Universe'.[80]

Or read Sheldrake's books, and the numerous other publications describing many of these 'interconnectedness' experiences. Jung mentions in his books several examples of ESP as well, and the Gaugelins have been vilified for proving that there is really something in astrology, but fortunately they have found an articulate advocate in Hans Eysenck.[81]

Other phenomena that defy a horizontal explanation are the so called 'anniversary symptoms'. In an interview David Corfield explains that this is a label for cases such as: '... a woman with no prior history of angina ... who suffered a heart attack on the anniversary of her husband's lethal heart attack. In another case, a man's multiple sclerosis always became severely exacerbated on the date that his brother had died in a concentration camp'.[82]

In *Seven Experiments That Could Change the World*, Sheldrake proposes a number of experiments which are all well within the range of a do-it-yourselver, and he is eager to receive your results, which he promises to publish in the future. The evidence of several dogs that know when their masters are on their way home has been shown by him on national television here in the UK, and all his case histories are indeed a strong support for communication via the interconnectedness of the vertical dimension. Some of these experiments deal with widespread human experiences as well, such as: 'The sense of being stared at' and 'The reality of Phantom Limbs'. Then he goes on to subjects such as the scientific illusions of 'The variability of the "fundamental constants"' and 'The effects of experimenters expectations'.

The amazement about the fact reported by Kacelnik in *Nature*[83] , that 'a hand-reared crow that had never seen a tool being used, spontaneously began to use twigs to reach food, and even began to make his own tools', only becomes understandable if you realise that *everything at any time* is present in the vertical dimension and can be 'tuned' into. Then you do not have to utter such an implausible proposition that 'At least some of the crow's abilities, then, seem to be hard-wired into their brains'.[84] A relevant book here is Bill Schul's *The Psychic Power of Animals*, subtitled, *Incredible True Stories about the Secret World of Animals*, in which he has collected a host of case histories with references for further investigation.[85]

At several places I have mentioned some of my personal experiences, which can only be explained by accepting the reality of the vertical dimension and its communication potential. Here I will just describe a couple of other personal experiences that again proved to me the reality of our interconnectedness.

In a field above our house, I was clearing up a pile of branches that had been trimmed from our trees and hedges by pushing them through our motor-driven shredder, which I had mounted on a trailer so that I could move the machine to where it was needed. While I was standing on the angle irons of the trailer's towing triangle, a youngster was helping me by passing branches on to me. Because of the noise we were both wearing ear protectors. Then in a moment of inattentiveness, my foot slipped off one of the iron bars and, losing my balance, I fell backwards and my other foot got trapped inside the triangle. While I was falling, I realised that the next thing would be that either my leg or ankle would break, because my foot was so trapped that it could not rotate further. Fortunately the sole of my shoe broke loose and I ended up still trapped but unharmed on my back in the grass.

When I looked around, I noticed that my young helper had not noticed anything because his back was towards me, but the next thing was that Emmy came rushing from the house in my direction. She had been ironing inside in front of the television, but suddenly she 'knew' intuitively that something was wrong with me and that she needed to investigate straightaway. Her action could not be reduced to 'just coincidence', because of the precise timing with which she came to my assistance.

Or take another occasion when we were sitting at our breakfast table in West Somerset and the telephone started ringing. While I was getting up to answer the call, Emmy simply said, 'It's Erik, and they have a daughter'. And that was exactly the case. When I lifted the receiver, our son Erik gave me the happy news from the middle of the Netherlands that his daughter had been born a few hours earlier.

~ RETROCOGNITION

I am convinced, after studying a representative part of the enormous mass of recorded evidence, that the Ψ-faculty—including telepathy, clairvoyance, and precognition—is an established fact.[86]

Raynor Johnson

Driving home on the A39 from Barnstaple to Porlock, I took the shortcut downhill through the hamlet of Parracombe because traffic on the main road was bogged down (my apologies to the people who live there). While climbing back towards the main road, I saw a 1930s-type car crossing our path from left to right and thought that it was driving on the main road. However, on arriving at the point where it had crossed our path, I found there was no road whatsoever and the main road was still some hundred metres ahead. A few minutes later back on the main road, I mentioned this strange experience to Emmy sitting next to me, and she responded that she had seen the car as well and was in a similar state of wonder.[87]

When I explored the same place at a later occasion, I noticed that the car had been proceeding along what had been the track of an abandoned railway. I also discovered that our experience is not unique and has amongst others been documented in the extensive files of the Society for Psychical Research. Raynor Johnson—who in his book *Psychical Research* gives a compact summary of the whole paranormal field—describes two striking examples of similar retrocognition events from these files.[88]

While the cases described in the previous section can be understood as our awareness shifting to a different location below the surface of our ocean at the present time, these retrocognition cases can be understood as experiencing the same location in the past.

- LEY LINES

Jeffrey Keen concluded that dowsable fields are created and maintained in an "Information Field that pervades the universe."[89]

Ervin Laszlo

Like other paranormal phenomena, I would have dismissed divining and ley lines as well. But here again I had to change my outlook completely because of personal experiences. It started when our friends Grace and Douglas stayed with us for several days. Douglas suffered from diabetes and asked me if I had some physical work for him that would help him in lowering his high blood sugar level. So I asked him to find an underground plastic water pipe, so that we could connect a drinking trough in one of our fields to it. I showed him the location—along a dry-stone wall—where I thought the pipe was running underground. He started after breakfast, and by coffee time had dug a trench some 3 metres long and 0.5 metre deep at 90 degrees to the wall without, however, encountering the pipe.

During coffee we discussed the next step concluding that we had to go deeper, when Grace joined in offering to help us find the pipe. I countered that it was very stony soil and that the digging was very hard work indeed. 'No, that's not what I mean', she said, 'Can you make me a pair of dowsing rods?' She explained how I could make these from a steel wire coat hanger, and I made her a pair.

With these she entered the trench and walked towards the wall. There the rods crossed over and she said: 'Your pipe is right there'. And indeed at the very end of the trench that Douglas had dug—he starting about 10 cm from the wall and digging some 3 metres in the other direction—the pipe was hard up against the wall, and could simply be uncovered by hand. Obviously, a very clear triumph of feminine sensitivity and intuition over masculine reason and muscle!

Another problem became evident a few years later during a rare very dry summer. The spring we relied on for our drinking water, located in a field some 500 m away, dried out completely; so we had to tell friends staying with us to shower somewhere else, while we provided some water in plastic cans for emergencies.

A solution had to be found, so I consulted a water-engineering firm. The scheme they proposed was to pump the water up to our property from a lower-lying spring, which was, however, located not only much lower, but also rather far away. The cost of the scheme would have been prohibitive as well.

Then someone gave me the name of a water-diviner in a village not far away, and I made an appointment with him. He came, and by using his divining rods he pointed to a spot where according to him water was to be found (MX). This MX location, and the ones described below, can be found in figure 8.2. However, I did not dare to engage myself on a costly drilling exploration on this rather flimsy evidence alone.

Joop van Montfoort

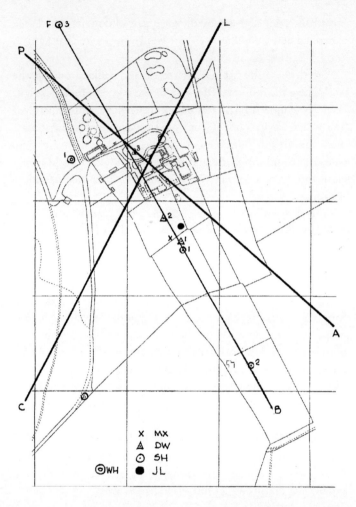

Figure 8.2 Ley lines at Halsecombe

Somewhat later, BBC television presented a series about the Cornish water diviner Donovan Wilkins. He seemed very confident, and several of his successful water finding exploits was shown during the series of programmes. So I wrote to the BBC, and Mr Wilkins replied that following the TV series he was very busy, but would come along in a couple of months. When he turned up, he told me that he had been a Cornish miner and that many of the successful members of that breed had been sensitives, so that they could locate ore by divining. He had changed his trade from finding ore to finding water.

I considered his 'ceremony' of placing little coloured discs, etc. on the ground, while he used his magic wand, a bit of mumbo-jumbo; but for a small fee he indicated three locations (DW1-3) where his son would drill for water in a few weeks, on a 'no cure, no fee' basis. The son turned up with a giant tractor with attached drilling gear, pulling an enormous compressor. At the first location he drilled some 80 metres down, but the only stuff that came to the surface was dust. At the second location it was the same story, and when he wanted to start on the third location, which was on the lawn in front of the house, Emmy stopped him and told him to find water somewhere else. Subsequently he took out his own divining rods and walked the field towards the main road, where he located a spot and started drilling until he broke his £1500 drill bit. He left rather upset and assured us that there was no water on our land. So we had still not come any closer to solving our water problem.

Some time later I saw an advert in our local paper by Peter Hedges offering to solve all water problems, also on a 'no cure no fee' basis. I rang him and told him about Mr Wilkins' exploits, but he could not be put off, because he told me that his wife Sheila had never yet failed to find water. They came, and she indicated a location close to where the Cornishman had been drilling. In fact the divining effect was so strong that her forked hazel branch was wrenched from her hands and broke, fortunately she had brought a spare one.

When they drilled (SH1), it was the same sorry story, just dust and no water. Peter told me that this was the first time Sheila had ever failed and as he is not a man to give up easily, they located a second place (SH2) to drill. There was a bit of water, but certainly not the promised quantity. So they tried again and drilled a third hole (SH3) in a field in front of our house. Some water, but not at all in accordance with Peter's projections and so Sheila indicated another possibility not far away.

Then the fact struck me that all the failed holes (SH1-3) were nearly on a straight line, as shown in figure 8.2. So I advised Peter and Sheila that she had obviously picked up something else; was it a 'ley line' that had interfered with Sheila's perception? So they got off that line, and the next attempt, in a small field north of Halsecombe Cottage (see chapter 10), yielded water in quantity. Subsequently cables and pipes were run to this hole, but when the pump was switched on a few weeks later, it turned out that the water had disappeared, perhaps the hole had been drilled too deep allowing the water to seep away.

So another borehole (WH1) was carefully sunk near it, and this has been our reliable source of drinking water for many years. Sheila and Peter are still friends, especially so because during the extremely dry summer of 2003 not only our spring but also this borehole dried up. They came again and located a new borehole (WH2), which supplied abundant water during the rest of that dry summer, while hosepipe bans were in place at many locations in the country, and while the water supply to a farm near us—which according to local legend had never before been without water—dried up.

Several years later, we asked my sons, who were staying with us on a holiday, to clear away a heap of broken corrugated roofing which was lying in a corner of a field west of Halsecombe House. They filled many bags and the outline of a hole 1.8 metres in diameter (JL) became visible. They persevered, and not only hundreds of glass bottles, but also an old cooker, a gas tank, gas light fittings, a spoked car wheel and a WW II US Navy gun-sight joined the growing heap of rubbish that emerged. The hole had initially been chiselled out very carefully, but deeper down it became rougher due to the fractured nature of the underlying rock.

The Exmoor Mines Research Group got interested, could it be a mineshaft? But although Paul Pickering (their chairman) maintains there is no evidence of minerals in this geology (nor is there water, in his opinion), a small group of us has been excavating, sorting and redepositing the household rubbish that filled the hole. At about 5 metres deep, the rubbish seemed to indicate that we are exploring the 1940s. We have no idea how deep the hole will turn out to be, which will only be known when someone decides to excavate it further.

Our local historian, Dennis Corner, told me later that this hole was dug as a well for a water supply in the 1890s by Jimmy Land, who farmed at nearby Westcott Farm. If Mr Land was a water diviner and believed as firmly in his divining evidence as his modern counterparts did, he had probably convinced Dr Potter (the owner of Halsecombe in that period), to dig for water where he indicated. The interesting fact is that also this hole is very close to the ley line as indicated in figure 8.2. If Mr Land was indeed a diviner, he was obviously fooled by something else as well, and after an enormous amount of unsuccessful effort, the hole was filled with rubbish.[90]

After all this evidence, I have to admit that a 'ley line' is at present the most likely explanation and when I told this story later to a local 'sensitive' Malcolm Wright, his immediate reaction was that Halsecombe was on the intersection of two ley lines! One of these runs from the stone circle on Almsworthy Common (A) via a burial mound to Porlock Church (P), the other one from Culbone Church (C) to those of Luccombe (L) and Timberscombe and then on to Croydon Hall (built on the location of an ancient monastery).[91] And as I have indicated in figure 8.2, the failed borehole evidence seems to point to a third one crossing St Agnes fountain (F) on North Hill and a couple of burial mounds on Exmoor (B).

When I gave a talk about these experiences in our local village hall, a question arose about 'negative ley lines'.[92] Malcolm Wright answered that there are no negative ley lines, their energy is neutral, how you experience it depends completely on your own disposition. I can only say that that statement fits in very well with my own experiences.

Later I found out that ley lines have been, and are, studied extensively. Alfred Watkins published a pioneering survey at the beginning of the twentieth century and many others have followed up his work.[93] Dowsing and ley lines seem even to have become respectable, witnessed by the opening sentence: 'Dowsing works, that much is now certain', in an article by Anthony Hopwood in *New Scientist* with the title: 'Dowsing, ley lines and the electromagnetic link'.[94] But that is barking up the wrong tree, as there is no electromagnetic link but instead a vertical association.

Another experience in relation to this ley line, confirmed for me that 'there is indeed more between heaven and earth than the eye can see'. In the 1999 Christmas period, a group of German friends stayed with us and I wanted to show them the above-mentioned stone circle on Almsworthy Common (crossed by one of our ley lines). However, when we arrived on the moor, cloud had descended and because of the dense fog we could not see any further than a few metres. So from Alderman's Barrow we walked south-east along a boundary hedge, and when I thought we had passed well beyond the stone circle, I lined our friends up at a few metres distance and we walked back in a north-easterly direction so that we could not miss it. Suddenly one of them shouted from far behind us that he had found it. He had not followed my obviously erroneous directions, but somehow 'knew' where the circle was and walked in the dense fog straight towards it. He had never been there before!

So all these experiences have further convinced me that there is much more between heaven and earth than can be explained horizontally. In particular the presence of something 'special' going on around these 'ley lines' has been verified by at least half a dozen independent witnesses.

- HEALING

For the performance of spectacular miracles there was no sect to rival the Quakers. Over 150 were attributed to their leader George Fox alone, and many other Friends boasted similar healing powers.[95]

Several attempts have been made to prove the reality of distance healing scientifically. Most of these have been rather unconvincing because we are all so different that there is no simple model that can be tested easily. In fact quite often it seems more to depend on the patient than on the healer. Take this humoristic case history related by Lawrence LeShan: 'However, all results must be evaluated cautiously. The most dramatic single result I had occurred when a man I knew asked me to do a distance healing for an extremely painful condition requiring immediate and intensive surgery. I promised to do the healing that night, and the next morning when he awoke a "miraculous cure" had occurred. The medical specialist was astounded and offered to send me pre and post healing X-rays and to sponsor publication in a scientific journal. It would have been the psychic healing case of the century except for one small detail. In the press of overwork, I had forgotten to do the healing! If I had only remembered, it would have been a famous demonstration of what can be accomplished by this method'.[96]

There have been numerous cases presented in books, articles and on television, but as I have no personal experience, I have to leave this subject to your personal discretion. If you have experienced that (distance) healing works, it can be fitted in and understood, in the light of our ocean model.

- Near-Death Experiences

There is no death, only a change of worlds.

Chief Seattle

But despite numerous attempts, no one has been able to scientifically explain all the elements of an NDE.[97]

Douglas Fox

I am not dying, I am entering into life.[98]

St Thérèse of Lisieux

With each LTP [Less-Than-Positive Near-Death Experience] we are reminded of the reasons why we are here. We are here to learn, to teach, to make a positive difference, and to be of service to others. We are here to learn and practice unconditional love and forgiveness, and to reconnect with our Creator.[99]

Barbara R. Rommer

This work with dying patients has also helped me to find my own religious identity, to know that there is life after death and to know that we will be reborn again one day in order to complete the tasks we have not been or willing to complete in this lifetime.[100]

Elisabeth Kübler-Ross

Raymond Moody, a medical doctor, was the first to have the courage to publish the experiences shared with him by some of his patients who had been 'dead'. Several of them, even after having had no discernible signs of life—such as heartbeat or brain wave activity—had sometimes, either spontaneously, or thanks to our modern revitalising techniques, revived from having been 'dead'. He coined the term 'near-death experience' (NDE) and published many case histories of what these patients told him of their experiences.[101] His first book triggered several more people, such as Elisabeth Kübler-Ross, Margot Grey, Kenneth Ring, Barbara Rommer and recently Brian Weiss, to record their own experiences, or those of their patients.

Margot Grey explains that '… the challenge to examine this phenomenon has until recently been largely ignored, as the medical and religious reaction to the experience seems generally to have been a denial of the possibility of its existence, and hence its consequent dismissal: 'It can't be true, therefore it isn't true'.[102] David Darling labels people with that attitude as 'intelligent people without brains',[103] but I would rather label them as with plenty of brains, but without open minds.

The recent experience of the difficulties I had—during my mother's last days, when I argued with the nurse and doctor to reduce the large amount of pills she was still with great difficulty supposed to swallow—is shared by others as well. This denial of death explains the often frantic activity to keep people alive instead of letting them die in peace and with dignity. Margot Grey shares my experience and writes (quoting Elisabeth Kübler-Ross): "The desire to be allowed to die in peace will be met with 'infusions, transfusions, a heart machine, or a tracheotomy'".[104]

In fact, the big surprise—the central mystery of many NDEs, is the reported expansion of consciousness as life shades into death. At just the moment we would expect awareness to close down, caused by the collapse of the body's life-support systems, and brain function becoming increasingly impaired, NDEers say that they experience startlingly brightened cognition. David Darling writes: '… In the words of one individual who went through this extraordinary, terminal transformation: "I felt as though I was awake for the first time in my life."' And a bit lower on the same page: 'One NDEer, speaking on Australian television, said: "I can't exactly describe it to you, but it was just all there. It was just there all at once. I mean, not one thing at one time, blinking on and off, but it was everything, everything at one time."'[105]

All this describes beautifully the experience of diving below the spacetime surface of our ocean. And if you think that the many NDE cases described in several books are difficult to check because you are convinced that these are just the result of realistic dreams, and that there is no 'hard scientific' evidence for them; take for instance this from an article in *The Lancet,* describing '... the case of a young woman "who had complications during brain surgery for a cerebral aneurysm. The EEG of her cortex and brainstem had become totally flat. After the operation, which was eventually successful, this patient proved to have had a very deep NDE." This included an out-of-body experience, during which she observed things that happened during the period of the flat EEG and that were subsequently verified'.[106]

Many NDE cases have shown that you can see without having to be inside your body, for instance floating above the scene and being able to report afterwards in great detail what happened e.g. during the operation while their body was lying unconscious with closed eyes on the operating table.[107] Or take that victim of a near fatal car crash in Switzerland, who during his out-of-body experience, noticed that while many of the other car drivers on their way to a football match were cursing, one woman was praying for the crash victim. He forced himself to remember her car registration number before returning to his body and, after he had recovered sufficiently, was able to trace her and thank her during their moving encounter.[108]

Kenneth Ring has done research on NDE cases involving people who have been blind since birth, 'Although congenitally blind, these people often describe things in tremendous detail as though they were sighted'.[109] And Brian Weiss even reports on a case of a blind woman who could describe in detail 'the pen, the clothes the doctors and nurses wore, the succession of people who came in and out the ICU [Intensive Care Unit] and what each did'. He concludes: 'Her *soul* had sight, not her body'.[110] Moody reports a similar case in a later book.[111]

There are also many reported NDE cases where patients hovering above the operating table describe, looking down on their unconscious bodies and even noticing items lying on ledges that they could never have seen from where their physical body was.[112] This seeing via the higher self rather than the body, is also the explanation for the mystery reported in *New Scientist* of the blind painter Esref Armagan who 'paints houses and mountains and lakes and faces and butterflies, but has never seen any of these things'.[113]

Brian Weiss is an example of a very courageous scientist, who as a 'Yale- and Columbia-trained psychiatrist … was so courageous to put his reputation and even livelihood on the line by publishing what he experienced with his patients when regressing them not only to past lives but also progressing them to future ones. He reports that we seem to have a choice of futures and by choosing the 'right' one we learn the desired lesson'.[114] How similar is this experience to that of the Greek soldier Er, reported on by Plato and whom I mentioned earlier. Moody reports on cases suggesting that the future is present as well, labelling it: 'The Flashforward'.[115]

An encounter with a 'being of light' was a frequent experience in NDE case histories, but how you identify that being, depends on your expectations. In Moody's American context, they ranged from an angel to Christ, while no one experienced 'a hell of flames and demons with pitchforks'. In his later book *The Light Beyond*, Moody reviews the NDE field and interviews a number of the other NDE researchers, some of whom have come across a few cases of people having dark experiences.[116] Generally the near-death experience changed people's lives profoundly, but he found that: 'No one has seen fit to proselytize, to try to convince others of the realities he experienced. Indeed, I have found that the difficulty is quite the reverse: People are naturally very reticent to tell others about what happened to them'.[117]

- BEFORE-BIRTH EXPERIENCES

... there is just consciousness floating free.[118]

Stephen Levine

I am disembodied. I am a point of floating consciousness.[119]

George Trevelyan

Her *soul* had sight, not her body.[120]

Brian Weiss

Reading about NDEs triggered in me a recollection of an experience I had when I was only a few years old. Lying in my crib before going to sleep, I remember that I could make something 'click' in my head. This transported me instantly into what I would now describe as interstellar space. All around me was total darkness, but there must have been light behind me because below me at an angle I could discern the vague outline of a vortex, a bit like a view of a tropical hurricane as seen from Skylab as shown in figure 8.3; but then observed at night with only some glistening of light reflecting from its funnel like outline.

Figure 8.3 Spacetime is at the end of the funnel? (NASA)

I was conscious, without having a body and obviously I could "think" without having a brain and "see" without having eyes, similar to the descriptions in the quotations I opened this section with and some of the NDEs described earlier.[121] Then I decided to float towards the edge of the vortex which, when I approached its edge, sucked me inside it with irresistible force.[122] I remember that this was followed by a very unnerving experience, like being squeezed through a funnel. The next thing I knew was that I was back in bed covered in goose pimples. Because I have always been a very curious investigator, I remember having repeated the experiment several times.

The soldier Er in Plato's tale, referred to earlier, explained that before being incarnated we have to drink from the 'River of Forgetfulness'. Obviously I had been naughty by not taking my full allocation, which explains why I had some recollection of my choice to 'incarnate'. This personal vortex experience of 'incarnating' seems to parallel David Ash's description of reality evolving from elementary particles to the universe as vortex based.[123]

My personal 'before-birth experience' (BBE) is confirmed by what Helen Wambach found when she researched the subject extensively. She stated: 'Of the 750 subjects reporting the birth experience, 81 percent said that they choose to be born and that it was their choice to make'. They often chose to be born reluctantly but did so because of the importance of learning certain lessons, while '90 percent of my subjects found that death was pleasant'.[124] Joan Grant confirmed these findings: 'No one is ever *sent* into incarnation'.[125] And if you are eager to know why people do make the choice to incarnate, consult Helen Wambach's or Barbara Rommer's books, in which they reproduce many of the individual answers.

It is certainly very interesting that not only their subjects, but also the persons having had an NDE reported on by Moody and others, had lost their fear of death completely. Barbara Rommer reports one of her subjects saying: 'It's easier to die than to be born, but the fear is built into us. People need to know that when they die they'll just be home with God'.[126] And one of Moody's subjects even remembering thinking, "Oh, I'm dead! How lovely!"[127]

In her book *Blessing in Disguise,* Barbara Rommer quotes the near-death researcher P. M. H. Arwater, who after describing his NDE research with children, indicates that: 'It is apparent to me that we, as a society, need to reconsider research findings of brain development in newborns and toddlers. Half of the child experiencers in my research base, for instance, could remember their birth, one-third had prebirth memory, and most of those that I could verify; via their mothers' testimony, began remembering at around seven months in utero, the same time medical science tells us that the fetus can feel and respond to pain'.[128]

We can deduce from these experiences that the real plight seems to be taking the decision of being born, but many also revealed that their choice of being incarnated in the second half of the twentieth century was deliberate because it is the time of 'enlightenment', 'spiritual awakening' and 'expansion of consciousness'.[129] They also found it often very hard to express their experiences: '... our world—the world we are living in now—is three-dimensional, but the next one definitely isn't. And that is why it's so hard to tell you this. I have to describe it to you in words that are three-dimensional. ... I can't really give you a complete picture'.[130]

But although we will always have difficulty gaining full insight while being in our bodies (remember Flatland), all these cases of transcendental experiences, whether NDEs or BBEs, can be understood in the context of our four-dimensional ocean model. It also explains the findings that children (and chimpanzees) beat adults at memory games.[131] There is simply less clutter (our layer of seaweed) between their conscious mind and the permanent unconscious (Akashic) memory. And if you think that NDEs or BBEs are rare, visit the amazing website: www.near-death.com for an extensive collection of these experiences.

8.3 DISCUSSION

We are not just highly evolved animals with biological computers embedded inside our skulls; we are also field of consciousness without limits, transcending time, space, matter, and linear causality.[132]

Stanislav Grof

... one thing I know, that, whereas I was blind, now I see.

John 9: 25

Matter is not that which produces consciousness, but that which limits it.[133]

Ferdinand Schiller

In fact, there is no paranormal or supernatural; there are only the normal and the natural—and the mysteries yet to be explained. It is the job of science, not pseudoscience, to solve those puzzles with natural, rather than supernatural explanations.[134]

Michael Schermer

If the hearer has the divine spark which makes philosophy congenial to him and fits him for its pursuit, the way described to him appears so wonderful that he must follow it with all his might if life is to be worth living.[135]

Plato

All the reported cases of phenomena that defy a horizontal explanation are for me supporting evidence for the reality of the vertical dimension, and confirm that we indeed live on the flimsy spacetime surface of an ocean of infinite energy, which some of us can tap into by going inside. Science accepts the fact of this vertical 'vacuum energy' as well—by, for instance, having accepted the reality of the Casimir effect, which manifests itself as a force exerted on two parallel plates at a minute distance.[136] The force between these plates is described as being derived from the energy present in the so-called 'vacuum'.[137] This vacuum, however, (as the word itself seems to imply) is not empty at all but, as we have seen, bristling with infinite (dark) energy.[138] With some artistic freedom, one could say that Eckhart was his time centuries ahead when he said 'The ground of the soul is dark'.

As had become clear to me from my personal BBE described above, our consciousness is not an 'epiphenomenon' of just having large and complicated brains, as is accepted by many scientists.[139] And if you believe that our personality is derived from hard-wired instructions in our genes while our brains are being built, this would imply that identical twins—having identical genes—would have identical personalities. That this is clearly not the case implies that our individual mind is independent of the body, which it needs to manifest itself in the spacetime realm only.[140] Just to quote one example from Judith Rich Harriss' book: 'Take Ladan and Laleh Bijani, conjoined twins from Iran who died in 2003 during an attempt to separate them. They were identical twins who had spent their entire 29 years joined at the head. And yet Ladan, the more outspoken of the pair told journalists before the surgery: "We are two completely separate individuals, we have different lifestyles, we think very differently about issues." Why did Ladan and Laleh have different personalities? We know the answer can't be in their genes because they had the same genes'.[141]

Similarly, the behaviour on the road of the same make and type of car does hardly depend on the car (body), but rather on the individual characteristics of their respective drivers (souls). Or read for instance the extensive, well-referenced study undertaken by Gary Lachman and presented in his book, *A Secret History of Consciousness*.[142] All of this warrants the conclusion that we are indeed spiritual beings, i.e. souls who do not need a body to be conscious. Dennis Kelsey states: '... in a human being there must be an element that exists and is capable of function even in the absence of a physical body!'[143] For reasons that are often beyond understanding—but have been explained in several traditions as a means of progressing towards enlightenment, we voluntary take the decision to incarnate (my decision to go to the edge of the 'vortex'), taking on a body to experience a life in the horizontal domain.[144]

Both Stanislav Grof and Rupert Sheldrake use the example of a television set to illustrate that horizontal biology behaves like the man from the depths of the jungle who is given a TV receiver. Because he has an investigative mind and has no idea that the images on his screen are derived from a remote transmitter, he takes the set apart to discover where the events and people on his screen come form. And if he is intelligent and careful he will be able to construct a reasonable model of what the results to the final image are of changes to the different components in his set. We, however, know that the set is only a passive transducer of the images generated in a studio and transmitted via electromagnetic waves from a transmitter that is often far away.

In a similar way, the soul uses the body to manifest itself in spacetime. Or to use the language of my trade again, the brain is not the computer hardware running the 'consciousness' software, but a very sophisticated interface driving our body and thus allowing our non-material self to manifest itself in the horizontal dimension.[145] After stating that 'our mental functions are linked to biological processes in our brains', Grof supports my view, writing: 'However, this does not necessarily mean that consciousness originates in or is produced by our brains. This conclusion made by Western science is a metaphysical assumption rather than a scientific fact ...'[146] He then uses the, above mentioned TV set example of how a television repair person is able to repair the set without this being seen as proof that 'the set itself was responsible for the programs when we turn it on'.

As I already indicated, my own BBE experience demonstrated to me that I could think without having a brain, or even a body, and this experience supports and explains what was described in an editorial in *New Scientist* about research in Britain that '... produced evidence that fetuses can remember music heard at just 20 weeks. What makes this so extraordinary is that fetuses this young don't yet have a cerebral cortex'.[147] Hence I fully agree with Ferdinand Schiller, whom I quoted at the beginning of this section: 'Matter is not that which produces consciousness, but that which limits it'. And indeed, defects in the body can seriously hamper the possibilities of expressing yourself in the physical dimension. Charles de Gaulle expressed this knowledge, when—after the death of his Down's syndrome daughter—he said, *'Maintenant elle est comme les autres'* (Now she is like the others).

Benjamin Libet and his team did some very interesting experiments, confirming the point I am stressing here, that the body is rather the executor than the initiator of physical actions: 'One of Libet's experiments involved connecting subjects to an EEG and asking them to flex their wrist spontaneously at any moment they felt the urge. He found that the subjects showed a readiness potential—a sharp drop in electrical activity in the brain that serves to clear the way for a neural event—a full half-second before any wrist flexions occurred. Even more surprising, this readiness potential showed up a good three hundred milliseconds before subjects reported consciously experiencing any impulse to make a move'.[148]

In the pages following this quotation from David Darling's book *After Life*, he discusses several similar research results, leading to him quoting a conclusion by Daniel Dennett that the factuality of these results 'demolishes the long-held concept of the Cartesian "I" inhabiting the brain'.[149]

I interpret this result as the 'software' (our non material self/soul) taking the decision, followed by the action in the 'interface' (brain), subsequently passing on the command to the 'peripheral' (body); again supporting the evidence that our actions are initiated—and our memories are stored—below the spacetime ocean's surface. Just to quote one other example in support of this model from a subject I was very much involved in; honeybees with 'a brain the size of a pinhead' do not only have the well known exceptional cell construction and navigational skills, but recent research seemed to demonstrate that: 'It has already been shown that they can count; now it seems they can recognise human faces'.[150]

The mystery of the development of a fertilised egg into its adult form can indeed be very well explained by what Sheldrake called 'morphic resonance'. Science tries desperately to find the blueprint for this development in the genes present in the chromosomes. Again comparing the building of a living being for the moment with the building of a house, for me the genes contain the recipes for the building materials. How to make bricks, pipes, roof tiles etc. translates into how to make amino acids, cells etc. needed in the different cells of the body that end up as bone, arteries, hair, etc. The architect's design of the completed building in his drawings corresponding to the design of the organism stored as a Form/Idea below the surface of our ocean.[151] Apart from many other examples, this model explains that—although the 'difference in the protein-coding sequences of DNA between chimps and man is only about one percent'—they are very different creatures indeed.[152]

Granted that scientists have often failed to recognise valuable new developments, I have on the other hand great sympathy for their conservative, restrictive attitude.[153] If indeed anything goes, imagine how many irresponsible people would set up shop to cure us and our world of all ills, while their hidden agenda would be to make a good living from people's credulity! Yet we have to take that risk and open our hearts, as one of Barbara Rommer's

NDE cases urged her: 'Please tell everyone, Doc, that the answer to everything is love'.[154]

Only after I had finished writing this book did I come across the series of books written by John Davidson, extolling in a much more extensive way the same message as I am trying to convey here.[155] He illustrates in detail the fascinating links with ancient Indian philosophy. However, when he advocates the fact that 'Free Energy' directly obtained from the vacuum will be generally available, I part company with him completely.[156] In all the cases listed by him and the cases I have described above, the crucial ingredient is always a particular person, i.e. someone who has her/his vertical channel open (remember the *chercher la femme* remark in my summary of Benviste's experiments described earlier). Without this 'sensitive' person present, the experiment will fail!

So I would like to end this chapter dealing with scientifically impossible phenomena with a falsifiable statement in the Popperian tradition: 'Unless there is a person involved having a channel open to the infinite possibilities of the vertical dimension, paranormal phenomena are not reproducible'. Hence in all 'normal' cases the laws of physics rule supreme and unless many of us are enlightened, 'free energy' will remain a *fata morgana*. This leads directly to the conclusion that initiating costly research programmes to tame these phenomena—whether it is cold fusion or space travel—for general use, is a waste of money.

The only way to achieve fulfilment is the path indicated by all spiritual teachers, i.e. towards enlightenment. Only then will we not have to sacrifice our beautiful planet to horizontal pursuits as we doing now, but then everything will be available to all of us without limitations. But if the message of the importance of the vertical dimension has been extolled so often, what has gone wrong over and over again, will be explored in the next chapter.

9 WHAT WENT WRONG?

9.1 EVERYTHING IS FINE, ISN'T IT?

I had also learned [attending a US school] that a person thinks with his head instead of his heart.[1]

Sun Chief

One of the principal factors that hinder us from fully appreciating our interdependence is our undue emphasis on material development.
We have become so engrossed in its pursuit that, unknowingly, we have neglected the most basic qualities of compassion, caring and cooperation.[2]

The Dalai Lama

When a civilization lacks rites of passage, its soul is sick. The evidence for this sickness is threefold: first, there are no elders; second, the young are violent; third, the adults are bewildered.[3]

Meladoma Some

In the last analysis, the psychological roots of the crisis humanity is facing on a global scale seem to lie in the loss of the spiritual perspective.[4]

Stanislav Grof

The economy grows by so many percentage points each year, the High Streets are full of shoppers—many in expensive designer clothes—carrying full shopping bags, cars are getting more and more refined, while the road network is growing apace. Consumerism now obviously fulfils the role of the 'bread', while TV, the Internet and so many of the latest gadgets provides the 'games' twenty-four hours a day. And didn't the Romans teach us that those in government could keep the people happy by giving them bread and games? Obviously we are doing something right, otherwise why would so many people from other parts of the world want to join in the fun, sometimes taking enormous personal risks to get into Western Europe or the USA? So it seems that we are very much on the right track.

No, we aren't, you only need to glance at a newsstand, listen to, or watch the daily news, to realise that—even allowing for the fact that 'good news is no news'—we seem to be in a terrible mess. Every opposition party decries what they think the party in government is doing wrong. But when the voters finally believe their remonstrations and vote them in to take the seat of power, it takes them only a brief period to stumble into similar pitfalls that they could so clearly point out before. Michael Wiederman puts our vain materialistic (horizontal) striving very much in focus: 'American capitalism rests on the assumption that we can achieve or buy happiness, a belief that fuels competition and consumerism. The research showing a lack of correlation between wealth and happiness casts doubt on this assumption. But competing for wealth is more than just an unproductive way to achieve happiness; it is a recipe for unhappiness'.[5]

In this book I do not want to linger on negative issues—which could easily fill a book on their own—so I will illustrate my concerns about what we are doing to this beautiful planet with just a few brief remarks and quotations relevant to (air) travel and diet.

If we are really serious about trying to save the planet from rising temperatures, then flying as little as possible should be one of our highest priorities. Instead of all our hectic rushing around horizontally, we would do much wiser to heed this testimony from the ancient vertical tradition of Taoism that:

> You can see the whole world without leaving your room.
> You can see the universe without even looking out your window.
> In fact, it is often true that the farther one travels the less one sees.
> By looking inside himself, the wise man sees with his heart and mind,
> And his heart and his mind see everywhere.[6]

This wisdom was powerfully articulated by a recluse—living in a Himalayan cave near a meditation retreat centre where he sometimes came in for a meal—when he expressed his refusal after being offered a fully paid-for excursion to England by one of the participants, with the reply: 'I am England'.

But what is often not widely advertised is that our eating habits are also a very important contributor to global warming. Not only the CO_2 contribution resulting from the production, processing and distribution of meat products, but also the enormous quantity of methane resulting from the raising of livestock is very important. Geoff Russel pointed out in a letter to *New Scientist* that 'the biggest source of methane arising from human activity is livestock'.[7]

Although I come very much from a meat eating tradition, and even in my teens was the butcher in the family (rabbits, chickens and geese), I was changed completely by a series of recurrent dreams, of which I remember the last one vividly:

I was witnessing the scene inside a cattle truck transporting a number of animals to the slaughterhouse. I was aware of the fact that the animals 'knew' they were going to die, and they wanted to prepare themselves for that momentous event. But their desire to have a moment of silence was made completely impossible by a couple of farmhands travelling in the back of that vehicle as well. Being Dutch, they wore wooden shoes and blue overalls and were indulging in horseplay, rolling around on the floor and repeatedly bumping into the animals. Consequently the animals arrived at the slaughterhouse without having found a moment of peace to prepare themselves for dying.

I woke up, deeply horrified and shocked about the farmhands' profound ignorance of the feelings of these animals, but soon realised that they just exemplified mankind's lack of insight. Waking up Emmy, I told her that I would never eat meat or its products again. So, against the whole tradition I grew up in, I became a vegetarian and I never have been in any doubt about the correctness of that spontaneous decision. Su Taylor comments: 'Everybody is trying to come up with different ways to reduce carbon footprints. But one of the easiest things you can do is to stop eating meat'.[8]

These are just two issues of the many problems facing mankind, but I do believe that they illustrate convincingly the appropriateness of the remark Dean Inge made a long time ago: 'The more man disbelieves in the next world, the more hideous he makes this one'.[9]

I will now discuss briefly what went wrong with our attitudes to healing and religion.

9.2 FROM HEALING TO MEDICAL SCIENCE

It is more important to know what kind of a person has a disease than to know what kind of disease a person has.

Hippocrates

One of the most dangerous errors in medicine is to treat symptoms and not get at the underlying pathology of the disease itself. Aspirin and ice packs may lower the fever but at the same time allow the underlying infection to destroy the vital organs of the body.[10]

Howard A. Rusk

As healers, then, we have to be able to transform people. We have to create in them the ability to reach out for their highest aspirations. We are not here merely to make organs function better. There are large issues at stake. Healing is meant to change the patient and, if necessary, his way of life.[11]

Lilla Bek and Philippa Pullar

Simply put, belief sickens; belief kills; belief heals.[12]

R A Hahn

In chapter 5, I have touched upon the subject of medicine already, illustrating it with examples from my own experience. Here I want to cast the net wider and show that there are many voices proclaiming the vitally important message that the intuitive vertical dimension has to be taken very seriously indeed.

If we look for instance at the evidence collected by Holger Kalweit in his book *Shamans, Healers and Medicine Men*,[13] we see that in every corner of the world there have always been men and women led by an inner vision, helping suffering mankind. He describes many instances of miraculous cures by the prescription of, for instance herbal remedies, some of them corresponding very much with my own personal experiences. If these shamanic healing stories are dismissed as coming from uneducated 'primitive' people; as a contrast I will now take a case history from, supposedly, the other end of our highly prized intellectual spectrum.

Michael Gearin-Tosh is an Oxford don who in 1994 was diagnosed with cancer, and was told that unless he started chemotherapy immediately, he had only a few months to live. Instead of following that seemingly reasonable advice, he followed his own intuition and—although quoting the medical maxim that 'the therapeutic benefit of hope cannot be overstated'—he subjected himself to a rigorous regime of diet and vitamins. After nearly ten years he is still very much alive and was able to tell the tale of his struggles and experiences.[14] At the end of his book, one of his many academic friends argues that his case still falls within the possibilities of survival statistics, and if you are interested in the fine details of his case, they are even available on the Internet.[15]

Michio Kushi and Alex Jack very much support Gearin-Tosh's thesis that a healthy diet is essential, writing: 'As many friends have declared after changing their lifestyle and eating macrobiotically, "Cancer was the greatest thing that ever happened to me. I learned that I had created it myself through years of wrong eating and wrong way of life. And what I made, I can unmake. After becoming macrobiotic, learning to cook and eat properly, and changing my view of life and way of living, I never felt better. My life is immeasurably enriched.'"[16]

These results are compatible with the experience Stephanie Matthews-Simonton, Carl Simonton and James Creighton report in their book *Getting Well Again*. They illustrate that '[cancer] is a disease associated with industrialised society' and reveal a straightforward connection with psychological factors such as worry and 'seeing no way out'.

Also in chapter 5, I have illustrated with several cases that it takes a lot of courage to stick your neck out and declare that you take the vertical dimension seriously. John Templeton had that courage and said: 'If governments encourage people to become more spiritual there will be a reduction in healthcare'.[17]

But it is not only scientists—who after all are supposed to defend their horizontal bastions frantically—who are vilified when they have the courage to ponder the possibility that there could be something beyond the confines of the horizontal dimension. Take for instance Hazel Courteney, who was maligned after she had the courage to write the book *Divine Intervention* about her spiritual experiences (starting of all places at Harrods in London).[18] In her follow-up book she writes: 'When *Divine [Intervention]* first appeared, media flak virtually destroyed my reputation as an alternative health columnist almost overnight. My credibility—and an excellent salary—were gone'.[19]

But in spite of all these risks, the experiences I have mentioned may have whetted your appetite and you might feel like investigating this very important medical field further. A good start could be Lynne McTaggart's book *What Doctors Don't Tell You*. It has as a subtitle: *The truth about the dangers of modern medicine.*[20] In this book she has collected a wide spectrum of well-documented medical case histories. Very much in parallel with my own experience as a gout patient (chapter 5), she asks—referring to another illness—the pertinent question: 'Is angioplasty being done for cardiologists or for patients?'[21] And after investigating the issue, she concludes: 'Modern medicine doesn't work because the very paradigm on which it is based is faulty—that germs or genes alone are responsible for illness and that our bodies are akin to complicated machines'.[22]

Of course I am fully aware that there are a great number of marvellous and caring doctors who wear themselves out in alleviating the sufferings of mankind, and I would be very grateful to be treated by one of them if the need arose. But especially in hospitals, doctors and nurses are often put under such pressures that there is hardly time to give serious attention to their patients. I was once rushed to the eye hospital in Oxford by ambulance and then had to wait for several hours before someone could look at my 'requires attention urgently' case. Fortunately there are now many positive signs of a move from mechanistic to holistic medical care to report as well. One, for instance, is that in recent years all our local surgeries have created space for complementary therapists.

9.3 FROM *RELIGARE* TO ORGANISING

I am for religion, against religions.[23]

Victor Hugo

It is one of the gifts of great spiritual teachers to make things simple. It is one of the gifts of their followers to complicate them again.[24]

Julia Cameron

I myself feel the Vatican has made me a post-denominational priest in a post-denominational era. I think denominations are passé. People in their twenties today, the post-modern generation, don't even *know* the difference between a Lutheran and an Anglican and a Roman Catholic, much less care.[25]

Matthew Fox

Religions usually begin as movements of radical liberation along spiritual lines but inevitably end up as pillars of the very societies which are the jailers of our souls.[26]

Stephan A. Hoeller

If Christianity cannot recover its mystical tradition and teach it, it should just fold up and go out of business, it has nothing to say.[27]

Bede Griffiths

To be a good Muslim we need to love not just our fellow Muslims but also Hindus, Christians, Jews and the rest. It may be a tall order, but without such vision religion has no meaning whatsoever.[28]

Maulana Wahiduddin Khan

As we have seen, practically all religious leaders proclaimed the simple but profound message that we will never find our life's fulfilment in the horizontal dimension and that our most important task should be the re-establishment of our inner, vertical connection. And as I pointed out before, this is poignantly expressed by the Latin verb *re-ligare* from which our word religion is derived. It appears that Eastern religions have in general remained much closer to that original message and that especially in the West we have lost our vertical pathway almost completely—which fact was so vividly illustrated by the triumphant intellect crowning a goddess of Reason in the cathedral of Notre Dame in Paris after the French Revolution.

Because so much of our western 'civilisation' is based on it, I will take Christianity as illustration of how a beautiful example and teaching has been corrupted for power political ends.[29] Napoleon Bonaparte expressed this fact clearly and honestly: 'A nation must have a religion, and that religion must be under the control of the state'.[30] Therefore, when participating in a church service, the reading of the creed gives me very much the creeps because I know that it was imposed upon the early church by great political pressure and was later tailored to fit current fashion.[31] Even little Anna writes: 'I don't like to go to cherch very much and I do not go becase I do not think Mister God is in cherch and if I was Mister God I would not go'.[32] I realise that it could be considered ironic, but I do see it instead as very refreshing that the foreword to the thirtieth anniversary edition of the *Anna* books containing this line was written by the Archbishop of Canterbury.[33]

As I outlined in chapter 6, Jesus' original message is clearly a vertical one, but one that can only be experienced rather than preached. And as we have seen as well, to bring about that experience you have to create the 'Be still and know that I am God' condition, which is clearly beyond the immediate possibilities of the millions in our hectic human society. Think of work pressure, the jostling and shopping in the streets of our cities, people with their mobile phones stuck permanently to their ears, surfing the World Wide Web glued to their computer screens, or any other of the countless distractions we are subjected to, all denying us the opportunity to 'be still and know'.

Often the original message is soon lost, and it is very understandable that many of the sensitives of the early centuries disappeared into the Middle-Eastern desert and became the fathers of several monastic traditions. Fortunately they left a copy of the Gospel of Thomas behind, of which Michio Kushi writes that 'The emerging consensus is that the *Gospel of Thomas* is not Gnostic at all but is the earliest of all the Christian gospels and preserves Jesus' teachings in the simplest, most original form'. It is interesting that Kushi analyses its sayings from his Japanese Buddhist background.[34]

In case you are in any doubt about the beauty of Jesus' original teachings, read Andrew Harvey's eye-opening *Son of Man*. Much of his book is based on early writings that have miraculously escaped the frenzy of destruction of all other texts than the approved New Testamental ones. Not only were the texts destroyed, but people—such as the Gnostics, having insights other than the official one—were eliminated as well.

It should be very clear that true religion does not focus on the (horizontal) dogmatic differences, but rather on the common (vertical) spiritual message! Krishnamurti puts it bluntly that '... religion has nothing to do with priests, churches, dogmas, or organised beliefs'. But the organisers took over very successfully indeed. The original pagan temple sites had already been converted into churches and the politicians (such as the emperor Constantine) also became involved.[35] Church leaders often wallowed in power and riches, completely ignoring the warning uttered by the founder of their religion: 'How hard it is for those who have riches to make their way into the Kingdom of God'.[36] That the head dominated the heart was put in sharp focus by Lin Yutang who described how one of the consequences of this 'horizontalising' is that '... I had already arrived at the position that the Christian theologians were the greatest enemies of the Christian religion'.[37]

Aldous Huxley explains in a similar vein—when discussing why it is so difficult to reconcile Mysticism and Christianity—that it is 'Simply because so much Roman and Protestant thinking was done by those very lawyers whom Christ regarded as being peculiarly incapable of understanding the true nature of things'.[38] Indeed, the true nature of things will only become clear when we 'make [our] way into the Kingdom of God', which way can, however, so easily be obstructed by accumulating possessions. Jesus expressed this fact concisely: 'It is easier for a camel to go through the eye of a needle than for a rich man to enter the kingdom of God'.[39]

The French scientist Blaise Pascal expressed the certainty resulting from his personal religious experience euphorically: 'FIRE. God of Abraham, God of Isaac, God of Jacob, not of the philosophers and scholars. Certainty. Certainty. Feeling of Joy. Peace'.[40] And from a lovely book about Leslie Weatherhead, written by his son, Kingsley—which is full of vivid stories of how Leslie ridiculed so much 'sacred' nonsense—I cannot resist quoting in full a beautiful "dream" '... in which an Anglican clergyman approached Heaven's gate when he died, understanding that the knowledge of the Athanasian creed was the important qualification for entry. Peter cups his ear and says, "Huh?" and the minister proceeds to recite it: "... neither confounding the Persons nor dividing the Substance—the Glory equal, the Majesty co-eternal—the Father eternal: the Son eternal: the Holy Ghost eternal. And yet there are not three eternals, but one eternal. And in this Trinity none is afore or after another. But the whole three Persons are eternal and co-eternal..." At length in the dream Peter looked up, shook his head, and said, "You carry on. I'm going fishing!"'[41]

We have seen how the Church so often simply became a tool in political power struggles, even becoming an instrument of the state, as Henry VIII did quite openly with the Church of England. It is then used to keep the populace in their 'proper' place, rather than being a tool for spreading the light.[42] We all know how much suffering the bloody suppression of anyone not following the party line has caused all over Europe. And I fully share the horror of Matthew Fox when he visited St Paul's Cathedral in London for the first time: 'I was shocked. I went up this aisle and here's some soldier who killed thousands of Indians in a battle in the Punjab and here's one who killed thousands in another battle. Right in the heart of a cathedral'.[43]

Instead you might expect that the Church following the teachings of Jesus—that 'he who draws the sword will be destroyed by it'—would stand up to the state or power-hungry dictators so obviously flouting these teachings; but that is often not the case at all. I remember having seen a photograph—taken in fascist Italy of the 1930s—of Roman Catholic priests goose-stepping in a parade for Mussolini's birthday, and other priests blessing the arms to be used in the invasion of Ethiopia.

The Jesuit William Johnston is similarly horrified: 'Yes. Some things in our history make me blush. How come the Church preached the crusades, encouraged wars, threw holy water on guns and battleships? And there is the scandalous fact that Christians have been fighting among themselves for centuries'.[44] And that this still happens today was shown on the TV news only a few years ago, when another Christian priest blessed Cruise missiles as they came off their production line in the USA.

Hence I agree completely with Andrew Harvey when he comments on Jesus' statement: 'Render to Caesar the things that are Caesar's and to God the things that are God's', with the observation: '... ironic has been the use of Jesus' statement as a justification for military service and the waging of one horrifying war after another, when it was precisely to prevent the use of military violence that the statement was made in the first place. One of the many obscenities of church history has been the only barely comprehensible denial that Jesus' teachings about love of enemies had any kind of political validity'.[45]

Or take these lines from that ex-soldier Laurens van der Post, noting that 'Fewer and fewer of us can find [religious awareness] any more in churches and temples and the religious establishments of our time. Much as we long for the churches to renew themselves and once more become, in contemporary idiom, an instrument of the pentecostal spirit, many of us now have to testify that, despite the examples of dedicated men devoted to their theological vocations, they have failed to give modern man a living experience of religion such as I and others have found in the desert and the bush of Africa'.[46] The American Indian writer, Ohiyesa underlines van der Post's statement: 'As a child I understood how to give; I have forgotten this grace since I became civilized'.[47]

Hence I envy the people who still have access to this type of ancient wisdom, such as for instance the ancient African traditions described by Adama and Naomi Doumbia in their book *The Way of the Elders*. This wisdom has been passed on by word of mouth, accompanied by appropriate ceremonies, through the generations, and could well date from the very beginnings of mankind. This is still going on, while we, in the so-called civilised West have been whitewashed, and the result of our lack of ancient roots and traditional wisdom is clearly expressed in the so often rowdy behaviour of our young men. They are not taught ancient wisdom by wise elders anymore, nor subjected to meaningful rites of passage, marking so clearly the passage from boyhood to manhood, which is so important for their self-esteem. The only way out of their purposelessness and hopelessness seems to be via posturing, as is often expressed in misuse of drugs, alcohol, fast cars, violence, vandalism, etc., to fill their emptiness and in being taken seriously by their gang mates.

I want this book to proclaim a positive message, so I will not dwell further on all the horrors that have been committed, not only by the RC 'Holy Inquisition', but also in, for instance, Calvinistic Europe and the Church of England's domain. The irony is that many of these crimes have been committed in Jesus' name, and I am sure that if he knew about them, he would turn in his grave.[48] If this remark shocks you, read Simcha Jacobovici and

Charles Pellegrino's book, *The Jesus Tomb*; or Andrew Harvey's book, which I mentioned earlier; or The *Myth of God Incarnate* by a group of Christian theologians.[49]

However, as I see it, in their urge to be taken seriously by their academic colleagues, many theologians have very much thrown the baby out with the bath water, because for me not only Jesus' body but everything physical is 'God incarnate'. And as Butterworth points out, if we make Jesus 'the object of our worship, He ceases to be the way-shower for our own self-realisation and self-unfoldment'.[50] We have indeed pulled God down to our level by remaking him in our image, making the Lollards' pithy observation still relevant today: 'God made man and not man God, as the carpenter doth make the house and not the house the carpenter'.[51]

I will illustrate this complete disregard of the original message with a few events that have stuck in my memory and which I experienced during my growing up in a Calvinistic church environment in the Netherlands. I can never forget, from when I was little, that during a church service a family was subjected to the formalised expulsion procedure of 'Cutting off from the Community'.[52] I experienced that ritualistic procedure as if the family concerned was pushed straight into hell. Another memory is of a minister pounding the pulpit while thundering, 'Our God is a God of wrath!' and that we were 'doomed miserable sinners, unless...'

Many people have argued appropriately that the present form of Christianity is not the religion of Jesus at all, but owes much more to the writings of Paul. This point of view is put concisely by Holger Kersten as: 'Out of the Good News brought by Jesus, Paul has made news that is dark and threatening, from the menace of which only he could show the way out'.[53]

When I was a teenager, heated debates went on in our church about an article in the church regulations. Which theology professor was right and which one was wrong? It led to our Calvinistic (*Gereformeerde*) church splitting into two, one half vividly accentuating the horizontal nature of the conflict by putting 'art. 31' behind the name of their church—thus proudly indicating that they kept to what was for them a crucial article of the church regulations. And when you counter that this all happened more than fifty years ago, and tolerance is now so much greater, let me just remind you of the recent 'excommunication' of Lord Mackay, the former Lord Chancellor, by the 'Wee Frees' (a breakaway Scottish Presbyterian Church) for attending the funeral service of a judge who happened to be a Roman Catholic.[54]

Or take this even more recent example from the US. Along with Neale Donald Walsch, I am deeply shocked that a Lutheran pastor was assailed by other 'Christians' because he participated with representatives of other religions in a memorial service for the victims of the 9/11 (11 September 2001) destruction of the World Trade Center in New York. Above and in chapter 6, I have described some of my own experiences of a similar intolerance, but with Walsch I had indeed believed that these shortsighted attitudes had been well left behind us. Walsch's comments on this 'Christian' attitude are worth quoting: 'How can we ask the world to heal itself when organized religion—the very institution that was meant to provide that healing—does nothing but inflict more and more damage, open wider and wider the wound, spread further and further its righteous indignation, its non-acceptance, its utter disdain, its total intolerance?'[55]

Heated academic theological debates have been going on and on, and when I walk into a bookshop in the small village in The Netherlands where my mother lived, I find the shelves filled with theological books. Particularly impressive is a hefty, 75 mm thick volume called *Gereformeerde Dogmatiek* (Calvinistic Dogmatics). I am sure that if Jesus were alive today, the only use he could see for it, and for a whole host of other similarly 'learned' books, would be to light a fire to fry his fishes.

Here again, we could have learned so much from Eastern wisdom, take this from China, for example: 'Do not criticize or argue about the scriptures and teachings. Do not detest the sage's writings. ... Always act as though you were face to face with the gods'.[56] Or this from the Indian sage Shankara: 'Talk as much philosophy as you please, worship as many gods as you like, observe all ceremonies, sing devoted praises to any number of divine beings—liberation never comes, even at the end of a hundred aeons, without the realization of the Oneness of Self'.[57] Walsch underlines this same point in a recent book, where he has God say: 'One of the biggest problems in the world today is organized religion. ... Not all religions, but most. And certainly, most of the largest'.[58] Eric Butterworth's brisk statement points to the solution for that problem: '... if the church is doing its job sincerely, it will be forever trying to put itself out of business'.[59] And Lenny Bruce puts the same message pithily: 'Every day, people are straying away from the church and going back to God'.[60]

Contrast our Western, often nitpicking academic attitude with the remark made by a Japanese Shinto priest when he was asked by a Western theologian: 'I've been now to a good many ceremonies and have seen quite a number of shrines, but I don't get the ideology; I don't get your theology'. The priest slowly shook his head before replying, 'I think we don't have ideology. We don't have theology. We dance'.[61]

The same message comes from ancient Chinese Taoism: 'Obedience to the letter must give way to the life of the spirit'.[62] And all of this is very much in line with what the Sufis practise, expressed by Rumi in one of his writings: 'Cross and Christians, end to end, I examined. He was not on the Cross. I went to the Hindu temple, to the ancient pagoda. In neither was there any sign. To the heights of Hera I went, and Kandahar. I looked. He was not on height or lowland. Resolutely, I went to the top of the mountain of Kaf. There only was the place of the 'Anqua bird. I went to the Kaaba. He was not there. I asked of his state from Ibn Sina: he was beyond the limits of the philosopher Avicenna ... I looked into my own heart. In that place I saw him. He was in no other place ...'[63]

The goal of Sufism has indeed been expressed as 'The teacher, the teaching and the taught have become one'.[64] And what about this very revealing statement from what we in our ignorance call a 'primitive' source—the Brazilian Macumba priestess, Maria-José: 'Our religion is practised, not studied'.[65]

As a rebellious teenager, while discussing with my father why I did not want to go to church anymore, I pointed out what I thought was wrong with our church. I used the 'toddler going to hell' argument (mentioned in chapter 2) and the 'art. 31' farce (highlighted above), as well as other failings in our church. His reaction was, 'Joop, you are right, but there is another side to the church and that is the important one'. Although I never forgot his words, I had no idea what he meant, and it took me some twenty-five years to discover the profundity of what he had been talking about.[66] Now I would reformulate his words as follows: all the things I had listed were unimportant aspects of the horizontal dimension, but that the real mission of the church (and temple, mosque, *vihara*, etc., etc.) is to teach people how to open up to, and experience the vertical one. I do indeed think that the prime importance of opening up to the vertical energy flow (in Christianity called the Holy Spirit) is the very reason why Jesus is quoted as warning '... that every sin and every slander can be forgiven; but whoever slanders the Holy Spirit can never been forgiven...'[67]

Then indeed can we understand what Wordsworth meant when he described our 'normal' condition as 'Our life's a sleep and a forgetting'; while Leslie Houlden summarises what went wrong in a few words: 'But today many of us are analysers'.[68] And if the essential message that the 'kingdom is within', and not in creeds and dogmas, is ignored further, John Templeman will certainly be proven right, claiming: 'I believe all religions are becoming obsolete, clinging to ancient concepts'.[69]

Carl Jung is also very much on the same wavelength when writing that '... creeds are codified and dogmatised forms of original religious experience'.[70] Further on in the same book, he confirms that personal experience is imperative, and that debating about this issue makes no sense at all: 'Religious experience is absolute. It is indisputable. You can only say that you have never had such an experience, and your opponent will say: 'Sorry, I have'. And there your discussion will come to an end'.[71]

Because Jesus is quoted in John's Gospel as having said, 'Other sheep have I which are not of this fold',[72] it keeps baffling me that Christianity is so often less wiser and less tolerant than other traditions. In our media, Islam is often portrayed as intolerant, but consider this saying attributed to Muhammad when he was asked to curse the infidels: 'I was not sent to curse the infidels but to have mercy on mankind'.[73] Supported by Gandhi: 'I do regard Islam to be a religion of peace in the same sense as Christianity, Buddhism and Hinduism are'.[74] In the same vein these ancient lines from the *Svetasvatara Upanishad* point to the one source of all:

Thou, Lord God, bestoweth all blessing, ...
Of all religions thou art the source ...
The source of all scriptures thou art,
And the source of all creeds.[75]

Roland Peterson's book *Everyone Is Right*, from which I have copied these lines, is a veritable treasure trove illustrating the many parallels between different religions. For me this is one of the books that should be part of the essential reading for every course dealing with religion.

In this book I have deliberately quoted extensively from little Anna. Did not Jesus say 'Let the little children come to me, and do not hinder them, for the kingdom of heaven belongs to such as these?'[76] Some children, like Anna, are born with their vertical channel open but, while in other societies their wisdom will be cherished and they can become treasured as shamans, our 'civilised' society will do its utmost to make them 'normal'.[77] Their mates and schoolteachers will often ridicule them and as apparent outsiders they will often feel very lonely and become so desperate that they might even end up in psychiatric institutions.

Fortunately there have always been children that did not fit the mould of conformity, from several of the early Catholic saints to Bernadette of Lourdes and the more recent case of the children of Medjugorje. And I have already mentioned Twyman's writing about his encounters with psychic children in the mountains of Bulgaria.[78]

Also George Bernard Shaw made it clear that we should look beyond the often so misleading surface phenomena, so that like him we become aware of the fact that 'There is only one religion, though there are a hundred versions of it'. And as Islam is very much in the news because of recent acts of terrorism by some of its misdirected young people, let me compensate for that negative image by ending this section with the words of the Muslim sage, Maulana Wahiduddin Khan:

Religion is to find who we are. A religion is no religion if it cannot teach us how to tap our inner source of peace.[79]

In chapter 10, I will describe some of the endeavours resulting from the application of a vertical attitude, but let us first consider the consequences of the foregoing in the next section.

9.4 AND THE CONSEQUENCES

Yes—we know that when you come, we die.[80]

Chiparopai

By 1973 I had realised that you can't teach spirituality in the Western model of education. This is why you don't get it in seminaries or any place else as such because our Western models of education, being Cartesian- or Enlightenment- orientated, are only about the left brain.[81]

Matthew Fox

If the Church saw only heathens when it encountered highly accomplished spiritual leaders and enlightened priests, scientists now see only black magicians when faced with masters of the human mind and psychophysical self-control. The witch hunt continues today, clothed in the mantle of science.[82]

Holger Kalweit

And there is no getting away from the fact that on-screen violence fosters off-screen violence.[83]

Helen Phillips

We have guided missiles and misguided men.

Martin Luther King

By limiting the values of our society mainly to the horizontal dimension, and by instilling that belief in our children via the educational system, we have created an outlook that measures success in life by irrelevant values such as titles, money, a big house in the right neighbourhood, expensive flashy car, luxurious holidays, being the top sportsman/woman, etc., etc.[84] So if you have not attained that level of abundant material wealth paraded in advertising and TV soaps, you can easily be convinced that you are a failure. And in trying to avoid having to face that hard fact, you are wont to divert your attention into one of the many forms of escape our society has on offer.

This escape can be in shopping till you are dropping; it can range from work alcoholism to drink alcoholism, or 'recreational' drugs from tobacco to heroin; it can mean being completely immersed in your favourite sport, from football to hunting; or spending your time in front of your TV or computer screen; or any of the many other distractions that our modern society has on offer. The activities that we have invented to prevent us from experiencing a moment of silence are simply too many to list.

Aldous Huxley summarises this continuous pandemonium very well and puts its outcome in sharp focus: 'Spoken or printed, broadcast over the ether or on wood-pulp, all advertising copy has but one purpose—to prevent the will from ever achieving silence. Desirelessness is the condition of deliverance and illumination. The condition of an expanding and technologically progressive system of massproduction is universal craving. Advertising is the organized effort to extend and intensify craving—to extend and intensify, that is to say, the working of that force, which (as all the saints and teachers of all the higher religions have always taught) is the principal cause of suffering and wrong-doing and the greatest obstacle between the human soul and its divine Ground'.[85]

Our children grow up in front of the TV bombarded with violence and adverts for all kind of non-essential rubbish, and it is now widely accepted that all this television and computer game violence, generates real violence.[86] The loss of heart-oriented education could very well explain the mystery of why our youngsters—who never had it so good—are experimenting with dangerous drugs and activities, sometimes leading to that most drastic action—suicide.[87]

After another murder spree in the USA, a *New Scientist* editorial with the despairing title 'Why are we so reluctant to accept that on screen violence is bad for us?' stated: 'By the time the average US schoolchild leaves elementary school, he or she will have witnessed more than 8000 murders and 100,000 acts of violence on television'.[88]

But should all of this not really be a profound warning against so called development, because it seems very much that—having passed a minimal standard of living threshold—the more capitalistic, i.e. materially wealthy, a country becomes, the more children's well-being seems to decline. Witness a 2007 UNICEF report, in which the US and the UK were 'at the bottom of an international league table examining the physical and emotional well-being of youngsters in the world's [21] wealthiest nations'.[89]

Sathya Sai Baba expresses the same message, making it clear that 'The idea of a high standard of material living has played havoc with society. The desire can never be satisfied. It leads to a multiplication of wants and consequent troubles and frustrations. We need morality, humility, detachment, compassion, so that the greed for luxury and conspicuous consumption is destroyed'.[90]

In T. C. McLuhan's moving book, *Touch the Earth*, Sun Chief—a Hopi Indian who received a Western education by attending the Sherman Institute in Riverside, California—gave a stunningly accurate assessment of what went wrong during this schooling: 'I had learned many English words and could recite part of the Ten Commandments. I knew how to sleep on a bed, pray to Jesus, comb my hair, eat with a knife and fork, and use a toilet ... I had also learned that a person thinks with his head instead of his heart'.[91] His last line expresses concisely what our whole educational system is about, and if you are unable to keep up with the Joneses intellectually, you might well be tempted to prove yourself to your mates—to improve your ranking in their pecking order—by acts of (racial) discrimination or vandalism. After all, if you behave like a Vandal in wartime, you might even be celebrated as a hero.

This reminds me of a court case in the Netherlands in the 1950s where someone had fallen foul of the law. His defence lawyer used the argument that the man had been a decorated war hero in our recent colonial war in Indonesia. In despair, the judge uttered something like, 'But surely you do not expect us to start a war for the benefit of this man?'

But fortunately we are still so sensitive that here in the UK half a million people are off work every day due to depression, while some forty per cent of university students have been reported to be affected by the same problem—and all this is very much part of what we call our normal society![92] Here again we could learn from what we in our ignorance consider less developed societies. Take Thailand, where it is not unusual for a youngster to spend a year as a Buddhist monk before embarking on further education and a career. The values instilled during that period are surely of a higher worth than those learnt on our streets or in front of the TV.

If we get rid of our worries about not being perfect, there is indeed no need anymore to prove ourselves with excessive spending or fighting to reach the 'top' and becoming depressed when we learn the hard way that all that triumphant reaching of the 'top' will not contribute to our happiness at all! So let me end this chapter with the very wise words from the Third Patriarch of Zen[93]

One in all,
All in One—
If only this is realized,
No more worry about not being perfect!

10 LISTENING TO A DIFFERENT MUSIC

10.1 A DIFFERENT MUSIC

Without inner peace, it is not possible to have world peace.[1]

Dalai Lama

Dogma and invoking dogma, is a classic sign of stupidity.[2]

Rupert Lay

We have to see that the spirit must lean on science as a guide in the world of reality, and that science must turn to the spirit for the meaning of life.[3]

Cary F. Baynes

The reaction which is now beginning in the West against the intellect in favour of feeling, or in favour of intuition, seems to me a mark of cultural advance, a widening of consciousness beyond the too narrow limits of a tyrannical intellect.[4]

Carl G. Jung

Imagination is more important than knowledge. For knowledge is limited, whereas imagination embraces the whole world.[5]

Albert Einstein

As I have illustrated in the foregoing pages, there have over the ages been many people who have insisted that we should listen to a different music. And this ancient message is being presented in many modern versions as well; but as I repeat again, you will only be open to that message if you either are a born sensitive, or like me have been tripped up by a personal experience. And that universal message—of experience being essential—can be found anywhere. Here are just a few examples, the first relating to one of the most ancient human races, the others from the frontiers of modern life.

In his storytelling about his experiences with the African Bushmen, Laurens van der Post starts chapter 10 in his moving book *The Heart of the Hunter,* with: "Thinking of all this afterwards, I recalled something written many years ago: 'Love is the aboriginal tracker, the Bushman on the faded desert spoor of our lost selves.' There was a great lost world to be discovered and rebuilt, not in the Kalahari but in the wastelands of our spirit where we had driven the first things of life, as we had driven the little Bushman into the desert of southern Africa".[6] And near the end of this book he uses the same dimensional imagery that I use: 'The image of the cross, in particular, remains a symbol of infinite mystery and power, as it was in the beginning of things in Africa, urging the first men to live not only horizontally but vertically as well'.[7]

A modern example is Peter Plichta challenging the most hallowed creeds of modern physics in his book *God's Secret Formula,* and explaining why it is so difficult to spread a different message: 'Revolutions are always accepted as having been necessary only after they have succeeded. You only have to have a thorough knowledge of the history of science to realize that it has been one vast human tragedy all along. If it turns out that my suspicions of the existence of a construction plan for creation are well founded, I won't be able to publish it just like that. Nobody would ever take me seriously. Nobody would help me, either. I would have to furnish the entire proof myself. But even if I managed it, my colleagues would only glance in my direction to show me how crazy they think I am'.[8]

In his book *Clairvoyant Reality*, Lawrence LeShan tries to explain why we still persist in our misguided belief that psi equals zero: 'In our present culture there have been three general explanations of these [paranormal] happenings, each accepted by some of us. The first explanation is that these things do not happen; they are nonsense, and reports of them are due to hysteria, softheadedness, or fakery. The second is that they do happen, but let's ignore them for sanity's sake and maybe they will go away. ... The third explanation is that they do exist, and let's use them for a little happy regression and get out an Ouija board and talk to our dead great-aunt Mary and play spooks and chills. None of these explanations is particularly constructive. Psychical research today is an unmitigated disaster area'.[9] A bit further on in this magnificent book, he stresses that 'The changes of viewpoint about the nature of man implied by these "damned facts" is a tremendous one. And we must not underestimate how terrible we need a new concept of man'.[10]

David Icke explains how difficult this embarking on a new concept actually is: 'Carl Sagan once said: "Intellectual capacity is no guarantee against being dead wrong". If, however, alternative explanations are systematically suppressed everyone else is encouraged to be dead wrong also'.[11]

But there are always exceptions, such as the young writer Gary Lachman, who obviously has not been brainwashed by a standard horizontal university education. In his book *A Secret History of Consciousness,* he quotes from a host of sources and presents a very wide and well-referenced portrayal of the reality of what I have called the vertical dimension. Take these lines for example: 'Beyond "our world" lies another world, the totality, the world of what Ouspenski called "the miraculous." Mystics, occultists, and metaphysicians have given it an assortment of other names: Gnostics speak of the *Pleroma,* Kabbalists of the *Ain Soph,* Neoplatonists of the One. Each, however, speaks of the same thing. Scientists, Moskvitin points out, will not be happy with this observation, because they want to get at the source of "the real world," which they believe is the world they see, and pin it down once and for all. But they cannot do this because, "There will forever remain an unknown zone of ultimate causation, created by, and coinciding with that in ourselves that will forever remain unknown—the blind spot in the mind."[12] In other words, there is some part of us that is not part of the phenomenal world, and it is this unknown part that is itself the cause of the phenomenal world. And since that is the case, the unknown part *cannot be explained* in terms of the phenomenal world of which it is the creator'.[13]

There have of course always been numerous initiatives illustrating in a practical manner that the solution to our many problems can be found in the vertical dimension only. Matthew Fox gives a long list of what he calls 'emerging base community groups in the "First World"'.[14] I will now explore one of these, i.e. Alcoholics Anonymous (AA), which since it foundation in the 1930s clearly fulfils a need. The full story of how the AA came into being can be found in their handbook; here I will just give a brief survey.[15]

The spark that was to flare into the first AA group was struck in Akron, Ohio, in June 1935, during a talk between a New York stockbroker and an Akron physician. It grew into an enormous organisation with groups meeting all over the world, and has helped many people in their efforts to successfully beat their addiction to alcohol. And what is so relevant for our story is that the 12 step recovery programme which is basic to AA's success, clearly indicates that recovery is only considered possible by taking a spiritual approach. The first seven steps of their recovery programme are:

1. We admitted we were powerless over alcohol—that our lives had become unmanageable.
2. Came to believe that a Power greater than ourselves could restore us to sanity.
3. Made a decision to turn our will and our lives over to the care of God *as we understood Him*.
4. Made a searching and fearless moral inventory of ourselves.
5. Admitted to God, to ourselves, and to other human being the exact nature of our wrongs.
6. Were entirely ready to have God remove all these defects of character.
7. Humbly asked Him to remove our shortcomings.

If the wording puts you off because it sounds too old-fashioned and churchy, try to accept it as a historical document and replace its wording with language that suits you better.

These steps express clearly that no solution can be found without (in our model's words) taking the primacy of the vertical dimension as imperative; and this message is confirmed by David and Susan Larson, writing: 'Alcoholics Anonymous invokes a higher power to help alcoholics recover from addiction. Those who participate in AA are more likely to remain abstinent after inpatient or outpatient treatment'.[16]

AA's success has spawned a whole host of similarly named organisations, but I have no idea whether the spiritual roots of AA have been followed by these others as well. A recent trawl with 'anonymous' as input for the *Google* search engine yielded a very long list indeed. They varied from Narcotics Anonymous via Overeaters Anonymous, Debtors Anonymous, Sexaholics Anonymous and Parents Anonymous to even Civilization Anonymous. There are in fact many more, and I have no idea how successful these other organisations are, but I have just mentioned a few to illustrate how a useful (vertical) idea behind the founding of the AA can have a significant influence and follow up.

10.2 MANY PATHS GOING UP THE SAME MOUNTAIN

I was raised in the Church of England, but since my [near death] experience I have become non-denominational. I now feel all religion is basically the same and I think there should be a world religion which would put an end to the religious divisions and problems that this causes.[17]

Woman having had an NDE

Like the bee gathering honey from different flowers, the wise man accepts the essence of different Scriptures and sees only the good in all religions.[18]

Shrimad Bhagavatam

Believe in God - for there is only one God for mankind, though He may be called by many names.

Sathya Sai Baba

He who does reverence to his own sect, while disparaging the sects of others wholly from attachment to his own, with intent to enhance the glory of his own sect, in reality by such conduct inflicts the severest damage on his own sect. Concord therefore is therefore meritorious, to wit, hearkening and hearkening willingly to the Law of Piety, as accepted by other people.[19]

Edict of Asoka

If we know that the solution can be found in the vertical dimension only, how do we go about to bringing that knowledge into practice? If we are enslaved to the 'fata morgana' glamour of the horizontal dimension, perhaps we should start a Horizontal Anonymous, or a Possessions Anonymous movement. You only have to look at the average levels of debt, not only of the various states, but also of the population in our Western consumer societies, to realise there is a real need for such an organisation.[20]

The various faiths should of course have been the fellowships that guided us onto the vertical spiritual path indicated by their founders, but as we have seen, their followers so often ignored the founder's basic message and became bogged down in horizontal pursuits from dogmatic squabbles to church property/portfolio management. Consequently there are only a few exceptions to the massive downturn in the number of devotees that religious organisations in the West have undergone in the last century, resulting in the large number of empty and deserted churches. The example of the AA shows that even in finding a solution for a seemingly unrelated problem such as alcoholism, their language is remarkably 'religious'; again confirming the theme of this book that the solution to all our problems can be found in the vertical dimension only. Here I will just give a few examples of faiths in diverse traditions that are undogmatic and not hung up on creeds and regulations.

On the European scene, the Unitarians have always been very open-minded and they describe themselves as a 'Religion without dogma'. They advocate the oneness of God, have no creed and are very much supporters of individual freedom. Then there are the Quakers, or the 'Religious Society of Friends', who have done away with all the externalities and meet in silence without priests or rituals. In that silence they are seeking the direct experience of God; or as their founder, George Fox, expressed it 'Silence is part of the worship'. And he also directed his followers to 'Be still and cool in thy own mind and spirit from thy own thoughts'. As that stillness can have as a result the opening up our inner channel, Fox made it clear that 'Each person has an inner light (part of God's spirit) inside them—so there is a unity between human beings'. A modern Quaker, Bernard Carter, expressed this old insight as: 'Religion is living with a God. There is no other kind of religion, living with a Book, living with or by a Rule, being awfully high principled are not in themselves religion, although many people think they are and that that is all there is to it'.[21]

As far as I am aware, the Quakers do not teach, or promote a specific meditation technique to help attain this experience of stillness; probably because Fox was a naturally gifted mystic and therefore he did not see the need to disseminate a technique that could open up the vertical dimension for those who are not so gifted. He made it quite clear, however, that 'Spiritual truth can only be known through direct revelation from God', and 'All human beings can have a direct experience of God—they don't need priests to help them'. Quakers are very tolerant indeed and are correct in claiming that the Kingdom of Heaven is to be experienced in the here and now.

Regarding meditation in the general Christian context, I have already mentioned amongst others the rediscovering and promoting of a 'lost' Christian meditation tradition by the Benedictine monk John Main in chapter 7.[22]

Within the Islamic family, the Sufis have always been a beautiful and important tradition; also pointing to the underlying oneness of the various religious traditions. In the Sufi tradition, the influence of the thirteenth century mystic, Muhyiddin Ibn 'Arabi, is at the basis of organisations such as the 'Beshara Trust' and 'The Muhyiddin Ibn 'Arabi Society' who actively try to follow his teachings.[23]

Geographically straddling the rich Hindu and Muslim traditions—and also very undogmatic—are the Sikhs, for whom outward observations, such as rites, pilgrimage and asceticism, are quite irrelevant. They rather stress opening up the heart by the chanting of a divine name as mantra.

Buddhism originated in the same subcontinent and in it there are many streams, ranging from the ancient Hinayana to the much later Japanese Zen traditions. This variation allows for the accommodation of widely varying attitudes and temperaments. After the seemingly disastrous occupation of Tibet by the Chinese, one of the positive results of this invasion was that the Dalai Lama became a very visible figure for the rest of the world as well.[24] Indeed, the Indian subcontinent has always been not only an abundant fount of ancient experiential wisdom, but also the cradle of a veritable host of techniques for opening up our vertical dimension; many of which have over the centuries been exported to the rest of the world.

To illustrate that a model should not be taken literally, I will now change our diving in the ocean model to one in which the many ways promising enlightenment are described as different paths going up the slopes of a mountain; all of them leading to the same summit and approaching that common objective from different directions.[25] And because we are all so very different keep trying until a path is discovered that appeals to, and works for you.

To explore some of these paths you could for instance follow 'The Interfaith Seminary' course described below, trawl your local library, 'New Age' bookshop or the Internet. But do remember that it is essential not to get bogged down in intellectual analysis, but to go for the experiential side, because only then will we understand the significant commonality between the many different religious paths. This has been beautifully illustrated by Huston Smith in his Foreword to the revised edition of Frithjof Schuon's book, *The Transcendent Unity of Religions*.[26] I have slightly modified his illustration in figure 10.1

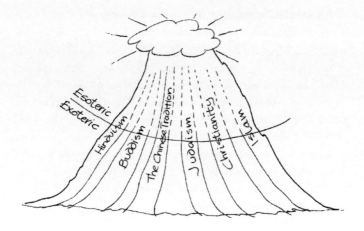

Figure 10.1 All paths leading up the same mountain

This insight into the underlying common message of the different religions has led to the many interfaith movements that have sprung up widely. One of the important aims of this movement is building bridges of understanding between the different faiths. What is needed, however, is not only bridging the gaps of misunderstanding, but realising that these faiths just represent different traditions of inner development, i.e. they illustrate diverse pathways going up the same mountain. And a mountain has been symbolically represented as the abode of the god(s) in many traditions, such as Mount Meru in the Hindu, Sinai in the Jewish, or Olympus in the Greek tradition.

But again, do not get trapped in external symbols or activities, and explore beyond these externalities which should be the aim of the many 'interfaith' groups. Perhaps, rather than 'interfaith', a better name for this movement expressing this moving 'beyond faith' would be 'metafaith' or the better sounding 'ultrafaith', rather than 'interfaith'. But let us now look into one of the exponents of this movement, i.e. 'The Interfaith Seminary':

Well before the term 'interfaith' was coined, a remarkable man made his mark in his new home in the US. Although Joseph

Gelberman, originally from Hungary, was a Hasidic rabbi, he 'hung out with swamis, priests and ministers'.[27] And this led in the 1970s—with the support of other religious leaders such as Swami Satchidananda, Methodist minister John Mundi and others—all of them wishing to bridge the gaps between the different faiths—to the establishment of the New Light Temple in New York.

In 1981 he helped to establish 'The New Seminary', an organisation set up to train Interfaith Ministers and Spiritual Counsellors. As witnessed by the following quotations, the attitude of its study programme is to accept all faiths as equally valuable, so that there is absolutely no need for any conversion effort: 'Many ways - one truth', 'Never instead of, always in addition to' and 'Serving all with an open mind and a loving heart'. Gelberman underlined this: 'God gave only part of his wisdom to each of all the religions' so that 'we must come together to understand it completely'.

The seminary has trained hundreds of people and has resulted in several offspring seminaries, such as 'The All Faiths Seminary', 'One Spirit Interfaith', and here in the UK, 'The New Seminary'. This last offspring, its name having been changed to 'The Interfaith Seminary', was started at the request of Gelberman by Miranda MacPherson (Holden) in 1996.[28]

The first year of its two-year course is dedicated to the study of the major religions, including recent spiritual developments such as 'A Course in Miracles'. Typically, during a particular month a major religion is not only studied, but its daily practices are engaged in. Of course, academically this can mean a very superficial sampling of these faiths only, but it is at least an exploration of the signposts pointing to the different paths up the mountain. And studying a particular tradition indicates where more information or support can be found.

The second study year focuses on personal development of the students, exploring issues such as our ego, shadow and higher-self; letting go what is unhelpful for yourself and for others. As well as the development of non-judgemental, respectful, helpful understanding and kindness towards other traditions (or none), and accepting their surface differences, but always emphasising their underlying oneness. This year also goes into details about services and ceremonies for milestones in people's lives, such as: wedding ceremonies, blessing and naming, to funeral and memorial-services.[29] A very important subject—which was only briefly introduced in year one—is the principles and practice of spiritual counselling.

Again, we have to keep very much in mind that the essence of every religion and its practices is to be found in the vertical rather than the horizontal dimension, so study on its own cannot give you the personal experience to make it become a reality. Accordingly in parallel with studying, an important aspect of the course is 'Opening to Direct Revelation' in which the various techniques for inner exploration are probed.

I will end this section by reproducing the statement published by 'The Interfaith Seminary' on its website: 'The Interfaith Seminary is an innovative training programme for Interfaith Ministers and Spiritual Counsellors, to serve the spiritual needs of people from all faiths and none. We train open-hearted men and women to become non-denominational ministers and counsellors, to support individuals, families and communities in living a direct, authentic spirituality that is relevant and helpful to our modern world. The Interfaith Seminary, believing that there is One God/Truth and many paths leading to the Source of All, is grounded in a universal and inclusive approach to spirituality. It is not designed as a rival to traditional religions or their seminaries. Rather, it serves as an addition, promoting an ethic of respect, reconciliation, forgiveness and fellowship, supporting peacemaking and the remembrance of our fundamental human unity'.

With such an inspirational mission statement it is no wonder that 'The Interfaith Seminary' is filling an obvious need, because here in the UK the number of students increases year by year, so that in England there are now (2006) faculties in London and in Manchester, while another one is in Perth in Scotland. And if you want to explore this interfaith movement further, or look for contacts in your area, just go to www.interfaithfoundation.org for the latest information.

At the end of my second Oxford course (see chapter 2), several of the participants expressed the wish to continue our getting together for further exploration on a more informal basis, which we were allowed to do several times in one of the other university buildings. But as these meeting places were so bland, we started to explore the possibility of finding a bigger house where we would be able to meet in more congenial circumstances, and have exchanges and meditations that could lead to deeper exploration of the vertical dimension. This led to us putting our semi-detached house on the market and looking at several properties in the Oxford area. We settled on an ancient house on the green of the lovely small village of Sutton Courtenay, where I explained our ideas to Fred Bloom, who was involved in similar activities at 'The Abbey' just across the road.

But as the sellers of that house wanted to delay their moving out, and following a number of amazing coincidences, we ended up buying a big house halfway up Porlock Hill in Somerset. When we came through its gate for the very first time, Emmy exclaimed, 'That's it, that's it!' And she explained that in the past months she had had recurrent dreams about a house, even once thinking it was a boat, because there seemed to be portholes; these turned out to be holes in the wall around the veranda, and the sea was indeed nearby, see figure 10.2. So when she entered the gate she had immediately recognised it as the house she had seen in her dreams.[30]

Figure 10.2 Halsecombe House

The house, dating from about 1900 was well built, but was in a serious state of neglect and needed loving attention urgently. Ceilings had fallen out, the roof leaked, etc. etc. But because Emmy was so sure that this was our place, we put in an offer, which was accepted. The house was owned by the 'Lord Bishop of Bath and Wells,' who obviously was so glad to have found a buyer that, although no deeds had been signed yet, allowed us to move in a few weeks later, just days before Christmas 1984. Later I heard that the reaction in the nearby village of Porlock was: 'That house needed a crazy Dutchman'—which I considered as a compliment.

When, much later, I pieced together the fascinating history of the house, I discovered that the property had been given to the Church of England by a Miss Wyld, and one of the most amazing discoveries was that in her will, dating from 1949, she had stipulated that the house should be used '...preferably as a residence for a religious community'. Nothing had come of that fine idea and as already mentioned, when we came here, everything was in a very decrepit and neglected state. The house and outbuildings are now fit for another hundred years, which has been a long and often arduous uphill battle.[31] We also restored it to its older name of Halsecombe House.[32]

For over twenty years we ran the house on interfaith principles as a retreat, a meeting place, for courses, as well as family holidays; initially on our own and later with the help of a small community trying to live there with an attitude of sharing and service, which was as much a blessing for us, as for the hundreds of people who visited Halsecombe. One of our neighbours, Richard Acland expressed this type of project as: 'There is a new spirit abroad, and increasingly people come together locally so as to 'do their own thing' for the sake of a more creative and sustainable life style. These local enterprises can be seen as living green shoots coming up through cracks in the concrete of a psychologically sick and disintegrating society'.[33]

In 2006, a few years after I wrote the above about Halsecombe, we had to come to the conclusion that we had been unable to find successors who—without our own full-time commitment—could run this big place successfully. Also it was not up to 21st-century standards, so we have passed it on to others and have retired to a lovely village on the coast of the Celtic Sea. 'Retire' is indeed the proper word, because Halsecombe was a lot of hard work over many years, therefore I will give the very appropriate last word to Sathya Sai Baba, who:

... asks no one to come and sit at his feet, and has often remarked that hands that work are holier than lips that pray. He is not decrying prayer—merely saying that that in many cases actions speak louder than words.[34]

10.3 HEALTH'S FORGOTTEN FACTOR

One can scarcely imagine such a revolution: Economism and the consumer society would die overnight. An entirely different set of values would emerge; for instance, quality of life would be primary, not the quantity of consumer goods. The criteria for the good life would be gauged in terms of happiness, health, and well-being—for *all* subjects.[35]

Sallie McFague

I ask the plant what it is good for. Some plants are only meant to be beautiful. Other plants are meant for food. Still others are to be used as medicine. Only a healing plant has spoken to me. I ask its permission to take it with me and add it to my medical pouch.[36]

Rolling Thunder

I tend to agree with a patient of mine who once observed that she knew a lot of Ph.D.s and M.D.s who were educated far beyond their intelligence![37]

Lawrence LeShan

What a cold and lonely place [this hospital is]. All the latest technology whirring away, but the most important life-saving device missing. The medical profession does not yet realise that love is one of the most important things to help us to return or cross the bridge called death.[38]

Julie Chimes

I have borrowed the title of this section from a review article by David and Susan Larson in a book that is highly relevant to my theme: *God, Science & Humility*.[39] The article is subtitled *Medical Research Uncovers Religion's Clinical Relevance* and it illustrates the trend that the influence of what I have called the vertical dimension, can indeed be of critical importance in the healing process. Their research, centred on the US situation, has uncovered that the medical profession has largely ignored the influence of anything that could be related to spirituality. This reflects the impact of such prophets as Freud, dismissing religion in many different ways, such as it being a 'borderline psychosis ... a regression to primitive narcissism'.[40] This led one of the Larsons to write: 'during my residency training in the mid-1970s, I heard that religion was general harmful to one's mental health'.[41] But when they embarked on a systematic programme of reviewing the literature in peer reviewed journals in the field of psychiatry, they discovered that this dismissal is completely unfounded, which they expressed in the carefully worded conclusion that '... the basis of psychiatry's negative views on the impact of religious commitment remained at best highly questionable'.[42] They also report that several medical schools now instruct their students to 'include a spiritual assessment as part of routine history in a respectful, non-judgemental, and non-imposing fashion'. Financial support for this work has been made available by the John Templeton Foundation. And that their experience is not an exception is witnessed by a whole host of books supporting similar views, such as Agnes Sandford's book *The Healing Light,* which is full of cases of healing 'at the command of faith'.

Another striking statistic—supporting the case that a change of attitude is urgently required—is that the suicide rate of young adolescents has soared 400% between 1950 and 1990 and is now the cause of death in 1 in 7 cases of all those in the age group between fifteen and nineteen years of age.[43] And as I already illustrated in chapter 6, isn't this a clear signal that although 'we never had it so good', there is in our society something seriously missing for sensitive young people.

The Larsons mention that: 'Nursing has a history of recognizing and affirming the importance of religion and spirituality that stands in marked contrast to the negative attitudes toward religion previously promulgated by psychiatry and psychology'.[44]

In this context I want to quote Harold Schilling's more general observation in full: 'Thus many of our youth sense keenly—and correctly, I think—that the scholarly and educational establishment has done serious damage to both science and religion, because for too long a time it has allowed itself to be unduly influenced by positivist doctrine and has worshipped too much at the shrine of the intellectually "hard" approach, the coercively logical deduction, the utterly dispassionate analysis, of the impeccably rational, the rigorously objective and conceptual, and the "realistic"—while contemptuously derogating the "softer" approach of the arts and the nonconceptual, subjective, nonrational, intuitive, creative, and idealistic. Certainly this is one way of effectively stifling, or even destroying, sensitivity to the reality of mystery and the gentle might of tenderness, and of constricting human consciousness'.[45] These observations are to a very large extent true for the system of education as is commonly practised elsewhere in the West.

In the US, Carl Rogers was very much a pioneer indicating the need to move in a different direction. He gives a very interesting list of symptoms, indicating spiritual growth: 'Let me indicate a few of these value directions as I see them in my clients as they move in the direction of personal growth and maturity'. And he itemises:

They tend to move away from facades. Pretence, defensiveness, putting up a front, tend to be negatively valued.

They tend to move away from "oughts." The compelling feeling of "I ought to do or be thus and so" is negatively valued.

The client tends to move away from being what he "ought to be," no matter who has set that imperative.

They tend to move away from meeting the expectations of others. Pleasing others, as a goal in itself is negatively valued.

Being real is positively valued. The client tends to move toward being himself, being his real feelings, being what he is. This seems to be a very deep preference.

Self-direction is positively valued. The client discovers an increasing pride and confidence in making his own choices, guiding his own life. ...

Perhaps more than all else, the client comes to value an openness to all of his inner and outer experience. ... This openness becomes the client's most valued resource. ... Sensitivity to others and acceptance of others is positively valued. ...

Finally, deep relationships are positively valued. To achieve a close, intimate, real, fully communicative relationship with another person seems to meet a deep need in every individual, and is very highly valued.[46]

In the same book, Barry Stevens underlines the abnormality of our so-called normal world by quoting a patient in a mental hospital: 'You want me to come in your world, but I lived there for twenty-three years and I don't like it'. She comments: 'The patient was a very mixed-up person, but I don't think he was mixed up about this'.[47] And further on: 'Perhaps all the sensitive and human people get scrapped and sent off to mental hospitals?'[48]

She describes exactly the same experience with the traffic in Hawaii in the 1930s as I had when moving to Italy in the 1960s, namely that it was so much less 'Highway Code' and much more person oriented. She writes: 'When I moved to Hawaii in 1934 and the traffic in Honolulu looked like madness—totally disorganized—this was because it was so different from the order that I was used to. ... The driving was very much person-to-person, with recognition on both sides'.[49] And when you have adapted your style of driving to watching other drivers more than traffic rules and regulations, you really appreciate this more person oriented behaviour'.

To return to the medical field, here in the UK Steve Wright teaches and has initiated courses and conferences covering 'vertical' subjects. He edits a peer-reviewed journal *Sacred Space*, which is dedicated to publishing 'papers, reports and other material in relation to spirituality of concern to all those involved in health care'.[50] Corroborating what I wrote above about the changing attitude at American universities, it reports that during an interview with him, Larry Dossey stated that 'Today, ... 80 of the 125 medical schools in the US have courses that have begun to deal with this area'.[51] What 'this' stands for, he explained earlier in the interview: 'The fundamental nature of what we're dealing with is the infinite nature of consciousness, what I call nonlocal mind. Nonlocal mind reaches out in time and space. It can insert information into the world, as in remote healing and intercessory prayer'. So there has indeed been a remarkable shift towards a more 'vertical' orientation by many of those engaged in teaching the new generation of health carers.

After having covered so much ground over such a vast field of human experience, my final chapter will deal with summing up the message I hope to convey in this book.

11 Summing up

11.1 REVIEW

There is, we are aware, a philosophy that denies the infinite. There is also a philosophy, classified as pathologic, that denies the Sun; this philosophy is called blindness.[1]

Victor Hugo

It is dangerous to be right in matters on which the established authorities are wrong.

Voltaire

Nyama is the energy that emanates from Spirit and flows throughout the universe. ... To recognize this energy is to appreciate that everything is interconnected, integral parts of a whole.[2]

African elder

Dogma and invoking dogma, is a classic sign of stupidity.[3]

Rupert Lay

Tell them what you're going to tell them,
Tell them,
Tell them what you have told them.

Speechwriter's aphorism

In this brief review there will again be some unavoidable reiteration and repetition of what went before, but perhaps we are now in a better position to answer the important question that I posed at the beginning, namely, was there in fact any purpose in writing another book about this subject at all. I do think that it should now have become clear that throughout the ages so many sages have completely agreed on the fact that the answer to all our questions—rather than being discovered in books or universities—can only be found in personal experience. However, Aldous Huxley, in the introduction to his brilliant *The Perennial Philosophy* advised: 'If one is not oneself a sage or a saint, the best thing one can do, in the field of metaphysics, is to study the works of those who were...'[4]

Another striking example of this open-mindedness to accepting the guidance of others is William James, who opened his lectures on mysticism with the warning: 'Whether my treatment of mystical states will shed more light or darkness, I do not know, for my own constitution shuts me out from their enjoyment almost entirely, and I can speak of them only at second hand'.[5] But although he can speak of these life-changing experiences 'only at second hand', he adds that 'No account of the universe in its totality can be final which leaves these other forms of consciousness quite disregarded'. Then he follows these remarks up with page after page of widely ranging (both in time and place) reports of mystical experiences. I wonder however, if his brave efforts are still taken seriously by our educational establishments, because as we can see so clearly, their priorities are so often limited to the horizontal dimension only. Just remember Richard Milton's reaction (quoted in chapter 5) to the vilification he was subjected to by one of our leading educators.

If we continue to educate our youngsters within a strictly 'psi equals zero' framework, and ridicule those having an inner knowledge that there is more to life, then this could very well be an explanation why suicide is so rife amongst young sensitive people. I vividly remember one of my colleagues telling me with delight about his beautiful bright daughter going to university.

When I asked him a year or so later how she was doing, he replied: 'Joop we don't have her anymore, she jumped off her flat's balcony'. And if you think that her's is an exceptional case, research published in 1993 revealed that 60 per cent of youngsters have contemplated suicide.[6]

As I pointed out in chapter 6, if your outlook is limited to the horizontal dimension only, there is indeed no other motivation for living than money, possessions, power, status, titles, thrills, sex etc., and you will discover in their pursuit that this is a very empty outlook indeed. Only after life has taught you that the vertical dimension is the realm of primary value (implying our underlying oneness), will you understand what Aldous Huxley meant with: 'Everything is ours, provided that we regard nothing as our property. And not only is everything ours; it is also everybody else's'.[7]

In chapter 1 I described that if you dare to advocate that inner (vertical) values are indeed of great importance, you might very well end up in a figurative prison comparable to Mr Square's in the so meaningful *Flatland* story (chapter 3); or be hauled before the Inquisition of your peers and being subjected to their worried looks or even vitriolic contempt. But for some it might very well come as a surprise that in this case one is in excellent company indeed; which fact can be deduced from the many quotations I have given to support my case. Take for instance the pronouncements of scientific geniuses like Einstein, Pauli, Jung and so many others about the importance of spiritual matters. Their remarks were heavily frowned upon by many of their colleagues who were firmly embedded in the horizontal dimension.

Although in the course of putting my personal experiences in a framework that works for me, you might very well think that I have quoted from and referred to other books very selectively. In fact, I have only used a small selection from the notes and books that I have collected over the years. I could have gone on and on, clobbering you with many more facts and quotations, but

I simply had to stop somewhere because the alternative would have been a hefty tome, something like the 600 plus page book with quotations on reincarnation that Sylvia Cranston collected so admirably.[8]

My aim has been to have a fairly compact book with a clear message, although I am very much aware that I can write as much as I like, but unless you, the reader, has a personal experience which necessitates you to accept that there is more to life than science can encompass, you can still dismiss all of it. Also the experimental evidence presented by others is often considered to be inconsistent; Glen Barclay puts it concisely: 'If one learns nothing else from the study of the occult, one at least learns not to expect consistency'.[9] However, a few pages further on he puts our minds at rest by stating: 'It is not usually necessary to multiply examples of the impossible; one verified instance is sufficient to prove any point worth making'.

As I have illustrated over and over again in the preceding pages, so many problems we are facing have their origin in the fact that there is simply no horizontal way out. Take as an example these confirming remarks from Jung: 'How often have I heard a patient exclaim: "If only I knew that my life had some meaning and purpose, then there would be no silly story about my nerves!" ... It is much more a question of this unreasoned need of what we call a spiritual life, and this he cannot obtain from universities, libraries, or even churches. He cannot accept what these have to offer because it touches only his head [horizontal], and does not stir his heart [vertical]. ... Not to recognize the spiritual source of such [dream] contents means faulty treatment and failure'.[10]

The implications of accepting that the vertical dimension is of such paramount importance still gives me the feeling that I have at least been able to put together many of the important pieces of life's jigsaw puzzle in a consistent framework. But it is a very sobering thought that even a prolific writer and great philosopher of the stature of Plato 'In a letter written during the last years of his life ... made the remarkable statement that he had never once revealed the secret side of his teachings. I have not written the true philosophy, he admitted. It must always be hidden, passed like a spark from teacher to pupil but never divulged in writing'.[11] But only this spark of personal experience can give the encouragement leading to gaining insight, and again I cannot refrain from referring to what others have written concerning this vitally important issue. Take for instance Thomas Merton: 'Zen clearly gives priority to experience, but so does Christianity if it is properly understood'.[12]

Harry Moody and David Carroll's book, *The Five stages of the Soul*, from which I took the above remark about Plato, is chock-full with tales and anecdotes illustrating the unceasing search for answers. Translated into the terminology I have used in this book, their tales very much confirm that we can find answers in the vertical dimension only.

Personal experience is the clue, expressed so succinctly by the Buddhist motto: 'To see with one's own eyes and be liberated'.[13] But instead of following this advice, we hide behind our protective fences and see the world through narrow slits only, as illustrated in figure 11.1.

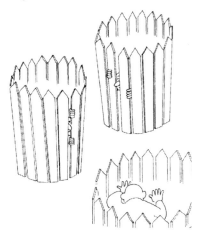

Figure 11.1 Our 'normal' behaviour

And if you think that this picture is exaggerated, just look around at the ubiquitous evidence—such as defensive mounds, towers, castles, walled towns and even whole countries (such as China and Israel)— all over our planet.

A very striking example can be seen in the amazing Italian city of San Gimignano with its thirteen towers, which are the modest remains of the original seventy-two that had been built there; some of which are sketched in figure 11.2.

Figure 11.2 San Gimignano

Of course these towers were not only defensive fortresses, but also dwellings, and they illustrate that we will also use our fences as status symbols, showing off our wealth by the size of one's tower. Nowadays we do not build our towers only of stone and bricks, but also of steel, and by putting wheels under these, we drive around in them. And the 'looking through slits in our fence' image we can see everywhere around us, particularly striking for those cars with dark tinted windows.

In the footsteps of Gandhi—who walked rather than travel in a posh car—when we are oriented vertically, we will feel embarrassed and ashamed rather than proud when exposing our material wealth in such a blatant way. And an additional indicator of something being seriously wrong with our society is the stark increase in the number of cases of autism, because autism seems such an extreme case of hiding inside our fence. Even if it really can help autistic people to have an Internet connection inside their fence, this is again a clear case of treating the symptom rather than the cause.[14] Fortunately, there is also some progress to report in removing fences, such as the recent clearing away of the 'Iron Curtain' and the 'Berlin Wall'.

As a horizontal dogmatist, the price you pay for ignoring all the evidence of so called paranormal phenomena, is that life has no meaning, apart from trying to excel in the horizontal pursuits I listed above; or just limiting yourself to the propagation of our species. But apart from what I have referred to already, there is an enormous amount of other evidence pointing in another direction. I have mentioned several of the courageous academics putting their careers at risk by daring to stick their necks out. People like Carl Jung defining (vertical) Synchronicity as an 'acausal connecting principle', or the later studies of Raymond Moody, Margot Grey, Kenneth Ring, Michael Sabom, Elisabeth Kübler-Ross and others of near-death experiences (NDEs), which so often describe experiences in the vertical realm.[15]

Or take for instance the books describing evidence published by scientists from behind the Iron Curtain, collected in Sheila Ostrander and Lynn Schroeder's books *Psychic discoveries behind the Iron Curtain* and *The ESP Papers*; or the books by Ken Wilber and so many others. Also the 'Afterlife experiments' seemingly conveying messages from the deceased, already reported on by Jung and later followed up and well documented by Gary Schwartz and Linda Russek.[16]

Likewise in the field of cancer research, where we find that the evidence for a vertical (psychological) cause is indicated many times by the personal experiences of the Simontons, and their review of the literature. Although many physical substances have been identified as contributing to the development of cancer; they write that a major factor remains '... being cut off from the resources of their unconscious processes'. Or as I have seen with my own father (dying of lung cancer at the age of fifty-four): 'They were simply wanting to die. For that seemed the only way out'.[17]

Also it is hard to ignore the evidence of the remote viewing experiments pioneered by Russell Targ, Harold Puthoff and many others, which have been published widely in books and peer reviewed scientific journals.[18] Stanislav Grof points to the critical fact that 'the process of developing this skill [remote viewing] does not involve new learning so much as it involves "unlearning" negative conditioning that claims these abilities are not "real"'. And on the same page he firmly puts the finger on the sore spot, stating that '... when confronted with a choice between accepting a new worldview and quelling our fears, we often choose the latter. But believe me, if you really decide to be open minded and start looking for it, there is such a truly vast host of evidence out there'.[19]

But do not be at all surprised that—even when you have presented solid and waterproof evidence that there is more to life than just the horizontal dimension—your evidence might be so misrepresented that you exclaim, like Gary Schwartz and William Simon did: 'What we later saw on air [about their experiments with a clairvoyant] knocked us off our feet'.[20] They open the section in their book titled *Diagnosing and Treating "Skeptimania"*, with: 'It's one thing to be skeptical—open to alternative hypotheses. It's another to be *devoutly* skeptical—always "knowing" that cheating, lying, fraud, and deception are the explanations for any not-yet explainable phenomenon.'[21] This sceptical attitude is so widespread that the manuscript of what later became an enormously valuable bestseller, i.e. Fritjof Capra's *The Tao of Physics*, was initially turned down by all the major publishers in London and New York.[22]

Grof expresses his hopeful belief: '... that unbiased study of psychoid phenomena and transpersonal experiences will eventually lead to a revision of our view of reality that will be equal in scope to the Copernican revolution or the shift from Newtonian to quantum-relativistic thinking in physics'.[23] I can say a wholehearted *Amen* to that, and can add the words of Robert Morris, who has run the Koestler Parapsychology Unit at the University of Edinburgh. He explained in an interview that what parapsychology needs to become acceptable are 'Two things. One, effects of sufficient strength and consistency, so you know something is going on that isn't readily understood by other means. And secondly, coming up with a mechanism'.[24]

His first requirement of consistency will be difficult because the vertical dimension is simply not subject to the power of our will, nor as I pointed out at the end of chapter 8, to the rules (such as reproducibility) of the horizontal dimension. His second requirement of a mechanism (model) is what I have tried in this book. I have given many examples of so-called paranormal phenomena, and have tried to present a model that—at least for me, and several others—has helped greatly to come to terms with these. Yet if we are so afraid that the seemingly solid foundations of our horizontal world-view are being undermined; we can still 'safely' follow the example of the engineer who was consulted by the editor of the *Proceedings of the IEEE*[25] when they were considering the publication of Russell Targ and Harold Puthoff's solid evidence of their remote viewing experiments.[26] He said:

This is the kind of thing that I would not believe in even if it existed.[27]

11.2 THE NEXT STEPS

No man can reveal aught but that which already lies half asleep in the dawning of your knowledge. ... For the vision of one man lends not its wings to another man.[28]

Kahlil Gibran

Whoever enters the Way without a guide will take a hundred years to travel a two-day journey.[29]

Rumi

"May I become your disciple?"
"You are only a disciple because your eyes are closed. The day you open them you will see there is nothing you can learn from me or anyone."
"What then is a master for?"
"To make you see the uselessness of having one."[30]

Anthony de Mello

Precognition is a demonstrated verity. It is a strange, paradoxical and seemingly absurd fact, but one that we are compelled to admit. ... The explanation will come (or will not come) later. The facts are none the less authentic and undeniable.[31]

Charles Richet

The five stages in our vertical development which Harry Moody & David Carroll identify in their book *The Five Stages of the Soul,* are: the Call, the Search, the Struggle, the Breakthrough and the Return. They illustrate and elucidate each stage and its possible choices extensively by taking examples from the many spiritual traditions we have on our planet. And the answer to my concern about the usefulness of me writing this book, which I opened this chapter with, can be identified in the 'Return' stage. They write of this stage that 'People who have been through the Breakthrough begin to understand that their relationships and activities, even the burdens and hardships they once thought were so intolerable, are necessary pieces in life's mosaic. ... Then ... we return to our everyday life. But this time we are charged with new tasks. What are these tasks? First, to integrate what we've experienced into our daily lives. Second, to continue making efforts in hopes of further spiritual growth. Third, to give back to others of something what we've learned'.[32] And that final task convincingly expresses the answer to my concerns.

The learning from experience should lead us to assist others in the opening up of their vertical channel, instead of—as happens so often—ridiculing those who are born sensitives. Would it, for instance, not be much more important if our schools taught children this opening up of their inner channel, rather than learning about the 'glorious battles' our 'heroic' forefathers fought? Sathya Sai Baba made it very clear that 'Education should be about how to live, not how to make a living'.[33] Indeed, we have to reinvent education completely so that, as in antiquity, schools can indeed become the '*wisdom schools,* as opposed to the *knowledge factories* that have characterised education during the industrial era', as Matthew Fox puts it so poignantly.[34]

Although the vertical approach to education is still being practised in the much older civilisations of South-East Asia, when students from that area are 'successful' and gain admission to a

Western university for their further education, they have to be very strong indeed not to be "brainwashed" by Western science, as Fritjof Capra's Indian colleague at Imperial College expressed it.[35] Jung supports that critical assessment: 'As a doctor who deals with ordinary people, I know that the universities have ceased to act as disseminators of light'.[36]

You only have to read how dismissive western professors often are about 'occult' phenomena to realise how much pressure is put on their students to dismiss their 'vertical' beliefs and join the 'horizontal' brotherhood; with the possible result of feeling so desperately alone that, as I already mentioned, suicide so often seems the only way out.[37] Lawrence LeShan remarks about this dismissiveness: 'The general refusal to deal scientifically with the material gathered in this [paranormal] field seems to be a phenomena *in itself demanding explanation*'.[38] However, rather than 'scientifically', I would have preferred the expression 'open mindedly' because the vertical dimension is by definition beyond science's strictly horizontal brief. In the East—after their studies and before embarking on a career—youngsters often spend a few years in a Buddhist monastery and here again I am on the same wavelength as Matthew Fox: 'The young have a special need today to be gifted by the elders. Why not a sabbatical for young people—a year off from the strife of adolescence (which psychologists tell us lasts until age twenty-seven in our culture)—to engage in spiritual exploration? This sabbatical year would relieve the job market as well as teach the young new ways of being themselves'.[39]

But again, do keep very much in mind that the search has to be conducted by *doing* rather than *reading*. Eric Butterworth expresses this same message poignantly: 'Many otherwise sincere students of "the way" *are overread and underdone*'.[40] Although in my own case, reading triggered my curiosity, which then led to me deciding to do the meditation experiment with its life changing results.

People who have listened to their inner voice are for instance Eileen Campbell, who was instrumental in the founding of the *Findhorn Community*,[41] Machaelle Small Wright, initiating a similar enterprise called *Perelandra* in the USA;[42] or in fact Emmy's intuitive 'knowing' that brought us to *Halsecombe* (chapter 10). Indeed, this doing should be the most important thing in life, as Ramakrishna knew intuitively; so that, when his brother admonished him to study so that he would be able to secure a decent job, he replied, 'Brother, what shall I do with a mere bread-winning education? What I want is that wisdom which will illumine my heart, and having won which I shall be satisfied for ever'.[43]

Another Hindu sage, Vivekananda, was so distressed by the agnostic doctrines of his Western college education that he too became suicidal. Francis Younghusband writes of him: 'He believed that the credo of Universal Reason called on him to suppress the yearnings of his artist nature'.[44] Fortunately for him, he found in Ramakrishna a teacher who could give him the guidance that his western education had so completely lacked. Or take this other thought provoking and deeply revealing tale, also told us by Younghusband: 'A wise Hindu sage, when a young Indian told him that he had become an atheist, congratulated him. And on the youth expressing his astonishment that a man of God should congratulate him on becoming an atheist, the sage replied: "Your becoming an atheist shows that you have begun to think. Go on thinking."'[45]

So thinking is not to be denigrated because, as we have seen, thinking and feeling are very much complementary, we need them both! Further on in his book *Modern Mystics,* from which I took these quotations, Younghusband supports that view: 'True it is that the intellect alone could not have taken these mystics to the heart of the universe. Feeling was then necessary; for feeling can penetrate deeper than thought. But use of the intellect, and use of the fruits of the intellect as shown in the results of science and philosophy, would have given them a wider and deeper comprehension of the universe with which they were striving more intimately to relate themselves'.[46]

Life goes on as before, but having become one of the 'Changed Ones', as the Sufis call them, you have to live and advertise the message that all that we do, amass and advertise in the horizontal dimension (beyond basic needs) is completely irrelevant when compared to the importance of opening up to the vertical dimension. There simply is no other solution than to embark on the inner voyage of discovery! But to embark on such an 'abnormal behaviour ' needs courage and perseverance, as Thomas Merton once told David Steindl-Rast: 'We will need the courage to do the opposite of everybody else'.[47] But courage and perseverance may not be enough, because what does not fit your view of the world, you cannot even see. Indeed so often you do not see what there is, but what you think there is, and if you are insisting of describing reality within the confines of horizontal factuality only, you have to realise that this fact discloses very much about you, rather than about reality.[48] And again this wisdom can be found in an ancient eastern text such as *The Tibetan Book of the Dead*, which puts it concisely, 'As a thing is viewed, so it appears'.[49]

If we limit our outlook to the horizontal dimension only, then that outlook is gloomy indeed, as Fritz Schumacher pointed out when discussing the consequences of that attitude for the appreciation of the work we do: 'If we continue to teach that the human being is *nothing but* the outcome of a mindless, meaningless and purposeless process of evolution, a process of "selection" for survival, that is to say, the outcome of nothing but *utilitarianism* —we only come to a *utilitarian* idea of work: that work is *nothing but* a more or less unpleasant necessity, and the less there is of it the better'.[50] And the message that *good* work should instead be a path to enlightenment is very ancient indeed, as we see in this quote Fox took from the *Bhagavad Gita*: 'Know therefore what is work, and also know what is wrong work. And know also of a work that is silence: mysterious is the path of work. The person who in his or her work finds silence, and who sees that silence is work, this person in truth sees the Light and in all his or her works finds peace'.[51]

The same ancient text makes it very clear that you do not work just for the money: 'Set thy heart upon thy work, but never on its reward'.[52] And in ancient China as well, it was made very clear by the sage Lao Tzu where focussing on horizontal pursuits rather than on vertical ones leads to:

> When rich speculators prosper
> while farmers lose their land;
> when government officials spend money
> on weapons instead of cures;
> when the upper class is extravagant and irresponsible
> while the poor have nowhere to turn -
> all this is robbery and chaos.
> It is not in keeping with the Tao.[53]

Also Rumi stresses the vitally important message: 'Work in the invisible world at least as hard as you do in the visible'.[54]

As an engineer who always wanted to know how things work so that I could understand their operation and eventually improve or repair them, I have in this book simply tried to construct a signpost indicating that the most important direction to explore is the vertical one; or in other words that religion (in the true sense of the word) is the most essential pursuit in life! And please do not—like so many believers do—fall into the trap of concentrating on the signpost, instead of following for yourself the direction it indicates.

I am not at all competent to give general advice about which of the many possible trails is right for you: you simply have to find that out for yourself, again keeping very much in mind that what worked for me or your friend, doesn't necessarily work for you. So don't lose courage, but keep trying.[55]

The tolerance and simplicity of the Buddhist approach appeals very much to me, and I will just quote a few lines from Aldous Huxley underlining my preference: 'Thus, in many Buddhist societies, the manufacture of arms, the concoction of intoxicating liquors and the wholesale purveying of butcher's meat were not, as in contemporary Christendom, rewarded by wealth, peerages and political influence; they were deplored as businesses which, it was thought, made it particularly difficult for their practitioners and for other members of the communities in which they were practised to achieve enlightenment and liberation'.[56] And his observation is underlined by the Jesuit priest William Johnston who, after having lived for many years in East Asia, wrote: 'But the longer I sat the more I realized that Zen has an important message for the monotheistic religions. For the fact is that Zen abhors all divisions, abhors all use of the discriminating intellect, abhors all words (*no dependence on words and letters* is the great slogan) whereas the divisions and wars and quarrels among the monotheistic religions have been caused primarily by our clinging to words, to letters, to dogmas, to formulas, to structures, to doctrines. ... If only we could move towards a mystical state of consciousness where all is one. ... And Zen goes not only beyond words and letters but beyond fear, anxiety, greed, pride, lust, envy anger. ... Now what I say of Zen is also true of Christian mysticism. It also leads to an altered state of consciousness where all is one in God'.[57]

But again, do realise, as Johnston did, that there is no substitute for personal experience, which was made very clear by Shih-t'ou when he replied to the question 'What is the ultimate teaching of Buddhism?' with: 'You won't understand until you have it'.[58]

However, if you are baffled by the enormous range of different Buddhist schools and practices, which are the healthy result of the absence of dogmas, doctrines and a central 'clearing house' (the Buddha alone is credited with 84,000 teachings), then a very forthright and helpful survey can be found in *The New Buddhism,* written by James William Coleman, from which I quote the Buddha underlining this very point:

> Nothing whatsoever is to be clung to as I or mine.
> Whoever has heard this teaching has heard all of the teachings.
> Whoever puts this into practice has put all of the Dharma into practice.[59]

But I also accept that the guru adulation and the gold and glitter often associated with the Hindu approach—while repelling me—might be just what your artistic soul was yearning for. And always keep in mind that you are definitely not alone in your explorations, and while you might often despair and think you are the only 'abnormal' one around; the statistics definitely give a very different picture: 'A study of religious and mystical encounters among the American population conducted by the National Data Program for the Social Sciences in 1988 and 1989 shows that almost *a third of Americans* have had a mystical or numinous experience in their lives, while *65 percent* have undergone paranormal experiences. ... Only a small percentage of respondents reported *never* having had a paranormal or mystical experience. ... There is, it turns out, a vast underground of people who have experienced a Call and yet are hiding their mystical lights'.[60] And in the case that you despair that the 'Call' hasn't been heard yet, that can be a very good thing indeed; as Bede Griffiths explains: 'Despair is often the first step on the path of spiritual life and many people do not awaken to the Reality of God and the experience of transformation in their lives till they go through the experience of emptiness, disillusion and despair'.[61]

Also remember that Jesus is reported to have expressed a similar praise of 'abnormality': 'That which is highly esteemed among men is abomination in the eyes of God'.[62] Yes, Jesus was far more radical than the churches founded in his name, which are so desperately trying to be respectable. In the *Gospel of Thomas*, he stressed the unimportance of external paraphernalia graphically: 'When you disrobe without being ashamed and take up your garments, and place them under your feet like little children and tread on them, then you will see the son of the living one, and you will not be afraid'.[63]

There have been movements such as the Modernists trying to fit religious faith inside the horizontal restrictions of science. By disposing of a transcendent God they hoped that their practitioners would be taken more seriously by the academic community. Don Cupitt comes to mind expressing on the *Sea of Faith* website that 'the church must get rid of all her supernatural beliefs'.[64] As I interpret this as advertising to get rid of beliefs that imply the existence of the vertical dimension, I wrote a letter to one of his admirers, John Spong, the author of the book *Christianity has to Change or Die;* and to attain that aim he is part of an organisation *Christianity for the Third Millennium*. In my letter I summarised the (vertical) message of this book, but I am still waiting for his reaction.

However, for those who have had a personal experience of the reality of the vertical dimension, the same message about its priority and critical importance can indeed be discerned everywhere, which issue I will deal with in the next section.

11.3 SIGNPOSTS ARE EVERYWHERE

Nothing in this life is more important than our relation with Spirit, and any behavior or attitude that places anything before Spirit will surely attract lessons to correct it.[65]

African elder

The happy man is not he whom the crowd deems happy, namely into whose coffers mighty sums have flowed, but he whose possessions are all in his soul.[66]

Seneca

Human beings can attain a worthy and harmonious life only if they are able to rid themselves, within the limits of human nature, of the striving of the wish fulfilments of material kinds. The goal is to raise the spiritual value of society.[67]

Albert Einstein

If there is any good to be found, it must be a spiritual good.[68]

E. F. Schumacher

You are the designer of your destiny. You are the author. You write the story. The pen is in your hand, and the outcome is whatever you choose.[69]

Lisa Nichols

Joop van Montfoort

In his book *The New Consciousness in Science and Religion*, Harold Schilling discusses the 'tremendous expansion and transformation of [man's] consciousness' and lists a number of general principles contributing to 'what human life ought to be like. Item three on his list is '... human life—individual and communal, national and international—should be dominated by the tender and persuasive elements of life, and most of all by the strongest of these, love'. And he follows this up by stressing that the vertical dimension should take priority over the horizontal one: 'In a truly human society the qualitative aspects and values of life should in man's strivings take priority over quantitative ones'.[70]

Indeed, very much like signposts, this same message can be discerned everywhere. Apart from the quotations going back to antiquity that I opened this section with, take these from two contemporary authors, First Gary Zukav: 'Feel your intentions in your heart. Feel not what your mind tells you. Rather than serve the fake gods of your mind, serve your heart, the real God. You will not find God in your intellect. Divine Intelligence is in the heart'.[71] Followed by Matthew Fox again: 'Our work must make way for the heart, that is, for truth and justice to play an ever-increasing role in our professional lives. Without that heart-food, we will surely die of starvation of the spirit and all the promotions and fat paychecks in the world will not assuage the feeling that we are dying in the soul'.[72]

As I mentioned in the Introduction, I have referred to many books and articles but I am very much aware that their selection results from my personal interests; again, what appeals to me does not necessarily appeal to you. The Dalai Lama said about religions that 'we have different tastes, [so] we must take that what is most suitable for us'. So never give up hope, and keep searching until you encounter a way that feels right for you. Rabbi Nahman of Bratislava expressed this so poignantly: 'God chooses one man with a shout, another with a song, another with a whisper'.[73]

It must have become obvious from the many quotations I illustrated my text with, that there are a multitude of books already out there conveying a similar message, which is, as we have seen, as old as mankind. For example, recently Emmy gave me a book with the remark that I should read it. It was one of the books she had picked up intuitively in a Glastonbury bookshop. When I started reading it, I could hardly put it down until I'd finished it, and I thought that it gave me the answer to my apprehensions. It made me realise that whatever I presented as a solid proof for the reality and importance of the vertical dimension, it would only appeal to someone who is on a similar track as myself and would leave others completely cold.

The book that gave me this insight is *My Grandfather's Blessings*, written by Rachel Naomi Remen. Like me, she was the child of working parents, and was also very much influenced by her grandfather. She became a medical doctor, and for me the whole book is a powerful testimony about how essential a vertical approach to a supposedly horizontal pursuit like medicine is, and that 'In our struggle towards freedom we are neither abandoned nor alone'. During her study she experienced this as 'Our focus was on cure and not healing' and further on 'I also used to believe that things that could be expressed in numbers were truer than things that could only be said in words. I no longer believe that...' She deduces from her experiences that 'After more than thirty-five years as a physician, I have found at last that it is possible to be a professional and live from the heart. This was not something that I learned in medical school'. To conclude with a last quote: 'But science can never serve unless it is first translated by people into a work of the heart'.[74] I could go on quoting from her very moving book, but again my taste is not necessarily yours, so get hold of it and see for yourself how the same message can be expressed in a completely different way.

If you are eager to be convinced by authors who may be more appealing to you personally, you only need to explore your local library or the 'Mind, Body and Spirit' shelves in a bookshop or the Internet. As we have seen, the same message of the primacy of the vertical dimension can be found in the writings by authors ranging from Plato to Einstein, Meister Eckhart to Anthony de Mello, Russell Targ to Fritjof Capra, Ken Wilber to Gary Zukav, Lynne McTaggart, etc., etc. But if you are not at all on my wavelength of reading mainly non-fiction books, then again Emmy pointed me to an amazing series of very readable novels by Susan Howatch. Superficially, her books are about the life stories of an interesting range of functionaries in the Church of England, but she gives a large number of quotations appropriate to the message I have been trying to convey in these pages. Take this one from Dean Inge, quoted by her: 'The mystical experience seems to those who have it to transport them out of time and place and separate individuality. This of course, brings us at once among the most formidable philosophical problems. Those mystics who are also philosophers generally hold that neither space nor time is ultimately real'.[75]

And to whet your appetite, I have lifted the following gems from her own writing:

... the mystical and the worldly, not in opposition but complementing each other...[76]

So many people fail to realise that the greatest journey one can ever take is the journey to the very centre of one's being.[77]

Strange how easily the past and present interweave nowadays, but time's all an illusion. ... Reality is beyond time. Reality is spiritual.[78]

By showing scepticism? Or resorting to ridicule? No, I leave that to the scientists—the ones who can't bear to admit they don't know all the answers.[79]

... the logical positivists prove only one thing: that it's possible to have a brilliant intellect and still wind up a spiritual ignoramus out of touch with ultimate reality.[80]

The same insight is clearly expressed by Cary Baynes in her introduction to Jung's *The Secret of the Golden Flower*: 'The solution cannot be found either in deriding ... spirituality as impotent or by mistrusting science as a destroyer of humanity. We have to see that the spirit must lean on science as its guide to the world of reality and that science must turn to spirit for the meaning of life'.[81]

The same message can indeed be found everywhere.

Scientists are proposing to make contact with other possible civilisations somewhere out there in the vastness of the universe; in fact some of them have already sent signals and probes. But even signals travelling with the speed of light of some 300,000 km per second will take years to reach our nearest star, while others are billions of light-years away. It would be a much more profitable pursuit to aim for spiritual enlightenment because in this way, by leaving the spacetime prison of our ocean's surface, we would be one with everything and everybody else, wherever in the universe they may be located.

However, a very basic issue is that neither I, nor anybody else, will ever be able to 'prove' with argumentation the reality of the vertical dimension, because that can only be experienced. But even though this search is so important do not, like I once did, try to force anything because that will only end in failure. Madame Guyon cautioned very appropriately 'I tried to obtain by effort that which I could only obtain by ceasing all effort'.[82]

In the first pages of this book, I quoted Victor Stenger advocating the belief that 'psi is zero', and I want to end this brief review with a few books by another scientist who firmly subscribed to that belief as well. Carl Sagan is one of the heroes of my generation, and although a couple of years younger than me, he died in 1996. From what I have read in his books, I assume that politically and socially we are very much on the same wavelength; therefore I will dedicate some space to him, putting him in the role of 'devil's advocate'. It is very much a pity that he cannot answer me back anymore.

His book *The Demon Haunted World*, which appeared in the year of his death, is a really captivating read. He vividly illustrates the dangers of even admitting that psi could be anything else than zero. And of course, he is right to warn us of even contemplating that possibility, because by opening this particular Pandora's box you can indeed be completely submerged by a flood of paranormal claims. Unfortunately there are not only deliberate cheats and crooks, who prey on the gullible to flog their wares (often for large amounts of money), but also very nice people who really believe in what they are trying to sell you, be it either wares or services, or indeed a sure method of opening up your inner channel.

So Sagan advises to subject everything to scientific scrutiny and declares anything that doesn't fit into the horizontal dimension as rubbish. He plays it safe, decreeing that psi is zero and that there is no vertical dimension. Even going as far as: "'Spirit' comes from the Latin word 'to breathe'. What we breathe is air, which is certainly matter, however thin. Despite usage to the contrary, there is no necessary implication in the word 'spiritual' that we are talking of anything other than matter (including the matter of which the brain is made), or anything outside the realm of science".[83] Indeed in this way everything is kept under tight horizontal control and all experiences should be subjected to the unforgiving tools of sceptical thinking.[84] But that attitude implies limiting yourself to an extremely tunnel-visioned approach to the world around you; ignoring the fact that many bookshelves can easily be filled with books documenting experiences that can only be fitted in if one accepts the reality of another dimension beyond the restrictions of the horizontal one. So even tunnel vision is too liberal because that attitude limits you to narrow horizontal-slit vision only.

But by taking that 'safe' approach (advocated by Sagan) of dismissing the host of claims that fail to meet scientific criteria without personal investigation, that will definitely result in throwing out the vertical baby with the horizontal bath water. Centuries ago, William Blake already cautioned against the result of this blinkered (scientific) approach: 'May God keep us from single vision and Newton's sleep...'

Sagan has subtitled his book, *Science as a Candle in the Dark,* but as I, and many others have experienced, the real 'candle' can only be experienced in the vertical dimension. Very much like Sagan, I was a boy who kept asking questions, and as we grow older that basic curiosity should not be compromised and put to sleep, even if it undermines all of our cherished certainties. And especially as a scientist you are obliged that if there is still any doubt in your mind, to keep experimenting until the matter is resolved to your own satisfaction instead of hiding behind horizontal dogmatism (after all, the word 'science' comes from the Latin *scire*, to know*)*.

Sagan denounces, for instance, Transcendental Meditation and its initiator, Maharishi Mahesh Yogi, and of course from the outside the TM claims seem indeed ridiculous.[85] But he does mention nowhere that he submitted the TM claims to the test of personal experimentation. At least I subjected my doubts about those claims to the test, and it definitely contributed to the fact that I had to completely revise my original dismissive attitude. Therefore his claim that '... the metaphysicist has no laboratory' is definitely erroneous.[86]

Yes, I do know that the non-replicability of experiments in the vertical dimension is considered to be a major problem, making them fall foul of horizontal scientific criteria; their importance is, however, that they can teach you personally a great deal.[87] And as Karl Popper rightfully argued, you have only to see one black swan to know that the law that 'all swans are white' is false.

Indeed, I also had great difficulty with the gold and glitter narcissism of the TM scene, its guru worship and the ranks of three-piece suited youngsters organised in a hierarchy with Maharishi as pope, very much paralleling that of cardinals, bishops, priests and deacons.[88] But looking beyond what is for me a ghastly surface shimmer, I learned that the basic teachings and claims are based on centuries of experience, and that they are derived from an ancient philosophy which has at least been preserved until today, while we in Europe seem to have lost most of our ancient 'pagan' wisdom.

In this book I have used many references to illustrate particular points of my narrative and I do hope that this has helped to whet your appetite. Even if you are a committed horizontalist, I do hope that my arguments and the quotations given have at least been able to uncover a soft spot and that you might be willing to read one more book about this 'dangerous' subject. Perhaps because he has so much in common with me (age, star sign, trade and personal experience), I advise you to read Russell Targ's *Limitless Mind*, from which I will quote just one paragraph: 'Our ability to share this experience of freedom, love, and spaciousness is what gives meaning to our lives. With our present technology of television, video games, e-mail, and computers, however, we run the risk of never having another quiet moment. This represents the greatest loss we could possibly experience'.[89] The well-referenced evidence summarised in his book, and in part published in leading peer-reviewed scientific publications, proves without a shadow of doubt that we are indeed interconnected, not only in space but in time as well.

I will end this brief review of the myriad signposts—each of which is pointing to one of the many trails that are out there—each of them promising inner revelation—with one appropriate quote from Konstantin Tsiolkovsky:

It is either one or the other, you know. If these scientists believe that such an [ESP] ability really exists in people, they actually have no right to call it supernatural. ... Everything that exists in nature is precisely what we call natural. ... if these scientists, contradicting their own logic, are inclined to believe a certain natural phenomenon to be supernatural, it means that they are simply incompetent and their opinion should be disregarded as unscientific.[90]

11.4 BE STILL AND KNOW

Those who do not seek the purpose of life are simply wasting their lives.[91]

Ramana Maharshi

Accustomed long to meditating on the Whispered Chosen Truths,
I have forgot all that is said in written and in printed books.
Accustomed long to application of each new experience to mine own growth spiritual,
I have forgot all creeds and dogmas.[92]

Milarepa

If you make a great effort to change people around you, your effort will be wasted.
If you want to change others, you must first begin to change yourself.[93]

Masami Saionji

It is only with the heart that one can see rightly; what is essential is invisible to the eye.[94]

Antoine de Saint-Exupéry

For ultimately, it is the spiritual and mystic side of life which provides us with its real meaning.[95]

John Davidson

Joop van Montfoort

As will have become clear from what I have presented before, we have to commit ourselves to a complete change in orientation, in electrical engineering terminology: to a ninety degrees phase shift, i.e. from horizontal to vertical.[96] But if we look around us, we see that the whole aim of our society, and hence its government, is to promote *having* rather than *being,* and that economic growth (i.e. money) is advertised as the only cure for all of society's problems.

We are so clever, 'yet knowledge which used without reference to compassion, may utterly destroy mankind', as Christmas Humphreys puts it so appropriately.[97] We desperately need to become wise and embrace the ancient message that wisdom is the head guided by the heart. We have to come to the realisation that the vertical dimension is the really important one, and this insight has to result in the sea change of not being obsessed with possessions and status, but with inner growth, even when the seemingly so glamorous trappings of the horizontal dimension are dangled continuously in front of our eyes, not only in shopping centres but via our TV screens in our very living rooms as well. Not that possessions are intrinsically wrong; it all depends on our relationship to them, as Swami Prabhavananda made crystal clear: 'But the man who has given up his sense of attachment experiences the advantages which possessions afford without the misery which possessiveness brings'.[98]

This abandonment of possessiveness can make us so free and so powerful that we do not need our materialistic fences to hide our insecurity anymore, as illustrated in figure 11.3. And that will only be possible when we have committed ourselves to going within, opening up our inner vertical dimension.

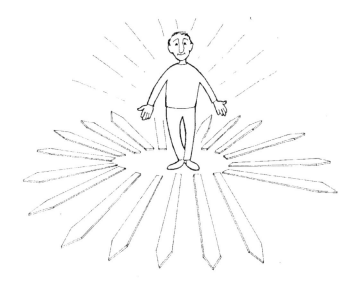

Figure 11.3 Not afraid anymore

Sathya Sai Baba describes the sequence of going within clearly: 'First comes knowledge, then skill, then balance, then wisdom—and then you go within'.[99] Then indeed can we experience that we are not alone, that we are all waves on the same ocean, or in other words, children of the same mother/father. Only then will the ancient title of this book become a living reality for you: *All is One* ... and not only *One* but *Now* as well, because we come to the realisation that the essence of our being is outside the prison of space and time; as Norman Friedman makes clear 'It is as though events do not occur [in time], they just are'.[100]

Of course, I do realise that all this is much easier said than done, after all, we have been brainwashed for so long in believing that success in life is identified with possessions and status. But as I have shown, more and more people are becoming aware of the fact that these pursuits are exactly the ones that cause the ruination of our beautiful planet. As always the Dalai Lama is optimistic that we will change our ways: 'Since even wild animals can gradually be trained with patience, the human mind also can gradually be trained, step by step'.[101]

I really think that instead of trying to 'convert' people who are already frozen in their ways and beliefs, it would be more profitable to initiate the process of accepting the primacy of the vertical dimension by presenting that essential message at an early age. Instead of ridiculing sensitive children, we should do everything possible to protect and stimulate that expression of their openness to the inner dimension. Again we can learn so much from the Eastern traditions, and Cardinal Joseph Ratzinger saw this clearly when he warned: 'Someone rightly predicted in the 1950s that the challenge for the Church in the twentieth century would not be Marxism, but Buddhism'.[102]

A notable voice from the East is Yu-Lan Fung, expressing the holistic synthesis of what we have called horizontal and vertical: 'This-worldliness and other-worldliness stand in contrast to each other as do realism and idealism. The task of Chinese philosophy is to accomplish a synthesis of these antitheses. That does not mean they are to be abolished. They are still here, but they have been made into a synthetic whole. How can this be done? This is the problem which Chinese philosophy attempts to solve. According to Chinese philosophy, the man who accomplishes this synthesis, not only in theory but also in deed, is the sage. He is both this-worldly and other-worldly'.[103] Or in other words, being both in the head and the heart, and as we have seen opening up the heart is what religion should be about, as again the Dalai Lama makes clear 'Western civilisations these days place great importance on filling the human brain with knowledge, but no one seems to care about filling the human heart with compassion. This is what the real role of religion is'.[104]

. You can dismiss all of these ideas as pipe dreams that are clearly impossible to realise, but I will keep insisting that there is simply no other alternative. And that every one of us is personally responsible, is beautifully symbolised by William Holman Hunt's painting of Jesus[105], sketched in figure 11.4.

Figure 11.4 No door handle on the inside

It is appropriate that Hunt called it 'The Light of the World', which in our tradition he depicts as Christ. For an ancient Persian, for instance, it would have been Mithras, their god of Light, the ritual of which was spread widely by the legions throughout the Roman Empire around the time of Jesus. If you inspect this painting carefully you will discover that there is no handle on Christ's side of the door, which can be interpreted as again underlining the message that it is up to us to take the initiative and open the door.

Indeed, Basil the Great advised to keep the inner dimension secret: 'The uninitiated are not permitted to behold these things', and 'Their meaning is not to de divulged by writing it down'.[106] But Meister Eckhart assures us that the 'Light' is eager to follow up our invitation: 'You do not need to call to Him far off. He waits much more impatiently than you for you to open to Him, He longs for you a thousand times more urgently than you for Him'.[107] So don't be afraid to correct statements dismissing the reality of the vertical dimension. Your colleagues might well look at you with a worried expression on their faces, uttering, 'You're not serious, are you?' But as has happened to me, they might come back to you years later, saying, ' When you told us about the importance of spiritual pursuits, I thought you had gone around the bend, but now I am beginning to think that you were right after all'. Then you will discover that you are not at all alone, as I did when two little old ladies came up to me telling me how glad they were that I had intervened when a fundamentalist Christian minister dismissed other religious approaches during a Lent meeting in a village I was then living in.

Of course, I have an understanding for rules and regulations which are often not only essential to keep an organisation together, but can be a very valuable safety net indeed. Also, William James wondered—around the end of the nineteenth century—why so many scientists deliberately keep their eyes shut: 'Why do so few "scientists" even look at the evidence for telepathy, so called? Because they think, as a leading biologist ... once said to me, that even if such a thing were true, scientists ought to band together to keep it suppressed and concealed'.[108] And he summarised their scepticism thus: 'Better risk loss of truth than chance of error'.[109]

Indeed if you allow psi to be anything else than zero, you open the door to all the 'silliness spouted by the world's weirdoes'.[110] But the whole purpose of life is of course to get our eyes open and indeed to get rid of the blindfold of creeds and dogmas. Henry Miller comments: 'We're asleep, don't you know, we're sleepwalkers'.[111] So please do wake up!

You might possibly think that taking paranormal phenomena seriously could very seriously hinder your academic career. On the other hand, a recent conference on 'Alternative Spiritualities and New Age Studies' hosted by the Open University attracted around 150 researchers from all over the planet; one of its protagonists declaring 'No matter what you think of religion, you cannot think it is irrelevant. There is a pressing imperative nowadays to understand how some people are seeing the world differently from others, so we might understand why people behave as they do'.[112]

To underline that the message I have tried to convey in this book is indeed an ancient and universal one, I will quote Sogyal Rinpoche's closing remarks in his book, *The Tibetan Book of Living and Dying*: 'More than anything, I pray that the book I have written could contribute in some small way to help awaken as many people as possible to the urgency of the need for spiritual transformation, and the urgency of the need to be responsible for ourselves and others. We are all potential buddhas ...' From his ancient tradition of Buddhism, the message is very clearly summarised in one line 'Cease to do evil; learn to do good; cleanse your own heart'.[113]

Indeed, cleansing our heart is what we are trying to realise in meditation practice; then you can indeed discover with many others that psi is infinite. You are free to dismiss this message, but give then at least the next generations the chance to be more open-minded. Roy Wilkinson makes this very clear: 'To learn of these things in our old age may perhaps be of limited use to us personally, but we can take care that children receive a proper education so that they avoid our difficulties'.[114]

I will repeat the advice I gave at the beginning of the book, namely that I will never be able to prove to you the existence of what I have called the vertical dimension, that you can only find out for yourself. But I do think that I have made my case: namely that the simple horizontal/vertical model has great explanatory power, making the many pieces of life's great jigsaw puzzle fall in their proper places. If we accept that our universe is just the space-time surface of an ocean of infinite energy, it also explains the baffling experimental results pointing to the profusion of dark energy and dark matter which seemingly surround us. And by exploring the vertical dimension yourself, you may well discover not only that you are a child of the One, but also that 'psi is infinite' and 'All is One'.

Following Victor Stenger's example (chapter 2), this life-changing conclusion can be expressed in two simple formulas:

$$\Psi = \infty \text{ and } \mathbf{All} = \mathbf{1}$$

But enough of formulas and words, because, as Father Thomas Keating expressed it so poignantly: 'God's first language is silence. Everything else is a bad translation'.[115] And because Jesus is reported to have said 'I tell you the truth, anyone who will not receive the kingdom of God like a little child will never enter it',[116] I want to give the last word to little Anna:[117]

'Fynn, you have to know much more to be silent than you do to keep talking.

NOTES

Preface

1. Kirk and Raven, *The Presocratic Philosophers*, Cambridge University Press, 1957, p 168
2. quoted in Aldous Huxley, *The Perennial Philosophy*, London, 1950, p 90
3. William Johnston, *Christian Mysticism Today*, Collins, 1984, p 146
4. George Trevelyan, *Exploration into God*, Gateway, Bath, 1991, p 8
5. Lawrence LeShan, *Clairvoyant Reality*, Turnstone Press, 1982, p 44
6. Lawrence LeShan, *How to meditate*, (1974) 1985, p 65

Chapter 1   Introduction

1. Chuang Tzu (369-286 BCE), chapter 2
2. Quoted in Deepak Chopra, *The Path of Love*, New York, 1997, p 296
3. Quoted in Aldous Huxley, *The Perennial Philosophy*, London, 1950, p 69
4. I started taking clocks apart when I was around five years old because I wanted to understand how they worked and I drove my elders potty by always asking, 'Why?' I vividly remember that my grandfather silenced me for a few minutes with the remark, 'One fool can ask more than seven wise men can answer'.
5. *The Essential Teachings of Ramana Maharshi*, Inner Directions, Carlsbad (Ca), (2001) 23003, p 87
6. in March 2006
7. J. Krishnamurti, *The Awakening of Intelligence*, London, 1973, p 207

Chapter 2   Background

1. www.templeton.org
2. C. G. Jung, *Memories, Dreams, Reflections*, Fontana, London, (1963) 1967, p 330

3.   L. Wittgenstein, *Tractatus Logico-Philosophicus*, Routledge, London, 1960

4.   quoted in L. L. Whyte, *Accent of Form*, New York, 1954

5.   Richard Bach, *Illusions*

6.   I gave the Tao and Physics course at the Department of External Studies of the University of Oxford, in 1985 and 1986.

7.   For instance, Matthew Fox writes: 'When Dominican missionary Bartholomew de las Casas proclaimed in the sixteenth century that the Indian civilization was far superior than that of Spain, he was speaking a literal truth that has yet to be understood in Europe or America'; in *Creation Spirituality*, Harper San Fransisco, 1991, p 116f

8.   Roland Peterson, *Every One is Right*, DeVorss & Co, Marina del Rey, CA, 1986

9.   'The Tao and Physics', Dept. of External Studies of the University of Oxford, in 1985 and 1986

10.   Victor J Stenger, *Physics and Psychics,* Buffalo, NY, 1990

11.   Wayne W. Dyer,*Wisdom of the Ages*, London, 1998, p 125

12.   G M A Grube, *Plato's Thought*, London, 1970 (1935), p 192

13.   Thomas Moore, *The Soul's Religion*, Bantam, 2003, p 192

14.   World Council of Churches, Assembly in New Delhi, 1961, quoted in Sallie McFague, *Super, Natural Christians: How we should love nature*, SCM Press, 1997, p 204

15.   Jenni speaking in Naomi Ragen, *The Sacrifice of Tamar*, London, 1995, p 339

16.   Albert Einstein, *The World as I See It*, Philosophical Library, 1949, p 24-28

17.   Ralph Waldo Emerson, 'Self-Reliance', in *Essays*, 1841 & 1844

18.   As an article in the *Los Angeles Times* of 1 December 2001: 'Lutheran Pastor Assailed', proved, sections of the Lutheran Church in the USA in the 21st century are still stuck in the attitude of asking for a pastor's expulsion from the church for participating in an Interfaith event; see Neale Donald Walsch, *The New Revelations: A Conversation with God*, London, 2002, p 43f. However, modern theologians have moved far away from this position, see e.g. John Hick (ed.), *The Myth of God Incarnate*, London, 1977, pp 9, 180, 183. In my opinion they have actually moved too far. In particular the title of the book is unfortunate, because I consider it as a reality rather than a myth, that not only Jesus but the whole universe is *God Incarnate*.

19.   Hugh Montefiore writes in *On Being a Jewish Christian*, London, 1998, p 169: 'I think it is a horrible religion which supposes that all those who do not believe in Christ are bound for hell'. E A Milne is quoted in Paul Davies in *Are*

We Alone?, Penguin, 1995, p 30: 'What then of the denizens of other planets, if the Incarnation occurred only on our own? We are in deep waters here, in a sea of great mysteries'. Joanna Macy 'found the Christian claims to "exclusivity of truth so absurd that [she] had a crisis of faith" and 'became an atheist'. Quoted in Catherine Ingram, *In the Footsteps of Gandhi*, Berkeley (Ca), 1990, p 144. In the same book on p 217, Diane Nash is quoted: 'When I was part of an organized religion, the beliefs actually interfered with my relationship to the creative force, which some might call God'. While Loran Hurnscot made the same point: ' ... that to hinge eternal salvation on one single, confused and handicapped lifetime seemed to me a diabolical idea. ... If this is orthodoxy, then may God save me from it'. Quoted in Joseph Head and S. L. Cranston, *Reincarnation an east-west anthology*, The Theosophical Publishing House, (1961) 1975, p 163

20. Then part of the Dutch East Indies, now called Irian Jaya.
21. His reply was in line with the Roman Catholic dogma: 'Extra ecclesiam nulla salus'. The much more tolerant attitude in the 1990s is illustrated by the comment the dean of one of the English cathedrals made when I told him the story of how I left the church I was brought up in; his reaction was: 'I would have walked out with you'. For a few years around 1960 I joined the church of the liberal minister in the village where I then lived.
22. quoted in Timothy Freke and Peter Gandy, *The Jesus Mysteries,* "London,2000, pp 129 and 90
23. M. K. Gandhi, *An Autobiography: The Story of my Experiments with Truth, Boston, 1957, p 136*
24. Steve Wright (ed.), *A Conversation with Miranda Holden, Sacred Space*, Vol. 3, 3, 2002, p 16ff
25. Later, together with my colleague, Joop van der Kam, who was very much a 'brilliant ideas' man, while I was more the 'doer' who got things operational
26. They had been designed by an electronics engineer who fled from Hungary during the 1956 uprising.
27. Regarding my stuttering, I seem to have been in the good company of: Isaac Newton, James Clerk Maxwell, Charles Darwin (*New Scientist*, 8 June 1991, p 53), Alan Turing ('Computers', BBC TV2, 17 December 1991) and the many others that can be found in the Wikipedia list of famous stutterers
28. Socrates, *Crito*, in Plato, *The last Days of Socrates*, Penguin, (1954) 1985, p 87

29.   Meladoma Some, an African spiritual teacher, quoted in
        Matthew Fox, *The Reinvention of Work*, New York, 1995, p
        253

30.   Quoted in G. I. Gurdjieff, *Meetings with Remarkable Men*,
        London, 1985 (1963), p 240

31.   B. Watson, *Hsün Tzu*, p 19, quoted by Raymond Dawson,
        Confucius, in Michael Carrithers, at al., *Founders of Faith*,
        Oxford University Press, 1989, p 106

32.   Much later I found research evidence that: 'Seventy-
        four percent of the complaints patients bring to medical
        clinics are of unknown origin and are probably caused by
        "psychosocial" factors' and 'Other studies indicate that
        between 60 and 90 percent of all our population's visits
        to doctor's offices are stress-related ...'; in Herbert Benson,
        M.D., *Timeless Healing*, Simon & Schuster, 1996, p 49f

33.   Herman Millikowsky, author of amongst others: *Sociologie
        als Verzet (Sociology as Resistance)*, Amsterdam, 1973

34.   C. G. Jung, *Modern Man in Search of a Soul*, London,
        (1933) 1985, p 261

Chapter 3 How I was tripped up

1.   Stanislav Grof, *The Holotropic Mind*, Harper San Franscisco,
        1990, p 34 describing his own experience

2.   Peggy Mason & Ron Laing, *Sathya Sai Baba: The
        Embodiment of Love*, Pilgrim, 1987(1982), p 226f

3.   C.G.Jung, *Memories, Dreams, Reflections*, Fontana, London,
        (1963) 1967, p 216

4.   Joseph L. Henderson, 'Ancient Myths and Modern Man', in
        Carl Jung (ed.), *Man and his Symbols*, Aldus, London, 1964,
        p 97

5.   Vernon Coleman, *Bodypower: The Secret of Self-healing*,
        Barnstaple, (1983) 2005, p 50

6.   Both come from the Latin *Mons Fortis* (strong mountain),
        which was a popular name for castles in the Middle Ages.
        In my case the name of the castle was transferred to a small
        town from which one of my forebears must have come from
        (*van*) when he was registered after the French invasion of
        Holland at the end of the eighteenth century.

7.   The Citroën HY van, which I had converted into a camper,
        had at the rear two half-doors with a top hinged flap above.

8.   Lac Noir was connected via an underground tunnel to the
        neighbouring Lac Blanc in an electrical energy management
        scheme. Water could be pumped from the lower lake to the
        higher one during off-peak hours and the potential energy

stored in the water could be converted back into electricity when required during periods of peak demand. Something had obviously gone wrong with the water control system, flooding the station and killing the operators.

9. During a visit in 2009, I noticed that these buildings were being knocked down.

10. C G Jung, *Synchronicity—An Acausal Connecting Principle,* London, 1955

11. David Icke, in his book *The Robot's Rebellion,* Gateway, Bath, 1994, which I read recently, writes on p 177f: 'When thought patterns are broadcast by people they stay in that area until they are balanced by other patterns. The spirits of the dead are often still there, too. ... We call then 'ghosts' or 'lost souls'. When you go to the scene of battles it can feel 'eerie'. ... Sensitive people who go to such places can hear battles or see them happening'. And James Van Praagh adds: 'When someone is thrown out of the physical body suddenly, as in a violent death, the spirit may not know for a while that it has passed over. It may wander around the earth realm as if in a dream'. in *Healing Grief,* Spiritual Horizons, Inc., 2000, p 96

12. When working at the Philips Research Laboratory in the 1950s, I designed an instrument using these two dimensions to quickly identify the composition of 'floating around' metal wires in the wire pulling plant.

13. Robert Graves, *Goodbye to All That,* quoted in Anthony North, *The Paranormal,* London, 1996, p 56

14. Anthony North, *The Paranormal,* London, 1996, p 72

15. Gary E Schwarts, *The Afterlife Experiments,* 2002, p205

16. Joan Grant and Dennis Kelsey , *Many Lifetimes,* London, 1976, p 163

17. Niels Bohr, 'The Unity of Human Knowledge', Copenhagen, 1960, in *Essays 1958 - 1962,* 1963, p 12

18. Douglas Dean, John Mihalasky, Sheila Ostrander & Lynn Schroeder, *Executive ESP,* Prentice Hall, 1974, p 13

19. Quoted in David Leavitt, *The Man who knew too much: Alan Turing and the invention of the Computer,* London, 2006, p 255f

20. Quoted in Gablik, *Reenchantment of Art,* p 57f

21. C.G. Jung, *Selected Writings,* Anthony Storr, London, 1983, p 355

22. Niels Bohr, 'The Unity of Human Knowledge', Copenhagen, 1960, in *Essays, 1958 - 1962,* 1963, p 12

23. Quoted in Lawrence LeShan, *Clairvoyant Reality* (formerly *The Medium, The Mystic and the Physicist*), Turnstone Press Ltd, 1982 (1974), p 26

24. Edwin A. Abbot, *Flatland,* Oxford, 1978

25.   Richard P Feynman, *Surely you're joking. Mr Feynman!*,
        Bantam, 1985, p 292

Chapter 4 The 'ocean' model

1.   Sir James Jeans, *The Mysterious Universe*, Cambridge
        University Press, London, 1930, p 148
2.   Albert Einstein, quoted in M Capek, *The Philosophical
        Impact of Contemporary Physics*, D. Van Nostrand,
        Princeton, 1961, p 319
3.   C. G. Jung, *Memories, Dreams, Reflections*, Fontana,
        London, (1963) 1967, p 330
4.   sometimes referred to as 'Minkowski space'
5.   A very simple example of proving this proposition has
        been done by taking a pair of very precise atomic clocks.
        One was left behind in the lab while the other was flown
        around the world on regular commercial flights. The result
        corresponded indeed to the predictions made by relativity
        theory.
6.   see Sir James Jeans, *The Mysterious Universe*, Cambridge
        University Press, London, 1930, p 116ff, and Richard P.
        Feynman, *QED: The Strange Theory of Light and Matter*,
        Penguin, 1990 (1985), ch 3
7.   Spacetime is often described as a thin membrane,
        abbreviated to 'brane', but as I think space-time peters out
        gradually when descending into deeper waters, I find that
        this gives the wrong impression.
8.   Sir James Jeans, *The Mysterious Universe*, Cambridge
        University Press, London, 1930, p 114
9.   *Contra Epistolam Manichaei,* cap. 3, quoted in Victor
        White, *God and the Unconscious,* London, 1952, p 214
10.   Friedrich von Schelling, *System des transzendentalen
        Idealismus*, p 600
11.   Parahamsa Yogananda, *Autobiography of a Yogi,* p 318
12.   C. G. Jung *Selected Writings*, Anthony Storr, London, 1983,
        p 329
13.   Eric Butterworth, *Discover the Power within You* , Harper
        San Fransisco, 1992, p 34
14.   Adama and Naomi Doumbia, *The Way of the Elders*, St.
        Paul, MN, 2004, p 76
15.   Expressed cogently in an ancient saying: 'Energy is all there
        is ... but is not known', in Roland Peterson, *Everyone Is
        Right*, DeVorss, Marina del Rey, 1986, p 133.
16.   George Trevelyan, *Exploration into God*, Gateway, Bath,
        1991, p 162 and 181f. God as Light is a very widely used

model indeed: 'God is light and in him is no darkness at all.' (1 John 1:15) 'He is the one light that gives light to all.' (Katha Upanishad), 'Primal energy is Brahman' etc. quoted in Roland Peterson, *Everyone Is Right*, DeVorss, Marina del Rey, 1986, p 133. While Pitirim A. Sorokin writes: 'The immortal divine element which is in every man, will not die with the death of the body, but will return into the ocean of cosmic, supremely creative energy (often called "God," "Brahman," "Purusha," "Tao," "Divine No Thing," etc.) In Joseph Head and S. L. Cranston, *Reincarnation: An East-West Anthology*, The Theosophical Publishing House, (1961) 1975, p 230

17.   Such as *Tao* in China, *Brahman* in India, *Godhead* by Meister Eckhart and *Dharmakaya* in Buddhism. In the Buddhist context I appreciate the description Evans-Wentz gave: 'Universal Divine Being' is not to be regarded as the Personal Supreme God of the Semitic Faiths, but rather as a figurative personification of all supra-mundane forces, powers or influences, that emanate from the Void, the Qualityless, the Unmade, the Unformed...' In W.Y. Evans-Wentz, *Tibet's Great Yogi Milarepa* , OUP, London, (1928), 1976, p 38. Henri Vaughan expressed this inner light as: 'I saw Eternity the other night Like a great Ring of pure and endless light...' In Michael Cox, *Mysticism,* The Aquarian Press, 1983, p 201

18.   Socrates uses the same model, i.e. comparing what the sun is for the material world to what the 'Form/Idea of the good' is for the world of knowledge, but making clear that '... just as it was right to think as light and sight as being like the sun, but wrong to think of them as being the sun itself, so here again it is right to think of knowledge and truth as being like the good, but wrong to think of either of them as being the good, whose position must be ranked still higher'. Plato, *The Republic*, London, 1979, p 309

19.   Ramakrishna was instructed by his guru Totapuri that 'Brahman is the only Reality, beyond the limits of time, space and causation'. Francis Younghusband, *Modern Mystics,* London, 1935, p 74f.

20.   Michael Newton, *Journey of Souls*, Llewellyn Publications, St Paul, 2000, p 197

21.   Respectively quoted in: Paul Davies and John Gribbin, *The Matter Myth* , London, 1992, p 76; quoted in Ken Wilber, *The Atman Project*, The Theosophical Publishing House, 1980, p 76; and T. S. Eliot 'Burnt Norton', in *Four Quartets*, London, mcmlxviii, p 16

343

22. Ignorance of this insight can lead to the cynical remark of how there could have been light before the sun, which was created only on the fourth day.

23. Quoted in Aldous Huxley, *The Perennial Philosophy*, London, 1950, p 282

24. All identification is symbolic only, as the One is beyond any category we could possibly imagine.

25. Plato, *The Republic*, London, 1979, p 305ff

26. Plotinus, *Comment in Somnium Scipionis*, I, 14, 15 quoted in Arthur O. Lovejoy, *The Great Chain of Being*, Harvard, 1960, p 63

27. Arthur Eddington, *The Nature of the Physical World*, Cambridge, 1933, p 276

28. Quoted in Arthur O. Lovejoy, *The Great Chain of Being*, (1936), Harper, New York, 1960. p 68

29. Quoted in Anthony Gottlieb, *The Dream of Reason*, London, 2000, p 418

30. Stephan A. Hoeller, *The Gnostic Jung and Seven Sermons to the Dead*, Quest, 1982, p 44

31. Richard Wilhelm, *The Secret of the Golden Flower*, (1931) 1972, p 21

32. Zeeya Merali, 'Faster, faster, time is running out!', *New Scientist*, 22/29 December 2007, referring to the work of José Senovilla

33. Quoted in Louis Fisher, *Gandhi: His Life and Message for the World*, Signet, 1954, p 108

34. Frederic Hedge, *Ways of the Spirit, and other essays*, quoted in Joseph Head and S. L. Cranston, *Reincarnation: An East-West Anthology*, The Theosophical Publishing House, (1961) 1975, p 239

35. C. G. Jung, *Memories, Dreams, Reflections*, Fontana, London, (1963) 1967, p 335

36. Plato, *The Republic*, Penguin, London, 1979, p 309

37. SCUBA: Self Contained Underwater Breathing Apparatus

38. June Singer, an analytical psychologist, writes, 'The ego is to the self as the earth is to the sun', in *Boundaries of the Soul*, Prism Press, (1972) 1995, p 238

39. Pir Viliyat Khan, 'The Quintessence of meditation: Awakening your real self', Caduceus,65, p 16

40. Joost A. M. Meerloo, *Along the Fourth Dimension*, New York, 1970, p 138

41. Quoted in Brian Inglis, *The Unknown Guest*, London, 1989, p 65

42. Quoted in Michael Cox, *Mysticism*, The Aquarian Press, 1983, p 99

43. Richard Wilhelm, *The Secret of the Golden Flower*, (1931) 1972, p 36

44. Many different labels have been stuck onto the *vertical* dimension, such as fourth or fifth dimension. As theoretical physics now routinely uses ten or more dimensions, I did not want to enter in the numbers game and have chosen to call it *vertical*.

45. see e.g. Vera Stanley Alder, *The Fifth Dimension*, 1970, and John Hicks, *The Fifth Dimension*, 1999

46. Amiotrophic Lateral Sclerosis, in the USA often referred to as Lou Gehring's disease

47. Mitch Albom, *Tuesdays with Morrie*, p 179

48. Rabindranath Tagore (transl.) *One Hundred Poems of Kabir*, 1961, p 14

49. quoted in: Eric Butterworth, *Discover the Power within You*, Harper San Francisco, 1992, p 219

50. W. R. Inge, *Lay Thoughts of a Dean*, London, Putnam, 1926

51. D. T. Suzuki, *Mysticism*, New York, 1957, p 122

52. Victor White in his *God and the Unconscious*, London, 1952, p 116f, summarises Thomas Aquinas: 'It is not God who is wrapped in veils; the veils are the ignorance and darkness, the unconsciousness, which normally envelops our own minds; and it is these precisely which the very fact of the prophetic vision removes'.

53. Quoted in David Heinemann, *Sufi Therapy of the Heart*, New Delhi, 2003, p 90

54. Quoted in Deepak Chopra, *The Path of Love*, New York, 1997, p 49

55. Chang Tsai, quoted in Fritjof Capra, *The Tao of Physics*, Fontana / Collins, 1979, p 224

56. B. G. Goodwin, *Biology and Meaning*, (1972) quoted in Jeremy Campbell, *Grammatical Man*, Pelican Books, (1982) 1984, p 91f

57. Jeremy Campbell, *Grammatical Man*, Pelican Books, (1982) 1984, p 97

58. Quoted in Paramahansa Yogananda, *Autobiography of a Yogi*, SRF, (1946) 1993, p 144

59. Rupert Sheldrake. *A New Science of Life*, Blond & Briggs, London, 1981, p 93

60. Gary Lachman, *A Secret History of Consciousness*, 2003, p270

61. Pierre Teilhard de Chardin, The Future of Man, in Let *Me Explain*, Collins, 1974, p 51

62. Stanislav Grof, *The Holotropic Mind*, Harper San Francisco, 1990, p 123

63. 'Short- and long- term memory doesn't reside in our brain at all, but instead is stored in the Zero Point Field. ... Erwin Laszlo, would go on to argue that the brain is simply the retrieval and read-out mechanism of the ultimate storage

medium.' In: Lynne McTaggart, *The Field*, Element, London, 2003, p 124

64. W. Y. Evans-Wentz, *The Tibetan Book of the Dead*, Oxford, (1927)1985, p 147

65. Take for instance the 'Seven Heavens' discussed in Michio Kushi and Alex Jack, *The Gospel of Peace*, Tokyo, 1992, p 44f, and the tables of 'planes of consciousness' in Roland Peterson, *Everyone Is Right*, DeVorss & Co., Marina de Rey, 1986, p 97

66. See e.g. Lila Bek and Philippa Pullar, *The Seven Levels of Healing*, Century, London, 1986.

67. William A. Tiller, 'Energy Fields and the Human Body', In *Frontiers of Consciousness*, p 229ff

68. Rudolph Steiner, details these stages in *Supersensible man*, see e.g.: Roy Wilkinson, *Descent to a New Incarnation,* 2004

69. William A. Tiller, 'Energy Fields and the Human Body', in *Frontiers of Consciousness*, p 229

70. Frances Young, *A Cloud of Witnesses*, in John Hick (ed.), *The Myth of God Incarnate*, London, 1977, p 25

71. When I mentioned 'Lac Noir' to an acquaintance recently, his immediate reaction was, 'That is a terrible place'. So obviously others pick up these negative vibes as well.

72. e.g. Neville Randal, *Life after Death*, Hale, 1975 (Corgi, 1984); Raymond Moody, *Life after Life,* 1975; and *Reflections on Life after Life*, 1977

73. Sallie McFague, *Super, Natural Christians: How we should love nature*, SCM Press, 1997, p 56

74. E. F. Schumacher, *Good Work*, Harper & Row, New York, 1997, p 113

75. Niels Bohr, 'Quantum Physics and Philosophy', Florence, 1958, in *Essays, 1958 - 1962*, 1963, p 7

76. John Tyndall, Presidential address to the British Association for the Advancement of Science, Belfast, 1874

77. Dr Hashimoto, *Introduction to ESP* and *Mystery of the Fourth Dimensional World*, quoted in Peter Tompkins and Christopher Bird, *The Secret Life of Plants*, London, (1973) 1991, p 34

78. Similar tables headed 'Yin' and 'Yang' can be found in Michio Kushi and Alex Jack, *The Gospel of Peace*, Tokyo, 1992, p 22 and 168f or in the C. G. Jung tradition on www.cgjungpage.org

79. Arthur O. Lovejoy, *The Great Chain of Being*, (1936), Harper, New York, 1960. p 147

80. Although I have been using this kind of table since the early 1980s, it was very interesting to discover in 2006 a very similar one in Jeremy Campbell, *Grammatical Man*, Pelican

Books, (1982) 1984, p 241f. Another case of morphic resonance?

81.   Frithjof Schuon, *Survey of Metaphysics and Esoterism,* World Wisdom Books, 1986, p 68

82.   Plato, *The Republic*, Penguin, London, 1979, p 316ff, in the simile of the Cave

83.   William Shakespeare, *A Midsummer Night's Dream*

84.   In his essay 'Mysticism and Logic', Bertrand Russell places these two realms erroneously in opposition

85.   Ivan Selman makes this point in an unpublished manuscript, *The Celtic Church and Celtic Spirituality*, 1994.

86.   A very interesting parallel is that the well-organised Germans are usually early starters, while here in England work usually starts later. When people ask me why I am living in England rather than on the continent, my tongue in cheek reply is, 'Because it is no fun living in a well organised country'.

87.   or reductionism

88.   W. R. Inge, *Mysticism in Religion*, Rider, London, 1989, p 35

89.   Sallie McFague, *Super,Natural Christians*, SCM, 1997, p 30ff

90.   'There is no place in this new kind of physics both for the field and matter, for the field is the only reality'. Quoted in M. Capek, *The Philosophical Impact of Contemporary Physics*, D. van Nostrand, Princeton, 1961, p 319

91.   Joel S. Goldsmith, *A Parenthesis in Eternity*, New York, 1986, p 17

92.   See his tabular comparison in Lawrence LeShan, *Clairvoyant Reality* (formerly *The Medium, The Mystic and the Physicist*), Turnstone Press Ltd, (1974) 1982 , p 86f

93.   David Bohm, *Wholeness and the Implicate Order*, London, 1980

94.   Pierre Teilhard de Chardin, *The Phenomenon of Man*, London, 1961, p 63ff

95.   Frithjof Schuon, *Survey of Metaphysics and Esoterism,* World Wisdom Books, 1986, p 68

96.   David R. Hawkins, M.D., Ph.D., *Power vs. Force*, London, 2006

97.   Peter Plichta, *God's Secret Formula*, Element, Shaftesbury, 1997, p 170f

98.   Neale Donald Walsch, *All About God : A Dialogue between Neale Donald Walsch and Deepak Chopra M.D.*, 2000

99.   Timothy Freke and Peter Gandy, *The Laughing Jesus*, O Books, 2006

100.   The drawing was reproduced from a photo I took in the hall of Fredericksborg castle in Denmark.

101.   Gill Edwards, *Living Magically: A New Vision of Reality*,
        Piatkus, London, (1991) 2006, p 43
102.   Stephen Jay Gould, *Rocks of Ages: Science and Religion in the
        Fullness of Life*, London, 2001, 6
103.   Ian T. Ramsey, *Models and Mystery* , New York, 1964, 21,20
        quoted in Harold K Schilling, *The New Consciousness in
        Science and Religion*, London, 1973, p 177
104.   Percy Bysshe Shelley, *Declaration of Rights*, art. 27
105.   "De uitzondering bevestigt de regel."
106.   Queen Elisabeth of Austria (1837-1898), quoted in Joseph
        Head and S. L. Cranston, *Reincarnation: An East-West
        Anthology*, The Theosophical Publishing House, (1961)
        1975, p 190
107.   Quoted in Harold K Schilling, *The New Consciousness in
        Science and Religion*, London, 1973, p 179

Chapter 5   Horizontal pursuits

1.   Albert Einstein, *Out Of My Later Years,* p 260
2.   Quoted in Alan W. Watts, *Psychotherapy East and West*,
      Jonathan Cape, London, 1971, p 92
3.   Matthew Fox, *The Reinvention of Work,* New York, 1995, p
      243
4.   World Council of Churches, Assembly in New Delhi, 1961,
      quoted in Sallie McFague, *Super, Natural Christians: How
      we should love nature*, SCM Press, 1997, p 204
5.   Henry H. Bauer, *Science or Pseudoscience*, University of
      Illinois, 2001, p 177
6.   Aristotle declared that 'life according to intellect is best and
      pleasantest, since intellect more than anything else is man',
      quoted in Anthony Gottlieb, *The Dream of Reason*, London,
      2000, p 270
7.   Quoted in Tobias Dantzig, Number: the Language of
      Science, 1962, p 136
8.   Beverly Rubik, *The Interrelationship of Mind and Matter*, p
      1. Brian Ingram lists a number of these: 'Some of the most
      highly regarded physicists in Europe ... had been psychical
      researchers: Fechner, Weber and Zöllner in Germany,
      Schiaparelli in Italy, Lodge and Crookes in Britain,
      Flammarion in France. They had ceased to be so highly
      regarded when their orthodox materialist colleagues realised
      that they accepted the reality of psychical phenomena'.
      In *Natural and Supernatural: A History of the Paranormal*,
      Prism Press, (1977)1992, p 11

9.   Quoted in Fritjof Capra, *Uncommon Wisdom*, Flamingo, 1990, p 228

10.   In the same spirit the University of Chicago's catalogue of 1898-99 points out: 'While it is never safe to affirm that the future of Physical Science has no marvels in store even more astonishing than those of the past, it seems probable that most of the grand underlying principles have been firmly established and that further advances are to be sought chiefly in the rigorous application of these principles to all the phenomena which come under our notice'. Quoted in Robert S Mulliken in *Physics Today*, April 1968, p 56

11.   Leonard Susskind, 'Because we're here', Interview with Amanda Gefter, *New Scientist*, 17 December 2005, p 50

12.   Quoted in Tobias Dantzig, *Number: the Language of Science*, London, (1930),1962, p 204

13.   Even in 1967, an article by L. W. Morley, supporting continental drift by the magnetically banded anomalies of the ocean floor, was rejected by both *Nature* and *The Journal of Geophysical Research*. And for just such a case in botany, take C. K. Spengler's discovery of pollination by insects, which he published in 1793. His work was received with derision and he was fired from his teaching job; also see Don Williamson's letter to *New Scientist*, 18 November 1995, p 75, and William Broad and Nicholas Wade, *Betrayers of the Truth: Fraud and Deceit in the Halls of Science*, Century, London, 1983.

14.   Winner of the 2003 Nobel Prize for Medicine, quoted in *New Scientist,* 11 October 2003, p 8

15.   Quoted in Amir Aczel, *God's Equation* , London, 2000, p 61

16.   For instance, by the German Nobel prize winner

17.   See e.g. Paul Davies, *Superforce*, p 43ff

18.   Alain Aspect, ibid., p 46ff

19.   By Nicolas Gisin and others. See the web, where speeds of 10,000 to 10,000,000 times the speed of light are mentioned.

20.   Paul Davies and John Gribbin, *The Matter Myth* ,London, 1992, p 298, and the description of a more recent experiment: Peter Rodgers, 'Double-slit effect seen over time too', *New Scientist*, 5 March 2005, p 14

21.   Quoted in Jason Ellis and Katherine Ketcham, *In the House of the Moon*, Hodder & Stoughton, 1996, p 18f

22.   If the expansion of the universe were to run out of steam, it would contract and end in a Big Crunch. As it seems that the expansion of the universe is speeding up, scientists are now talking about the Big Rip. Mary Hesse cautions: 'Clearly the whole imperialistic aim of theoretical science

to be the royal and single road to knowledge has been a profound mistake. ... Scientific theory is just one of the ways in which human beings have sought to make sense of their world ...' Quoted in Stephen S. Hall, *Mapping the Next Millennium*, Vintage, 1993, p 397. And as Sheldrake points out, another factor is that the 'fundamental constants' used in our 'Laws of Nature' may be more like habits than constants, so they might have varied over time, which would allow many present day mysteries to be solved (Rupert Sheldrake, *Seven Experiments That Could Change the World*, London, 1995).

23.   Eric Lerner expressed this as: 'What we may find is a universe that is very different than the increasingly bizarre one of the big bang theory'. Quoted in Marcus Chown, 'End of the beginning', *New Scientist*, 2 July 2005, p 30ff

24.   Paul Davies and John Gribbin, *The Matter Myth* ,London, 1992, p 169

25.   Paul Davies, *Superforce*, London, 1984, p 5

26.   Walter Sullivan , 'Smallest of the Small', *New York Times*, 5 February 1967, quoted in Harold K Schilling, *The New Consciousness in Science and Religion*, London, 1973, p 110

27.   Quoted in David Shiga, 'Something for Nothing', *New Scientist*, 1 October 2005, p 37, in a discussion on the Casimir effect.

28.   Vladimir V. Shkunov and Boris Ya. Zel'dovich, 'Optical Phase Conjugation', *Scientific American*, December 1985

29.   Peter Rodgers, 'Double-slit effect seen over time too', *New Scientist*, 5 March 2005, p 14

30.   See e.g. Harald Frisch's essay 'The Magic Furnace' in *The World Treasure of Physics, Astronomy, and Mathematics*, Timothy Ferris (ed.), 1991

31.   Such as, for instance, the fleeting appearance of a Pentaquark which has been announced recently, *New Scientist*, 12 July 2003,p 16

32.   Quoted in Anthony North, *The Paranormal*, 1996, p 149

33.   Quoted in Harold K Schilling, *The New Consciousness in Science and Religion*, London, 1973, p 108

34.   David Bohm, quoted in Renee Webber, *Dialogues with Scientists and Sages*

35.   Quoted in: David A Ash, *The New Science of the Spirit*, 1996, p 127

36.   Robert J Oppenheimer, *Science and the Common Understanding*

37.   C. G. Jung and W. Pauli, *The Interpretation of Nature and the Psyche*, London, 1954

38.   Sir Oliver Lodge, *Phantom Walls*, London, 1930, p 107

39.   ibid., p 126

40. Sir Oliver Lodge, *The Substance of Faith*, London, 1907, p 106

41. Kurt Gödel, *An Example of a New Type of Cosmological Solution of Einstein's Field Equations of Gravity*, 1949

42. Quoted in Denis Brian, *Einstein: a Life*, 1996

43. Henry Margenau, *Yale Alumni Magazine* ,Feb. 1963 quoted in Harold K Schilling, *The New Consciousness in Science and Religion*, London, 1973, p 178f

44. Paul Davies, *God and the new Physics*, London, 1983, p ix and 229

45. Albert Einstein, *The World as I see it*

46. Quoted in Brown, *The Metaphysical Society*, p 106

47. Michael Bond, 'The longest journey', *New Scientist*, 31 May 2003, p 47

48. In response to a letter I wrote to Sue Blackmore about my before-birth experience (chapter 8), she wrote to me: 'As for the paranormal—perhaps it will hit me between the eyes one day! Until then I practice awareness and argue vociferously!' (postcard 23 October1993)

49. Kaibara Ekken, quoted in T. C. McLuhan, *The Way of the Earth* ,New York, 1995, p 132

50. Jan Ehrenwald, *The ESP Experience*, New York, 1978, p 228

51. Robert Jastrow, interviewed by and quoted in Denis Brian, *Einstein: a Life,* John Wiley, 1996, p 200

52. ibid., p 104. Buckminster Fuller replied to the question: 'Was there any common denominator, any one thing that great scientists had in common?' "The one thing they found common to all of them," Fuller says, "was... intuition ..." In Douglas Dean, John Mihalasky, Sheila Ostrander & Lynn Schroeder, *Executive ESP*, Prentice Hall, 1974, p 97

53. *Wall Street Journal*, October 10,1994

54. Quoted in Stephen Jay Gould, *Rocks of Ages*, London, 2001, p 35

55. E. F. Schumacher, *A Guide for the Perplexed*, London, (1977) 1978, p 127

56. Karl Stern, *The Flight from Woman*, New York, 1965, ch. 12

57. Stanislav Grof, *The Holotropic Mind*, Harper San Franscisco, 1990, p 18

58. John Maynard Smith declares '... the vitalist theories of Bergson and Teilhard de Chardin, to be untestable and therefore to be judged as myths rather than as scientific theories'. *The Theory of Evolution*, Penguin, Harmondsworth, 1985 p 12

59. Rowan Hooper, 'Inheriting a heresy', *New Scientist*, 4 March 2006, p 53 and Fern Elsdon-Baker, *The Selfish Genius*, London, 2009

60.   Richard Dawkins in *The Blind Watchmaker* strongly
        advocates complete randomness, while Fred Hoyle
        illustrated 'the high degree of improbability of the
        formation of life by accidental molecular shuffling ... to a
        whirlwind passing through an aircraft factory and blowing
        scattered components into a functioning Boeing 747'.
        Quoted in Paul Davies, *Are We Alone?*, Penguin, 1995, p 19

61.   Quoted in John D Barrow and Frank J Tipler, *The Anthropic
        Cosmological Principle*, Oxford, 1986, p 84

62.   John Peacocke, *God and the New Biology*, cc, 1986, p 39

63.   Quoted in Harold K Schilling, *The New Consciousness in
        Science and Religion*, London, 1973, p 185

64.   See Michael Hayes, *High Priests, Quantum Genes*, London,
        2004, p 190ff

65.   Jeffry Mogil at McGill University, Montreal, Canada,
        mentioned in: Richard Hollingham, 'In the Realm of your
        senses', *New Scientist*, 31 January 2004, p 40ff

66.   *Nature*, 293, p 245 (1981). In a later review John Maddox
        called his previous judgment 'injudicious' but remained
        sceptical, see *Nature*, 401, p 849 (28.10.1999) I cannot resist
        quoting what he wrote there: Many years later, Sheldrake
        told my wife that his children routinely prayed for the soul
        of the editor of *Nature*, believing that such a wicked person
        could only come to a bad end.

67.   Rupert Sheldrake, *A New Science of Life* , Blond & Briggs,
        London, 1981

68.   Plato, *Protagoras and Meno*, Penguin, Harmondsworth,
        1982, p 130

69.   *morphe* translates as form; an excellent summary can be
        found in Rupert Sheldrake, *Dogs that know when their
        Owners are coming Home*, London, 1999, Appendix C, p
        266ff

70.   Rupert Sheldrake, *Dogs that know when their Owners are
        coming Home*, London, 1999, p 23

71.   Rupert Sheldrake, *Seven Experiments That Could Change the
        World*, London, 1995, p 34

72.   Rupert Sheldrake, *A New Science of Life* , Blond & Briggs,
        London, 1981, p 186ff

73.   Eric Butterworth, *Discover the Power within You* , Harper
        San Francisco, 1992, p 51

74.   Gerald Edelman, *Bright Air, Brilliant Fire*, London, 1992,
        p 224

75.   M. -L. von Franz, 'Science and the Unconscious', in Carl
        Jung (ed.), *Man and his Symbols*, Aldus, London, 1964, p
        384

76.   ibid., p 381

77. Frithjof Schuon, *Survey of Metaphysics and Esoterism,* World Wisdom Books, 1986, p 68f

78. St George Jackson Mivart, *The Genesis of Species,* London, 1871

79. Danah Zohar & Ian Marshall, *The Quantum Self,* London, 1994, p 139

80. Robin Orwant, 'What makes us human?', *New Scientist,* 21 February 2004, p 37

81. Stephen Jay Gould, *Rocks of Ages,* London, 2001, p 198

82. Michael Newton, *Journey of Souls,* Llewellyn Publications, St. Paul, 2000, p 186f

83. Stephen Jay Gould, *op. cit.,* p 149

84. Stephen Jay Gould, ibid., p 159

85. Richard Milton, *Shattering the Myths of Darwinism* ,Park Street Press, Rochester, Vermont, 1997, p ixf

86. Aldous Huxley, *The Doors of Perception,* Harper & Row, New York, 1954, p 74f

87. Quoted in James Roose-Evans, *Passages of the Soul,* Element Books, 1994, p 108, who writes on the next page: 'The loneliness which Dickson learned to confront is to be found among thousands of students on the campuses of America, although College authorities often conveniently choose to deny this. I know because I have listened to so many of these students'.

88. Victor E. Frankl, *Man's Search for Meaning,* New York, 1984, p 129

89. Joseph Campbell, *Myths to Live by,* Condor, 1972, p 208

90. Emma Whitelaw quoted in 'Toxic effects can pass down the generations', *New Scientist,* 11 June 2005, p 7

91. 'Slime mould', *New Scientist,* 18 June 2005, p 54

92. Paul Davies and John Gribbin, *The Matter Myth* ,London, 1992, p 6f

93. Quoted in Richard Grossman, *The Other Medicines,* London, 1986, p 111

94. William A. Tiller, *Energy Fields and the Human Body,* see Fig. 3: 'Schematic illustration of tuning and transducing aspects of a chakra/endocrine pair for tapping power from the cosmos'. See also chapter 14 in *Frontiers of Consciousness.*

95. Dennis Mc Callum,*The Death of Truth,* Bethany House, Minn., 1996, quoted in Henry H. Bauer, *Science or Pseudoscience,* University of Illinois, 2001, p 195

96. Supported by several case histories in Vernon Coleman, *Why Animal Experiments Must Stop,* London, 1991, p 89

97. Henry H. Bauer, *Science or Pseudoscience,* University of Illinois, 2001, p 48f

98. Roger Highfied and Paul Carter, *The Private Lives of Albert Einstein,* London, 1993, p 262

99.   Paul Davies and John Gribbin, *The Matter Myth* ,London, 1992, p 303

100.   Quoted in Dr W. Ll. Parry-Jones (1883), see Dorothy Rowe, *Beyond Fear* ,London, 1987, p 184f

101.   A recent report disclosed 'that drug firms have spent $ 800 million since 1998 buying influence, including $ 675 million on direct lobbying of Congress'. *New Scientist*, 16 July 2005, p 4

102.   If you think my judgment is too harsh, read Jörg Blech's article 'The Illness Industry' in *New Scientist* 22 July 2006, p 24, or his book *Inventing Disease and Pushing Pills*, Routledge, 2006

103.   Quoted in: Martin & Karen Fido, *The World's Worst Medical Mistakes,* Sevenoaks, 1996

104.   David Healy of Cardiff University, quoted in: Marianne Barriaux, 'GSK [GlaxoSmithKline] rebuts Panorama claims it distorted Seroxat trial results', *the Guardian*, 30 January 2007, p 23, referring to a BBC TV *Panorama* programme, 'Secrets Of The Drugs Trials', of 29 January 2007. Also see, for the disastrous consequences of extrapolation of animal testing results such as of TGN1412 antibodies to humans, Andy Coghlan, 'What really happened in drug trial disaster?', *New Scientist*, 19 August 2006, p 9,

105.   Vernon Coleman, *Why Animal Experiments Must Stop,* London, 1991, p 48

106.   Joan Grant and Dennis Kelsey , *Many Lifetimes*, London, 1976, p 67

107.   ibid., p 194. An interesting parallel with the dream that made me a vegetarian, chapter 9.1, 'Diet'.

108.   Elisabeth Kübler-Ross, *Death: the Final Stage of Growth,* Prentice-Hall, 1975, p 23 and 15

109.   Quoted in David Darling, *After Life* ,London, 1995, p 180

110.   Vernon Coleman, *Bodypower: The Secret of Self-healing,* Barnstaple, (1983) 2005, p 43

111.   British Medical Association

112.   'Today', BBC Radio 4, 13 June 2005

113.   Rupert Sheldrake, *Dogs that know when their Owners are coming Home*, London, 1999, p 73

114.   Pat Rattigan writes regarding similar cancer treatment: 'The oldest prong of the lethal trident, cynically known as modern cancer therapy, is surgery. The notion being that the removal of a tumour cures the patient: ignoring the fact that cancer is a whole body, systemic constitutional disease which eventually manifests in a tumour ...' In *The Cancer Business*, Chesterfield, 1998, p 4

115. see e.g. www.medicinenet.com/gout/article.htm. An alternative for nettle tea are nettle capsules available in wholefood shops
116. Quoted in G M A Grube, *Plato's Thought*, London, (1935)1970, p 122
117. 'Consuming Needs' in *New Scientist*, 24 January 1998, p 12, and see for an extensive survey confirming the vital importance of diet: Collin Barras, 'Time to drop cancer from the menu', *New Scientist*, 3 November 2007, p 10
118. 'Softenon' was a trade name for a medication prescribed to pregnant women in the 1960s resulting in a number of children born without arms or legs.
119. Pat Thomas, 'Metal Madness', *Caduceus*, issue 62, Spring 2004, p 26ff
120. BBC TV2 documentary, broadcast on 29 February 2004: 'The Health of the Prime Minister'
121. Take this quotation from *New Scientist* of 29 July 2006, p 5, for example: 'Medication errors by hospitals and clinics in the US harm at least 1.5 million Americans every year and cause around 7000 deaths, according to a study by the US National Academy of Sciences. The mistakes cost the US healthcare system $ 3.5 billion a year'.
122. Matthew Fox, *The Reinvention of Work*, New York, 1995, p 199
123. Plato, *Charmides*, 156
124. J R Worsley, *Is Acupuncture for You?*, Longmead, 1985, p 2
125. ibid., p 100
126. Richard Grossman, *The Other Medicines* , London, 1986, p 165
127. Quoted in Matthew Fox, *The Reinvention of Work*, HarperCollins, (1994) 1995, p 10

Chapter 6 Vertical pursuits

1. Quoted in Deepak Chopra, *The Path of Love* , New York, 1997, p 49
2. Stanislav Grof, *The Holotropic Mind*, Harper San Francisco, 1990, p 83f
3. L. Wittgenstein, *Tractatus Logico-Philosophicus*, Routledge, London, 1960
4. 'Debating the Unknowable', *Atlantic Monthly*, July 1981, p 49, quoted in Henry H. Bauer, *Science or Pseudoscience*, University of Illinois, 2001, p 79

5.   'Myths and Realities of Space Flight', *Science* 232, (30 May) 1986, p 1075, quoted in Henry H. Bauer, *Science or Pseudoscience*, University of Illinois, 2001, p 228

6.   Quoted in *Caduceus*, 52, p 6

7.   John A. Sanford, *The Kingdom Within, The Inner Meaning of Jesus' Sayings*, 1987, p 118

8.   Anthony Gottlieb, *The Dream of Reason*, London, 2000, p 284

9.   ibid., p 366

10.   Quoted in Aldous Huxley, *The Perennial Philosophy*, London, 1950, p 33

11.   No one knows exactly where Socrates ends and Plato begins. David J Melling refers to Aristotle's testimony that 'Socrates never held certain doctrines Plato has him expound at length in his dialogues'.*Understanding Plato*, Oxford, 1988, p 11. A medical rationalist like F Lélut came to the conclusion that Socrates was *'un fou'* i.e. insane, quoted in Brian Inglis, *The Unknown Guest*, London, 1989, p 30

12.   Plato, *The Republic*, Harmondsworth, 1979 (1955), p 317ff. Immanuel Kant called it *"Das Ding an Sich"* (the thing-in-itself).

13.   Take e.g Black Elk, a holy man of the Oglala Sioux Nation: 'Crazy Horse dreamed and went into the world where there is nothing but the spirits of all things. That is the real world that is behind this one, and everything we see here is something like a shadow from that world ... I knew the real was yonder and the darkened dream of it was here'. Quoted in T. C. McLuhan, *The Way of the Earth* ,New York, 1995, p 437

14.   Plato, *The Republic*, Harmondsworth, 1979 (1955), p 312ff

15.   Quoted from Porphyry's, 'To Marcella', in Anthony Gottlieb, *The Dream of Reason*, London, 2000, p 283

16.   Sheldon Kopp, *If You Meet the Buddha on the Road, Kill Him!*, Palo Alto (Ca), (1972)1988, p 46

17.   Quoted in Ken Wilber, *The Atman Project*, The Theosophical Publishing House, 1980, p 76

18.   Alan W. Watts, *Psychotherapy East & West*, Jonathan Cape, London, 1971, p 2

19.   John Eccles, *Evolution of the Brain*, p 238

20.   Anthony Storr, *Jung*, London, (1973) 1974, p 97

21.   Deepak Chopra, *The Path of Love* , New York, 1997, p 10

22.   Peter Watson, 'Not written in stone', *New Scientist*, 27 August 2005, p 44

23.   C.G.Jung, *Memories, Dreams, Reflections*, Fontana, London, (1963) 1967, p 178

24.   Lee Lawson, *Love letters from the Infinite*, Thorsons, 2000, p vii

25.   Anthony Storr, op. cit., p 90 (see also pp 37f and 117)
26.   See e.g. Jung's similar lifelike experiences during a dream in C.G.Jung,op. cit., p 256
27.   'A visitation dream is nothing like an ordinary dream. The only commonality is that the body is asleep. A visitation dream is what Carl Jung called a "big dream", a mythic experience that comes to us from the archetypal realm'. So writes Lee Lawson in: *Love letters from the Infinite*, Thorsons, 2000, p 8
28.   In a letter to Dr Selig of 25 February 1953, quoted in: June Singer, *Boundaries of the Soul*, Prism Press, Sturminster Newton, (1972) 1995, p 407. Many examples of 'Nominative Determinism' have been published in the pages of *New Scientist* starting in 1994; a selection of these was published in Alun Anderson and Mick O'Hare (eds), *Bizarre: Tales from New Scientist*, London, 21 March 1998, p 59ff
29.   Anthony Storr, op. cit., p 105f
30.   C. G. Jung, op. cit., p 60. And when discussing 'the Aristotelian intellectualism of St. Thomas', on p 87 He describes his thought: 'They all want to force something to come out by tricks of logic, ... They want to prove a belief to themselves, whereas actually it is a matter of experience. They seemed to me like people who knew by hearsay that elephants existed, but had never seen one, and were now trying to prove by arguments that on logical grounds such animals must exist ...'
31.   C. G.Jung,op. cit., p 222
32.   Victor White, *God and the Unconscious*, London, 1952, p 238
33.   Jeffrey Goodman writes: What was the source behind Edgar Cayce? And how did he contact it? More than any other psychic, Cayce seems to have been able to make contact with some memory bank of the past which he called the Akashic Records.
34.   Quoted in Brian Inglis, *The Unknown Guest*, London, 1989, p 70
35.   Is this an interesting parallel with the 'many universes' solution to the problems posed by quantum physics proposed by Hugh Everett? In the vertical dimension there is indeed 'room' for an infinite number of universes.
36.   Many similar accounts are reported on by Franklin Loehr, 'The Woman who discovered 2,100 "Bridey Murphys"'. In Brant House (ed.), *Strange Powers Of Unusual People,* New York, 1973, p 88ff
37.   R. Wilhelm , *The Secret of the Golden Flower*, Routledge, London, (1931) 1972, p 86

38.   Brian Inglis, op. cit., p 35

39.   Eliot Slater and Martin Roth, *Clinical Psychiatry* , quoted in
         Dorothy Rowe, *Beyond Fear* ,London, 1987, p 282

40.   Victor White, *God and the Unconscious*, London, 1952, p
         250

41.   Plato, *The Symposium*, Penguin Books, (1951) 1985, p 64,
         attributed to Aristophanes, see Grube, *Plato's Thought*, p 99

42.   Roberto Assagioli, *Transpersonal Development*, London,
         1991, p 37

43.   Roberto Assagioli, *Act of Will*, p 17 quoted in: Roland
         Peterson, *Everyone Is Right* , DeVorss, Marina del Rey, 1986,
         p 207; and if your appetite has been whetted, there is a
         veritable host of similar quotations in Peterson's book.

44.   C. G. Jung, 'Psychotherapies on the Clergy', *Collected
         Works, Vol 2*, 1969, p 327ff

45.   Victor White, *God and the Unconscious*, London, 1952,172

46.   From a letter dated 22 September 1944, quoted in Victor
         White in his *God & the Unconscious,* London, 1952, p 236

47.   Victor White, *op. cit,*, p 117f

48.   Erich Fromm, *Psychoanalysis and Religion*, Yale University
         Press, 1950, p 6

49.   Quoted in Jason Ellis and Katherine Ketcham, *In the House
         of the Moon*, Hodder & Stoughton, 1996, p xiv

50.   John Snelling, *The Buddhist Handbook*, Rider, London,
         1989, p 94

51.   T. S. Eliot, 'Little Gidding' from *Four Quartets*, London,
         1968

52.   Percy Bysshe Shelley, *The Defense of Poetry*, 1821

53.   Frederick Franck, *The Zen of Seeing*, London, 1973, p x

54.   Matthew Fox, *The Reinvention of Work*, New York, 1995, p
         214

55.   Frederick Franck, *Art as a Way,* New York, 1981

56.   Jean Renoir, *Renoir My Father*, London, 1962 quoted in
         Michael Gearin-Tosh, *Living Proof* ,London, 2002, p 236

57.   E. H. Gombrich writes in *The Story of Art*: "Imagine an
         open-minded and eager critic in 1890 trying to bring the
         history of art 'up to date'. With the best will in the world
         he could not have known that the three figures who were
         making history at the time were Van Gogh, Cézanne and
         Gauguin; the first a crazy middle-aged Dutchman working
         away in southern France, the second a retiring gentleman
         of independent means, who had long ceased to send his
         paintings to exhibitions, and the third a stockbroker who
         had become a painter later in life and was soon off to the
         South Seas". Phaidon, (1950)1979, p 477

58.   Quoted in Oswald Hanfling in an Open University Art
         course, UAA, p 132

59.   Athena S Leoussi, 'Appreciating the arts', in Digby
        Anderson, *The War on Wisdom*, The Social Affairs Unit,
        2003, p 113
60.   Quoted in Sir Herbert Read, *Concise History of Modern Art*
61.   Peter Wolff, *City of the Mind*, Playhouse performance, BBC
        Radio 4 on 2.5.1998
62.   Shen Tsung-ch'ien, *The Art of Painting*, quoted in Jennifer
        Oldstone-Moore, *Understanding Taoism*, London, 2003, p
        104
63.   Musical scales are another illustration of the
        interconnectedness of humanity: 'It is an interesting
        phenomenon that the pentatonic or five-tone scale, a pre-
        Pythagoran system albeit in various forms, can be found
        in nearly all ancient music cultures in Asia, Africa, North
        and Latin America, Europe and even Australia'. Gunter
        Pulvermacher, 'Carl Gustav Jung and Musical Art', in Renos
        K. Papadopoulos et al. (eds), *Jung in Modern Perspective*,
        Bridport, (1984) 1991, p 259
64.   Quoted in Brian Inglis, *The Unknown Guest*, London, 1989,
        p 63. A modern example is the Dutch film music composer
        Laurens van Rooyen, who expresses the same experience: I
        do not compose music; it is passed on to me ...('*Ik componeer
        geen muziek; die wordt mij doorgegeven ...*') in *Prive*, 2
        May1981, p 8
65.   He is quoted on www.brittanica.com with: 'The war, the
        rotten times under communism, our life today, the starving,
        Bosnia ... This sorrow, it burns inside me. [and] I want to
        express great sorrow'.
66.   Frederick Frank, *Art as a Way*, p 25
67.   Plato, *The Republic*, Penguin, 1997, p 162
68.   Samuel Taylor Coleridge, *The Stateman's Manual*
69.   Samuel Taylor Coleridge, *Religious Musings,* 1794
70.   Thomas Carlyle, *Sign of the Times*
71.   Richard Bach, *Illusions*
72.   Joseph Campbell, *Myths to live by,* 1992, p 120
73.   ibid., p 209
74.   ibid., p 220
75.   Daito, quoted in Frederick Franck, *Art as a Way*, New York,
        1981, p 119
76.   Maximus of Tyre, *Dissertations*, xxxix.5
77.   Abdu'l-Baha, *Paris Talks*, Bahai Publishing Trust, London,
        1979, pp 130, 142
78.   Albert Einstein, *The World as I See it*, New York
79.   Quoted in Sarvepalli Radhakrishnan, *Religion of the Spirit*,
        in: Whit Burnett (ed.), *This is my Philosophy*, London, 1958,
        p 360

80.   Therefore I am very reluctant to sacrifice the word religion
        and replace it with spirituality, as e.g. Harry R Moody &
        David Carroll specify in: *The Five stages of the Soul* , Rider,
        London, 1998, p 132: 'Boiled down to essentials, religion
        applies to the outer aspects of worship: ritual, doctrine, and
        congregational practice. Spirituality, on the other hand,
        pertains to a person's deepest and innermost relationship
        with the sacred, with a Higher Power, with something that
        cannot be easily defined when the Search begins'.

81.   Joseph Campbell, op.cit., p 264

82.   His Holiness the Dalai Lama, *The Little Book of Wisdom*,
        Random, 1997, p 130 and 134

83.   Roland Peterson, *Everyone Is Right* , DeVorss, Marina del
        Rey, 1986

84.   *Rig Veda*, 1.164.46

85.   P Murray (ed.), *The Deer's Cry: A Treasure of Irish Religious
        Verse,* p 15

86.   Ivan Selman, *The Celtic Church and Celtic Spirituality*,
        unpublished manuscript, 1994

87.   Victor White, *God and the Unconscious*, London, 1952, p
        192

88.   John 10:30

89.   John 10:34

90.   See e.g. Michael Cox, *Mysticism,* The Aquarian Press, 1983,
        p 99f

91.   Fynn, *Mister God this is Anna,* HarperCollins, 1974, p 91ff

92.   Quoted in Satish Kumar, *YOU ARE Therefore I AM*, Green
        Books, 2002, p 89

93.   Matthew Fox, *Creation Spirituality*, Harper San Francisco,
        1991, p 74

94.   See for a brief description Paramahansa Yogananda,
        Autobiography of a Yogi, SRF, (1946) 1993, p 169

95.   Alan Ereira, *The Heart of the World*, London, 1990

96.   Michio Kushi and Alex Jack, *The Gospel of Peace*, Tokyo,
        1992, p 83

97.   Take into account that really you should not put a label on
        the One such as 'Father' or 'God'. The One is *Nothing* as
        well as *Fullness*, see e.g. what Jung wrote about this problem,
        calling 'it' the *Pleroma* in his *Seven Sermons to the Dead*,
        quoted in Stephan A. Hoeller, *The Gnostic Jung*, Wheaton,
        Ill, USA, p 44ff

98.   The word 'spirit' is indeed a very apt one; like 'prana' it
        translates as 'breath', which is a common way of illustrating
        the modern concept of 'energy flow'. Therefore, as is often
        done, it should not be confusingly used for 'mind'.

99. If you key in 'mana' in Wikipedia it produces amongst others a list of some twenty 'Analogies to mana in other societies'.

100. Adama & Naomi Doumbia, *The Way of the Elders*, 2004

101. Voltaire, quoted in Joseph Head and S. L. Cranston, *Reincarnation—an east-west anthology*, 1975, p 202

102. See Elaine Pagels, *The Gnostic Gospels*, 1988

103. '*nafs* , the Arabic and Sufi word for self, is akin to *nafas* (breath)', see David Heinemann, *Sufi Therapy of the Heart*, New Delhi, 2003, p 29. Also described as the 'Breath of God' or 'Primal Energy Flow'.

104. Gary Lachman, *A Secret History of Consciousness*, Lindisfarne Books, 2003, p 22ff

105. Holger Kalweit, *Shamans, Healers, and Medicine Men*, Shambala, 2000, p 228f

106. C. G. Jung, op. cit., p 237

107. Raymond Hostie, *Religion and the Psychology of Jung*, London, 1957, p 126

108. Christmas Humphreys, *Exploring Buddhism,* London, (1974) 1980, p 92

109. Anne Bancroft, 'A Crowning Clarity', in *The Light of Experience*, BBC, London, 1977, p 69

110. Alan Watts, *Buddhism: The Religion of No-Religion*, Boston, (1995) 1999, p 6

111. Dating from c. 330, in the Lateran Museum in Rome

112. *filioque* meaning 'and of the son', was a word added at the Synod of Toledo of 447 to the original Nicene Creed of 325, to express the Roman teaching that the Holy Spirit emanated not only from the Father but from the Son as well. And this creed had become mandatory for the Church as: The Emperor Theodosius, one of the last to rule an undivided empire, issued a decree in 380 prescribing the Nicene Creed as binding on all subjects. From: Piers Paul Read, *The Templars*, London, 1999, p 29. The Anglican Church now agrees with the Orthodox Church, because at the 1988 Lambeth Conference, it was decided not to print this addition to the Creed anymore (Res. 6.5).

113. 'The emerging consensus is that the *Gospel of Thomas* is not Gnostic at all but is the earliest of all the Christian gospels and preserves Jesus' teachings in the simplest, most original form'. In Michio Kushi and Alex Jack, *The Gospel of Peace*, Tokyo, 1992, p 18. In this book both the Gospel of Thomas and the Sermon on the Mount are extensively reviewed

114. 1 John 3:2

115. John 10:34

116. e.g. St Paul writes: "To prove that you are sons, God has sent into your hearts the Spirit of his Son, crying 'Abba!

Father!' You are therefore no longer a slave but a son, ...",
and "For through faith you are all sons of God in union
with Christ Jesus". Galatians 4:6-7 and 3:26. A very
revealing book covering the origin of many Christian beliefs
such as Jesus' divinity and the Trinity, is Timothy Freke
and Peter Gandy's *The Jesus Mysteries*, London, 2000, from
which I have quoted earlier.

117. Quoted in Sarvepalli Radhakrishnan, *Religion of the Spirit*,
      in Whit Burnett (ed.), *This is my Philosophy*, London,1959,
      p 363
118. Swami Prabhavananda, *The Sermon on the Mount according
      to Vedanta*, Hollywood, 1963, p 43
119. Joseph Campbell, *Myths to Live by*, New York, 1992, p 9
120. Matthew Fox, *Creation Spirituality*, Harper San Francisco,
      1991, p 83
121. T. C. McLuhan, *Touch the Earth* , London, 1982 (1972), p
      49
122. Barbara Wood, *Alias Papa*, Oxford University Press, 1985,
      p 244
123. Michael Wiederman, 'Why It's So Hard to Be Happy',
      Scientific American, February/March 2007, p 38
124. Of course I am very much aware of the good and the relief
      of suffering that many missionaries have been responsible
      for, but Edward Marriott's *The Lost Tribe*, London, 1996 (see
      e.g. p 10), is a testimonial that the race for converts is still
      going on today. Sylvia Cranston reproduces in her book,
      Reincarnation, Pasadena, 1994, p 69, a very revealing crime
      in India statistic published in a British census of 1881.
125. Quoted in *Lucifer*, London, April 1888, III, p 147
126. Red Jacket quoted in: T. C. McLuhan, *Touch the Earth* ,
      London, 1982 (1972), p 63 and 60ff
127. Swami Prabhavananda, op. cit., p xi
128. ibid., p 62
129. *The Zen Teachings of Hui Hai*, quoted in Peter Lorie and
      Manuela Dunn Mascetti (eds), *The Quotable Spirit,* London,
      1996, p 204
130. *The Upanishads: Breath of the Eternal*, Swami
      Prabhavananda and Frederick Manchester (trans.), New
      York, p 125f, quoted in Roland Peterson, *Everyone Is Right*,
      DeVorss & Co, Marina del Rey, 1986, p xi
131. Quoted in Roland Peterson, op. cit., p 82 and see the
      quotations from the Koran on p 80
132. Quoted in Don Cupitt, *The Sea of Faith*, London, 1985, p
      167
133. Neale Donald Walsch, *The New Revelations: A Conversation
      with God*, London, 2002, p 97f
134. ibid., p 18

135.   John Templeton at www.templeton.org
136.   Quoted in Richard Acland, *Hungry Sheep*, Basingstoke, 1988, p 58
137.   Deepak Chopra, *The Path of Love* , New York, 1997, p 307
138.   Richard Acland, op. cit., p 75
139.   Quoted in Peter Spink, *Spiritual Man in a New Age*, London, 1980, p 13
140.   Matthew 6: 33
141.   John 18: 36
142.   Luke 17: 21 Leo Tolstoy wrote a very interesting book, *The Kingdom of God is within You*, University of Nebraska Press,1984
143.   Matthew 13:11
144.   Stephen Levine, *Who Dies?*, Gateway, Bath, (1986) 1997, p 49
145.   Deepak Chopra, *op. cit.*, p 74
146.   Albert Einstein, *Strange is Our Situation Here upon Earth* and Veblen Thorstein, *The Theory of the Leisure Class*, 1899
147.   Quoted in Timothy Freke and Peter Gandy, *The Jesus Mysteries*, Thorsons, London, 2000, p 86f
148.   But keep in mind that one of his great supporters, the Indian industrialist Tata, once said: "It cost me a fortune to keep Gandhi simple." quoted in Catherine Ingram, *In the Footsteps of Gandhi*, Berkeley (Ca), 1990, p 247
149.   Referring to a study: A. J. Edmunds, *Buddhist and Christian Gospels*, Philadelphia, 1908 in: W. Y. Evans-Wentz, *The Tibetan Book of the Dead*, Oxford, 1985 (1927), p 4
150.   Hazel Courteney, *The Evidence for the Sixth Sense*, London, 2005, p 45
151.   Emmet Fox, *Sermon on the Mount* , Harper San Francisco, (1934) 1998, p 6. In the same spirit I have avoided in this book (which should very much extol a vertical message), all those irrelevant horizontal qualifications such as Sir, Reverend, Lord, Majesty, His Holiness etc, etc. If you are desperate to know how 'important' my sources are, the place to look is in '*Who's Who*' or on the Internet.
152.   Raymond A. Moody, *The Light Beyond*, ,Bantam,1988, p 39
153.   ibid., p 68
154.   C. G. Jung, op. cit., p 113
155.   U.S. Commissioner of Indian Affairs, *Annual Report*, 1873, p 527, quoted in Dee Brown, *Bury my Heart at Wounded Knee*, London, 1972, p 318
156.   Dee Brown, op. cit., p 421
157.   Quoted on www.brainyquotes.com
158.   Quoted in Stephen Jay Gould, *Rocks of Ages,* London, 2001, p 61

159.   Quoted in Aldous Huxley, *The Perennial Philosophy*,
         London, 1950, p 13

160.   Herbert Benson, M.D., *Timeless Healing*, Simon & Schuster,
         1996, p 213

161.   Alan W. Watts, *Psychotherapy East and West*, Jonathan Cape,
         London, 1971, p 87f

162.   ibid., p 176

163.   Christmas Humphreys, *Exploring Buddhism*, London,
         (1974) 1980, p 106

164.   ibid., p 128

165.   ibid., p 124

166.   Sigmund Freud, quoted in: James C. Livingston, *Anatomy
         of the Sacred*, New York, 1993, p 6 and in: *The Future of
         an Illusion*, in Jaroslav Pelikan (ed.), *The World Treasure of
         Modern Religious Thought*, Little, Brown and Co,, 1990, p
         73f

167.   Interview in *Caduceus*, 52, p 8, about the book *How to
         Know God*

168.   Peter Spink, *Spiritual Man in a New Age,* London, 1980, p
         42

169.   ibid., p 44

170.   Gabriel Marcel, *The Universal against the Masses*, in: Whit
         Burnett (ed.), *This is my Philosophy*, London, 1958,p 317

171.   Quoted in Reinhold Niebuhr, *On Freedom, Virtue and
         Faith*, in: Whit Burnett (ed), *op. cit.*, p 265f

172.   Quoted in Peter Spink, op. cit., p 21

173.   C. G. Jung,op. cit., p 162

174.   Quoted in Joseph Campbell, 'Jung and the Power of Myth',
         BBC2 TV programme, 2 September 1990, 21:35

175.   Harry R Moody & David Carroll, *The Five Stages of the Soul*
         , Rider, London, 1998, p 166

176.   Eric Butterworth, *Discover the Power within You* , Harper
         San Francisco, 1992, p ix

177.   *The Essential Jung: Selected Writings*, Anthony Storr,
         London, 1983, p 355 and quoted by Joseph Campbell in a
         BBC2 TV programme, 2 September 1990: 'Jung and the
         Power of Myth'

Chapter 7 How to open up the 'vertical' dimension

1.   Thomas Aquinas, *Summa theologica*, I, 1, 5 ad 1

2.   Quoted in C. G. Jung, *Memories, Dreams, Reflections*, 1967,
         p 388

3.   Quoted in Aldous Huxley, *The Perennial Philosophy*,
         London, 1950, p 227

4. Rudolf Otto, *The Idea of the Holy*, Oxford University Press, 1923
5. I am thinking of the schools based on Rudolf Steiner's ideas
6. Quoted in Michael Hayes, *High Priests, Quantum Genes*, London, 2004, p 217
7. Gilbert Wright, quoted in Dr Harlow 'The man who transported objects through space' in Brant House (ed.), *Strange Powers Of Unusual People*, New York, 1973, p 181
8. R. C. Johnson, *Psychical Research*, London, 1955, p 168
9. Luke 2: 49ff
10. Harvey Cox, *Turning East*, London, (1977) 1979, p 136
11. Matthew 18:1-3, see also 19:14 and Mark 10:15
12. Fynn, *Mister God, this is Anna*. Note that in 2004 the three books Fynn wrote about his experiences with Anna have been issued together in a jubilee edition, *Anna and Mister God*.
13. Fynn, *Anna and the Black Knight,* Collins, London, 1990, p 102
14. St Ignatius of Antioch is reported to have said, 'It is better to be silent and real, rather than to talk and be unreal'. Quoted in John Main, *Awakening*, London, 1997, p 88
15. James F. Twyman, *Emissary of Love: The Psychic Children speak to the World*,Walsh Books, 2002
16. Further information on the websites: www.emissaryoflove. com or www.jamestwyman.com
17. Fynn, *Anna and the Black Knight,* Collins, 1990, p 19
18. Fynn, personal communication. Daisetz Suzuki expresses a similar advice as: 'Man is a thinking reed but his great works are done when he is not calculating and thinking'. Quoted in T C McLuhan, *The Way of the Earth*, New York, 1995, p 141. This book is a true mine of wisdom from all over our planet.
19. Fynn, *Anna's Book*, Collins, 1986. p 45
20. Eric Butterworth, *Discover the Power within You*, Harper San Francisco, 1992, p xv
21. Christmas Humphreys, *Exploring Buddhism,* London, (1974) 1980, p 134
22. Quoted in David Heinemann, *Sufi Therapy of the Heart*, New Delhi, 2003, p 275
23. Gary Zukav, *The Seat of the Soul*, London, 1990, p 243
24. in his Foreword to: Lounsberry, *Buddhist Meditation*
25. Dalai Lama, *The Little Book of Wisdom*, 1997, p 11
26. Drs F.W. Blase, 'Transcendente meditatie', *Intermediair*, 12, 36, 3 september 1976, p 11ff
27. Became well known after the Beatles' exploits with him.
28. R.K. Wallace and H. Benson, 'The Physiology of Meditation', *Scientific American*, 1972, pp 84 - 90, and that

meditation still passes the grade is confirmed by the results of recent research of a 'Chinese meditation technique', see: 'Meditation passes strictest test so far', *New Scientist*, 13 October 2007, p 21

29. Frits Staal refers in his book *Exploring Mysticism* (Penguin, 1975), to research by Th. Brosse stating that yogis can not only influence their breathing, but also pulse and heart rate and even brainwaves.

30. Much later, I realised that the psychological effect of having paid a substantial sum of money is that you are directed to take what has been offered more seriously than when it had been given for free.

31. *TM Vrienden Vereniging* (TM Friends Society)

32. Reginald A. Ray, *Indestructible Truth*, Shambala, 2002, p 207

33. See chapter 2

34. A very good preparation could be the reading of chapter 4 'Beginning the Search' in Harry R Moody & David Carroll, *The Five Stages of the Soul*, Rider, London, 1998, p 127ff

35. Dalai Lama, *Stages of Meditation*, London, 2001, p 94

36. In Michio Kushi and Alex Jack, *The Gospel of Peace*, Tokyo, 1992, it is argued that the Old Testamental prophet Daniel and Jesus' brother, James, were vegetarians; see pp 40, 46 and 100, and the more general food discussion on p 73.

37. Totapuri, Quoted in Francis Younghusband, *Modern Mystics*, London, 1935, p 75

38. Quoted in Aldous Huxley, *The Perennial Philosophy*, London, 1950, p 150

39. D T Suzuki, *On Indian Mahayana Buddhism*, quoted in Fritjof Capra, *The Tao of Physics*, Fontana//Collins, 1979, p 35

40. Hui Neng, quoted in Aldous Huxley, *op. cit.*, p 160

41. Marqah, quoted by Michael Goulder in John Hick (ed), *The Myth of God Incarnate*, London, 1977, p 69

42. Masahisa Goi, *God and Man*, Shizuoka-ken, Japan, (1953) 200, p 42

43. David Heinemann, *Sufi Therapy of the Heart*, New Delhi, 2003, p 136f

44. W. R. Inge, *Mysticism in Religion*, Rider, London, (1947) 1969

45. Miranda Holden, *Boundless Love*, London, 2002, p 20

46. John E Coleman, *The Quiet Mind*, London, 1971, p 19

47. Krishnamurti, quoted in John E Coleman, *The Quiet Mind*, London, 1971, p 75ff

48. Krishnamurti, ibid., p 93

49. Krishnamurti, ibid., p 114

50.   Joel S. Goldsmith, *A Parenthesis in Eternity*, New York, 1986, p 45
51.   Similarly, *Kriya Yoga* initiates are required to sign a pledge not to reveal the technique to others; see Paramahansa Yogananda, *Autobiography of a Yogi*, SRF, (1946) 1993, p 366
52.   Dr David Fontana, *Meditator's Handbook*, Element, 1992
53.   Coleman writes: 'So far as my own researches were concerned I concluded that drugs are no substitute for the arduous process of true meditation in the search for a quiet mind for they do not bring about the necessary and lasting personality changes'. John E Coleman, op. cit., p 230
54.   ibid., p 171
55.   Deepak Chopra, *Return of the Rishi*, 1988
56.   J. Krishnamurti, *The Awakening of Intelligence*, London, 1973, pp 22, 25, 95, 100
57.   Reginald A. Ray, *Indestructible Truth*, Shambala, 2002, p 87
58.   Buddhasa Bikkhu, Quoted in Reginald A. Ray, *Indestructible Truth*, Shambala, 2002, p 148
59.   Dr Suzuki, quoted in Reginald A. Ray, *op. cit.*, pp 151 and 194
60.   Quoted in Andrew Harvey, *Son of Man,* New York, 1999, p 264
61.   Raymond Hostie, *Religion and the Psychology of Jung*, London, 1957, p 171
62.   ibid., p 220
63.   Quoted in: Swami Prabhavananda, *The Sermon on the Mount according to Vedanta*, Mentor, (1963) 1972, p 62
64.   Quoted in Peggy Mason and Ron Laing,*Sathya Sai Baba: The Embodiment of Love*, Sawbridge Enterprises, 1982, p 215
65.   But hang on to your critical faculties. Some disturbing statistics are given about meditation teachers taking advantage of their pupils in the sexual, health or financial spheres in Harry R Moody & David Carroll, *The Five Stages of the Soul*, Rider, London, 1998, p 160ff.
66.   John Main,who was instrumental in reviving the Christian meditation tradition, was, when he became a monk 'told to stop' the meditation practice he had been taught by a 'holy Indian teacher in Malaya'; see Laurence Freeman, *Light Within: The Inner Path of Meditation*, London, (1986) 1989, p 5. What can be considered as positive news for a more meditative approach is the recent press report that the 'Pope opens way for the return of Latin Mass', in *The Times*, 11 October 2006, p 40.
67.   L. Bernardi et al., 'Effect of rosary prayer and yoga mantras on audiovascular rhythms: comparative study', *British Medical Journal*, 2001; 223: 1446-9

68. Peter Spink, who founded the Omega Trust running a retreat centre near Bristol, in: *Spiritual Man in a New Age*, London, 1980, p 46

69. see e.g. Bede Griffiths, *The Golden String*, London, 1954 and *A New Vision of Reality*, London, 1989

70. John Main,e.g. *Christian Meditation*, Montreal, 1976. His meditation movement is widespread and contact addresses can be found at www.wccm.org

71. John Main, Quoted on the website of 'The World Community for Christian Meditation', www.wccm.org

72. John Main, *The Heart of Creation*, New York, 1998, p 90f

73. ibid., p 37

74. ibid., p 72

75. Laurence Freeman, *Light Within*, London, 1986

76. ibid., p 8 f

77. ibid., p 77

78. Rowan Hooper, *New Scientist*, 3 September 2005, p 9

79. Laurence Freeman, op. cit., p 49

80. ibid., p 85f

81. Christmas Humphreys, *op. cit*, p 136

82. Francis Younghusband, *Modern Mystics*, London, 1935, p 305

83. Christmas Humphreys, op. cit., p 84

84. ibid., p 98

85. *The Cloud of Unknowing*, anon. trans. Clifton Walters

86. Andrew Harvey, *Son of Man*, New York, 1999, p 201ff

87. John Snelling, *The Buddhist Handbook*, Rider, London, 1989, p 302f. A more recent survey by John Snelling is his *Way of Buddhism*, Thorsons, London, 2001

88. Reginald A. Ray, *Indestructible Truth*, Shambala, 2000, p 231

89. David Fontana, *The Meditator's Handbook*,Shaftesbury, 1992

90. Aryeh Kaplan, *Meditation and Kabbalah*, Weiser, York Beach, 1985, p 11ff

91. Chris Griscom, *Zeit is eine Illusion*, Goldmann, 1986, p 192

92. Miranda Holden, in Martin Nathanael, 'Interview with Miranda', *Gracevine Online*, February 2007

93. Quoted in Victor White, *God and the Unconscious*, London, 1952, p 139

94. Quoted in Anthony Gottlieb, *The Dream of Reason*, London, 2000, p 314

95. *Institutes*, I.v.11, quoted in Keith Thomas, *Religion and the decline of Magic*, Penguin, 1984, p 92

96. Joel Goldsmith, *The Thunder of Silence*, San Francisco, 1993, p 182

97.   Raymond A. Moody, *Life after Life*, followed by his later
       Reflections on Life after Life, 1977, and e.g. Margot Grey,
       Return from Death, London, 1985
98.   David Darling, *After Life*, London, 1995, p 50
99.   Deepak Chopra, *How to Know God*, Rider, London, 2000
100.   In the Hindu tradition it is written as 'Siddhis', here with
       one 'd' as a TM 'trademark'.
101.   A very similar experience is described by Larry Peters who
       was taught by his Nepalese teacher Bhirenda ; in Holger
       Kalweit, *Shamans, Healers, and Medicine Men*, Shambala,
       2000, p 73. On p 76 the problem of why it is so difficult for
       Westerners to participate is discussed: 'Foreigners often have
       a barrier in their heads, preconceptions that block them,
       which prevents them from really letting themselves go, ...
       In general foreigners are too hampered by their education'.
       (Remember Jesus and children: '... for of such is the
       kingdom of heaven'. Matthew 19: 14)
102.   The same is reported of the levitations of St Joseph of
       Cupertino by his biographer, Bernino: '..it was always
       noticed how little were his clothes and vestments
       disarranged during his aerial flights. It was almost as
       though an invisible hand were controlling his garments
       ..' Eric J Dingwall, 'The monk who could fly at will' in
       Brant House (ed), *Strange Powers Of Unusual People*, New
       York, 1973, p 24. In an interview, Dr Lozanov, who has
       studied psi phenomena extensively, dismisses levitation
       as being 'a distinctive jump': Victor Popovkin, 'Yogis,
       Supermemory, and Levitation', in Sheila Ostrander and
       Lynn Schroeder, *The ESP Papers*, Bantam, 1976, p 78f
103.   Only many years later did I come across the following:
       'Passing through solid metal or stone, walking in the
       midst of fire or on the surface of water - all these things are
       possible to him who is in harmony with *Tao.*' In Joseph
       Gear *How The Great Religions Began*, New York, 1956,
       p 101. Paul Davies writes: '... but some physicists - most
       notably John Wheeler - have long speculated that the
       laws of physics might not be fixed "from everlasting to
       everlasting" and insisted they are "mutable" and in some
       manner "congeal" into their present form as the universe
       expands ...' Paul Davies, 'The sum of the parts', *New
       Scientist*, 5 March 2005, p 37. I also remember a colleague
       who went to a holiday cottage to relax after a nervous
       breakdown telling us afterwards that his nervous tensions
       caused all the electrical equipment to break down. His case
       is confirmed by: 'If I get too little sleep for a few days in a
       row, then my electrical energies must get out of whack. I've
       been known to blow the transformer out totally, like three

or four times. Of course the electrical company wouldn't be happy to know it's me'. in Barbara R. Rommer, *Blessing in Disguise*,St. Paul, 2000, p 176

104.   Quoted in Michael Hayes, *High Priests, Quantum Genes,* London, 2004, p 195

105.   Most likely it was a vision, because if I had been dreaming, having fallen asleep while sitting upright, I would probably have fallen over.

106.   Julie Chimes reports a similar experience, described by her guardian spirit: 'As you watch, you will become aware of the space between these restless creatures. And, in that space, you will be amazed at what you know'. In Julie Chimes, *Stranger in Paradise*, Bloomsbury, London, 1995, p 121

107.   Lyn Andrews reports on her experience of transcending: 'Different layers of reality revealed themselves to me as though I was suddenly gifted with a new type of vision. As I progressed through each level during the process of self-realization, I came to understand that each one, though apparently separate, interconnects and affects the others. However at the level of spirit my mind went blank. It was only later that I came to realize that at that level of consciousness relativity had been transcended and unity with all that is, is enjoyed. See www.psyspiritstory.co.uk, quoted in Chris Clarke, *Living in Connection*, Warminster, 2002, p 215.
         Similar levels are described in the Hasidic tradition as climbing the spiritual ladder from one Universe to the next. They identify 'four universes, Asiyah, Yetzirah, Beriyah, and finally to Atzilut, the Universe of the Sefirot'. ... 'The level above Beriyah, ... must be considered "Nothing." ... Azilut is often referred as "Nothingness." ' See Aryeh Kaplan, *Meditation and Kabbalah,* Weiser, York Beach, 1985, p 293 and 299

108.   Mark 9:1 and Psalm 46:10 resp. See also Psalm 4:4: Stand in awe, and sin not: commune with your own heart, and in your chamber and be still'. Also: *The Essential Teachings of Ramana Maharshi*, Inner Directions, Carlsbad (Ca), (2001) 2003, p 43

109.   Caroline Chartres (ed.), *Why I am Still an Anglican*, London, 2006, p 2

110.   Aldous Huxley, *The Perennial Philosophy*, London, 1950, p 299

111.   But note Huxley's comment: 'The masters of Hindu spirituality urge their disciples to pay no attention to the *Siddhis,* or psychic powers...'; while the Buddha's comment on 'a prodigious feat of levitation performed by one of his disciples' was: 'This will not conduce to the conversion of

the unconverted, nor to the advantage of the converted'. In Aldous Huxley, *The Perennial Philosophy,* 1950, p 299

112. Maharishi Mahesh Yogi in e.g. Jack Forem (ed.), *Transcendental Meditation*, Bantam, 1976, p 28
113. Quoted in Sophy Burnham, *The Ecstatic Journey*, Ballantine, 1997, p 173
114. Brian Inglis, in *The Unknown Guest,* reports on several similar cases.
115. Herbert Benson, *The Relaxation Response*, Collins, London, 1976, p 113
116. John Main, *The Heart of Creation*, New York, 1998, p 91
117. Dalai Lama, *Stages of Meditation*, London, 2001, p 75
118. Quoted in Aryeh Kaplan, *Meditation and Kabbalah*, Weiser, York Beach, 1985, p 79
119. ibid., p 81
120. ibid., p 82
121. Quoted in Joseph Campbell, *Myths to Live by*, New York, 1992, p 230
122. Swami Prabhavananda, *The Sermon on the Mount according to Vedanta*, Hollywood, 1963, p 105
123. Masanobu Fukuoka Quoted in T C McLuhan, *The Way of the Earth,* New York, 1995, p 149
124. Quoted in T C McLuhan, op. cit., p 163
125. Bede Griffiths, *The Golden String,* London, 1954, p 11
126. Neale Donald Walsch, *The New Revelations: A Conversation with God*, London, 2002, p 97f
127. Andrew Harvey, *Son of Man,* New York, 1999, p 107
128. Matthew 6: 31-33
129. Andrew Harvey, op. cit., p 142
130. Diane Eisler, *The Chalice and The Blade,* Quoted in Andrew Harvey, *Son of Man,* New York, 1999, p 130
131. Andrew Harvey, op. cit., p 177ff
132. Quoted in Paramahansa Yogananda, *Autobiography of a Yogi*, SRF, (1946) 1993, p 377
133. Kahlil Gibran, *The Prophet*, Penguin, London, (1926) 1992, p 38
134. Dorothy Rowe, *Beyond Fear,* London, 1987, p 392

Chapter 8 Recapitulation and applications

1. Gary E Schwartz, *The Afterlife Experiments*, Atria, New York, 2002, p 205
2. Paul Davies, 'Laying down the laws', *New Scientist*, 30 June 2007, p 30
3. Peggy Mason & Ron Laing, *Sathya Sai Baba: The Embodiment of Love,* Pilgrim, 1987 (1982), p 108

4.   If you need to be convinced of the overwhelming improbability of random natural selection, see John T Barrow and Frank J Tipler, *The Anthropic Cosmological Principle*, Oxford UP, (1986)1996, p 565

5.   For instance, in Bill Schul's *The Psychic Power of Animals*, we read on p 66: 'Mesmer called it animal magnetism. Reichenbach referred to it as odic force. Keely named it motor force. Blondot called it N-rays. Soviet scientists have entitled it bioplasmic energy; and Czech scientists call it psychotronic energy'. While Richard Grossman in his *The Other Medicines*, London, 1986, gives on p 135 a list of forty-seven different names for this vertical energy flow.

6.   Quoted in Richard Grossman, *The Other Medicines*, London, 1986, p 44

7.   Matthew 7: 7

8.   Plato, *Phaedrus and Letters VII and VIII* , London, 1985, p 136

9.   Yes, of course, I do realise that one has to have food and shelter but again I can quote Plato, now from his *Eighth Letter* : 'First of all, men of Syracuse, give your adherence to laws which it is plain will not turn your thoughts towards moneymaking and wealth. Soul, body, and wealth are three separate things; range them in order in which the highest honour is paid to excellence of soul, and the third and lowest to wealth, which should be the servant of body and soul alike'. in Plato, *Phaedrus and Letters VII and VIII* , London, 1985, p 155f

10.   Quoted in Peter Haining, 'Introduction' to *Ancient Mysteries*, New York, Taplinger, 1977, in Henry H. Bauer, *Science or Pseudoscience*, University of Illinois, 2001, p 235

11.   Stanislav Grof, *The Holotropic Mind*, Harper San Francisco, 1990, p 127

12.   Referring to comments made by John Maddox, in Philip Ball, *H_2O: A Biography of Water*, Phoenix, (1999) 2003, p 298

13.   Paramahansa Yogananda, *Self-Realization*, Fall 2003, p 5

14.   Harold K Schilling, *The New Consciousness in Science and Religion*, London, 1973, p 207

15.   None of the scholars—Archbishop Dr Rowan Williams, Professor Tariq Ramadan and Rabbi Sir Jonathan Sacks—could come up with a reasonable answer to a similar question: 'Humphrys in Search of God', BBC Radio 4, 31 October, 7 November and 14 November 2006.

16.   Rowan Williams, 'Of course this makes us doubt God's existence', *the Telegraph*, London, 2 January 2005

17.   Homer, *the Iliad*, Book XXIV, Penguin Classics, 1972, p 451

18. Homer, *the Odyssey*, Book I, Penguin Classics, 1964, p 26
19. Plato, *The Republic*, Book X, Penguin Classics, (1955) 1979, p 451f
20. Quoted in Anthony Gottlieb, *The Dream of Reason*, London, 2000, p 320
21. Quoted in Victor White in his *God & the Unconscious*, London, 1952, p 255
22. Quoted in M. O'C. Walshe, *Meister Eckhart Sermons and Treatises Vol. II*, p 332f
23. Lao Tzu, *Tao Te Ching*, Stephen Mitchell, London,1989 (I am aware that this translation is challenged by Ian P. McGreal (ed.) in *Great Thinkers of the Eastern World*, Harper Collins, 1995)
24. Stephan A. Hoeller, *The Gnostic Jung and the Seven Sermons to the Dead*, 1982, p 44f
25. Michael Newton, *Journey of Souls*, Llewellyn Publications, St Paul, 2000, p 274
26. Hugh Montefiore, *On Being a Jewish Christian*, London, 1998, p 96f
27. Quoted in Leslie D. Weatherhead, *The Christian Agnostic*, London, 1966, p 3
28. Seth Lloyd and Y Jack Ng, 'Black Hole Computers'. *Scientific American*, November 2004, p 32
29. Rupert Sheldrake and Matthew Fox, *Natural Grace*, London, 1997, p 21
30. Mason Inman, 'Spooks in space', *New Scientist*, 18 August 2007, p 27
31. Steven Weinberg, *The First Three Minutes*, Glasgow, 1977, p 148
32. see Martin Rees, *Just Six Numbers*, Weidenfeld and Nicholson, 1999
33. John D Barrow, *The Origin of the Universe,* HarperCollins, New York, 1994, p 8, and see also Martin Rees, op. cit., p 88
34. John D Barrow, *The Origin of the Universe,* Harper Collins, New York, 1994, p 27
35. Amir Aczel, *God's Equation,* London, 1999, p 175
36. Philip Ball, *H_2O: A Biography of Water*, Phoenix, (1999) 2003, p 177ff
37. Editorial by J. Maddox (1988) in *Nature*, 333, p 787
38. Philip Ball, op. cit., p 294
39. J. Maddox, J. Randi & W. W. Stewart (1988): *Nature*, 334, 375, quoted in Philip Ball, op. cit., p 306
40. Michael Brooks, '13 things that don't make sense', *New Scientist*, 19 March 2005, p 30ff
41. For a revealing interview with the psychiatrist Patrick Lemoine on techniques and examples of the placebo effect,

see: Laura Spinney, 'Purveyors of mystery', *New Scientist*, 16 December 2006, p 42f

42. See also Martin Rees, *Just Six Numbers*, London, 1999

43. Marcus Chown, 'Dark-matter particles could 'X-ray the sun', *New Scientist*, 25 November 2006, p 15

44. In a letter to *New Scientist*, 7 May 2005, p 29, Rudi Van Nieuwenhove points to a theory 'to explain the rotation curves of galaxies based on minor deviations of the vacuum energy density, with no need for dark matter at all'.

45. Tom Shanks, 'That's not all, folks', *New Scientist*, 14 February 2004, p 19

46. Quoted in Anthony North, *The Paranormal*, 1996, p 113

47. Amir Aczel, *God's Equation*, London, 1999, p 203

48. For a survey of what is going on 'horizontally' in the field of 'dark energy' research, see: Stuart Clark, 'Heart of darkness', *New Scientist*, 17 February 2007, p 28ff

49. F.W.J. von Schelling Quoted in Joseph Head and S. L. Cranston, *Reincarnation: an east-west anthology*, The Theosophical Publishing House, (1961) 1975, p 184

50. Michael Le Page, 'The ancestor within', *New Scientist*, 13 January 2007, p 29

51. Rupert Sheldrake, *A New Science of Life*, London, 1981, p 104f

52. Isn't it striking that a parallel process seems to happen in following a meditation routine?

53. Peter Greig-Smith, 'The trees bite back', *New Scientist*, 1 May 1986, p 33f

54. or to 17x365? The *Magicicada septemdecula* emerges after 17 years, another species after 13.

55. Richard Milton, *Shattering the Myths of Darwinism* ,Park Street Press, Rochester, Vermont, 1997, p 222

56. Keith Ward, *God, Science and Necessity*, Oneworld Publications, Oxford, 1996, p 83

57. Mark Buchanan, 'Charity begins at Homo sapiens', *New Scientist*, 12 March 2005, p 33ff

58. Andy Coglan, 'Mendel will be turning in his grave', *New Scientist*, 26 March 2005, p 8f. Also: "Lamarckian" mechanisms should now be integrated in evolutionary theory, Emma Young (quoting Jablonka) in: 'Strange inheritance', *New Scientist*, 12 July 2008. p 29ff

59. Michael Le Page, 'The ancestor within', *New Scientist*, 1 January .2007, p 28ff

60. Quoted in Michael Hayes, *High Priests, Quantum Genes*, London, 2004, p 195

61. Lawrence LeShan, *How to meditate*, (1974) 1985, p 49

62. A compact survey of the field is e.g. R. C. Johnson, *Psychical Research*, London, 1955, while *The Inner Bookshop*,

Magdalen Street, Oxford, Oxon is one of the specialised 'alternative' bookshops

63. Anthony North, *The Paranormal: A Guide to the Unexplained*, London, 1997 (1996), p 203

64. see e.g. Hazel Courteney, *The Evidence for the Sixth Sense*, London, 2005

65. Anthony North, op. cit., p 140

66. W.Y. Evans-Wentz (ed.) comments: ' [Milarepa] thus acquired the *siddhi* of levitation and flying', in *Tibet's Great Yogi Milarepa*, Oxford, (128) 1976, p 212

67. Deepak Chopra, *How to know God*, Rider, London, 2000, p 171

68. Examples of vivid manifestations of that infinite energy are cases of spontaneous human combustion, see e.g. Jenny Randles and Peter Hough, *Spontaneous Human Combustion*, (Roy Herbert, 'In Search of the Fire Within', *New Scientist*, 12 September 1992, p 41), John Heymer, 'A case of spontaneous human combustion?', Forum, *New Scientist*, 15 June 1986, p 70; and see the case of Madame Kulagini in Lila Bek and Philippa Pullar, *To the Light*, London, 1985

69. Michael Hayes, op. cit., p 59f

70. ibid., p 220ff

71. Angus McGill, 'The healing hum ...', *Evening Standard*, 20 February 1990, p 29. It is interesting that Jill Purce is married to controversial biologist Rupert Sheldrake—again a case of *cherchez la femme*?

72. Quoted in Graham Hancock, *Fingerprints of the Gods*, Mandarin, 1996, p 166, from: *The Mythology of Mexico and Central America*, p 8. *Maya History and Religion*, p 340. Interesting is that both the Mayas reputedly carried gigantic stone blocks through the air, and the ancient Hebrews destroyed the walls of Jericho, with the sound of a trumpet.

73. Graham Hancock, op. cit., p 352

74. Brian Inglis, *Natural and Supernatural: a History of the Paranormal*, Prism Press, Bridport, 1992

75. *New York Times* editorial on Uri Geller and children tested in Stanford, referring to an article in *Nature* October 1974, quoted in: James F. Twyman, *Messages from Thomas: Raising Psychic Children*, Findhorn Press, 2003, p 150

76. James F. Twyman, *Messages from Thomas: Raising Psychic Children*, Findhorn Press, 2003, p 179

77. Rupert Sheldrake, *A New Science of Life*, London, 1981

78. Rupert Sheldrake, *The presence of the Past*, 1988; *The Rebirth of Nature*, 1990, *Seven Experiments That Could Change The World*, 1994; and *Dogs that Know when their Owners are coming Home*, 1999

79.   Rupert Sheldrake, *Dogs that Know when their Owners are coming Home*, London,1999, p 114
80.   J. Allen Boone, *Kinship with All Life*, HarperOne, New York, 1954, p 76
81.   H. J. Eysenck and D. K. B. Nias, *Astrology*, Penguin Books, 1982 and Hans J. Eysenck and Carl Sargent, *Explaining the Unexplained*, London, 1997, p 238ff
82.   Laura Spinney, 'Is there a psychoanalyst in the house?'. *New Scientist*, 17 February 2007, p 46f. Interview with Darian Leader and David Corfield about their book *Why Do People Get Ill?*, Hamish Hamilton, 2007
83.   Kacelnik, *Nature*, 433, p 121
84.   Editorial, *New Scientist*, 15 January 2005, p 3
85.   Bill Schul, *The Psychic Power of Animals*, Coronet, GB, 1987
86.   R. C. Johnson, op.cit., p 32
87.   Another occasion when I witnessed an 'apparition' was while on a business trip to Brussels in the 1970s, when I was woken up in the middle of the night by a female figure walking past the foot of my bed and disappearing throught the wall to my right. When leaving the next morning, I mentioned this to the receptionist but provoked no reaction.
88.   R. C. Johnson, *op. cit.*, p 55f
89.   Ervin Laszlo,*Science and the Akashic Field*, Rochester, Vermont, 2004, p 98
90.   The Maharaja of Jodhpur, was with his servants, a guest at Halsecombe in this period. Did they dig it? An Indian water engineer told me that the hole was typical of water holes dug in his tradition.
91.   Culbone Church has a very ancient history, both in legend and fact
92.   Joop van Montfoort, 'Leylines at Halsecombe', Porlock Village Hall, 23 January 2004
93.   Alfred Watkins, *The Old Straight Track*, Methuen, London, 1925
94.   *New Scientist*, 20/27 December 1979, p 48f
95.   Keith Thomas, *Religion and the decline of Magic*, Penguin, 1984, p 149, referring to George Fox, *Book of Miracles*, p ix, cf Fox, *Journal*, ed. N Penney, Cambridge, 1911, pp 108, 140-41, 420-21, 433; pp 234, 310, 342.
96.   Lawrence LeShan, *Clairvoyant Reality* (formerly *The Medium, The Mystic and the Physicist*), Turnstone Press Ltd, 1982 (1974), p 125
97.   Douglas Fox, 'Light at the end of the tunnel', *New Scientist*, 14 October 2006, p 48
98.   Quoted in Michel Quoist, *Prayers of Life*
99.   Barbara R. Rommer, *Blessing in Disguise,* Llewellyn, St Paul, 2000, p xx

100.   Elisabeth Kübler-Ross, *Death, the Final Stage of Growth*, Prentice-Hall, 1975, p 119
101.   Raymond Moody, *Life after Life*, 1975; *Reflections on Life after Life*, 1977
102.   Margot Grey, *Return from Death*, London, (1985) 1986, p 5
103.   David Darling, *After Life*, London, 1995, p 82ff
104.   Margot Grey, op. cit., p 10
105.   David Darling, op. cit., p 155
106.   Erik Kvaalen, letter to the *New Scientist*, 2 September 2006, p 18 referring to The *Lancet*, December 2001, Vol 358, p 2039
107.   Raymond A. Moody, *The Light Beyond*, ,Bantam,1988, p 14f
108.   Interview with Elisabeth Kübler-Ross, in *Kindred Spirit*, 1989, Vol 1, no 9, mentioned in Gill Edwards, *Living Magically*, Piatkus, London, 2006 (1991), p 8
109.   Barbara R. Rommer, *Blessing in Disguise*, St. Paul, 2000, p 7
110.   Brian Weiss, *Same Soul, Many Bodies,* London, 2004, p 10
111.   Raymond A. Moody, *The Light Beyond*, Bantam,1988, p 134f
112.   see e.g. Susan Blackmore, *Beyond the Body*, London, 1983
113.   Alison Motluk, 'Seeing without Sight', *New Scientist*, 29 January 2005, p 37
114.   This ties in well with Hugh Evered's solution to the Schrödinger's cat conundrum mentioned on p xx.
115.   Raymond A. Moody, *The Light Beyond*, ,Bantam,1988, p 22ff
116.   ibid.
117.   Raymond A. Moody, *Life after Life,* (1975), Bantam, 1976, p 89
118.   Stephen Levine,*Who Dies?*, Gateway, Bath, (1986) 1997, p 271
119.   George Trevelyan, *Exploration into God*, Bath, 1991, p 147
120.   Brian Weiss, *Same Soul, Many Bodies,* London, 2004, p 10
121.   Note that Richard Bergland is quoted thus: 'Can thinking go on outside the brain? Much scientific evidence points to that disturbing, previously unthinkable possibility'. In Stephen S. Hall, *Mapping the next Millennium*, Vintage, 1993, p 172. David Darling reports in *After Life* on several cases of people having normal or even superior intelligence without having a detectable brain. All this explains the consciousness and the 'even trickier "free will" problem', discussed by John Searle, 'Between a rock and a hard place\, *New Scientist*, 13 January 2007, p 48f.
122.   A very similar description was given by Chris Griscom, she mentions the *klick* (click) and going through a *Trichter* (funnel) or a dark *Strudel* (whirlpool), in: *Zeit is eine Illusion*, Goldmann, 1986, pp 20f and 152. A significant

difference is that she remembers what was at the other end
of the funnel, while I have no recollection of that at all.
My 'vortex' image also corresponds well with what one of
Moody's subjects described in this way: 'It looked almost
like the clouds of cigarette smoke you can see when they
drift around a lamp'. In Raymond Moody, *Life after Life*,
(1975), Bantam, 1976, p 102. Obviously my experience
is not unique at all and similar to those reported on by
Michael Newton, e.g. 'I ... am floating towards the Ring
... it's circular ...' and 'I'm being sucked inward ... through
a funnel ...'. He concludes that 'The hollow tube effect
described by my cases is apparently not the mother's birth
canal. It is similar to the tunnel souls pass through at
physical death and may be the same route'. [but in the other
direction]; see *Journey of Souls*, Llewellyn Publications, St.
Paul, 2000, p 207f and 266. Others have also reported
my experience of movement caused by just willing it, for
example: 'I had complete freedom, and anything I wanted
I could create by just thinking about it! In other words,
if I thought "go faster," then I went faster. If I thought
"slow down," then I could've slowed down'. In Barbara R.
Rommer, *Blessing in Disguise*, St. Paul, 2000, p 139

123.   David A. Ash, *The New Science of the Spirit*, London, 1995
124.   Helen Wambach, *Life before Life*, New York, (1979) 1981, p
         41f
125.   Joan Grant and Dennis Kelsey , *Many Lifetimes*, London,
         1976, p 203
126.   Barbara R. Rommer, *Blessing in Disguise*, St. Paul, 2000, p 3
127.   Raymond Moody, *Life after Life*, (1975), Bantam, 1976, p
         41
128.   Quoted in Barbara R. Rommer, op. cit., p 208
129.   Helen Wambach, op.cit., p 68ff
130.   Raymond A. Moody, *Life after Life*, (1975), Bantam, 1976,
         p 26
131.   Rowan Hooper, 'Chimps beat people at memory game',
         New Scientist, 8 December 2007, p 10
132.   Stanislav Grof, *The Holotropic Mind*, Harper San Francisco,
         1990, p 18
133.   Ferdinand Schiller, *Riddles of the Sphinx*, Quoted in David
         Darling, *After Life*,London, 1995, p 160
134.   Michael Shermer, 'Demon-Haunted Brain', *Scientific
         American*, March 2003, p 25
135.   Plato, *The Seventh Letter*, 340 in *Phaedrus and Letter VII
         and VIII*, Penguin Classics, 1985, p 135
136.   He was the director of the Philips Natuurkundig
         Laboratorium when I worked there in the 1950s.

137.   When I was taught quantum physics a long time ago, the vacuum was also called 'Fermi's sea'

138.   The vacuum is discussed in many books. For a short introduction, see e.g. "The vacuum as the 'All'" in Danah Zohar & Ian Marshall, *The Quantum Self*, London, 1994, p 194ff

139.   Hence, however complicated we make computers they can never become conscious or have souls. But see the soul being defined as 'the program which controls the body' in John T Barrow and Frank J Tipler, *The Anthropic Cosmological Principle*, Oxford UP, (1986)1996, p 659

140.   Helen Wambach, in *Life before Life*, New York, (1979) 1981, p 157 writes: 'I believe it has been established beyond reasonable doubt that the personalities of identical twins and indeed of quadruplets and quintuplets are different, even though the genetic material is the same'.

141.   Judith Rich Harris, author of *No Two Alike*, interviewed in *New Scientist* 25 February 2006, p 48

142.   Gary Lachman, *A Secret History of Consciousness*, Lindisfarne Books, 2003

143.   in Joan Grant and Dennis Kelsey , *Many Lifetimes*, London, 1976, p 53

144.   The vortex image goes at least back to Anaxagoras describing the influence of a "cosmic 'Mind'. This 'Mind' (*nous*) intervened to eradicate the state of primeval chaos by the induction of a vortical motion in space, ..." In John D Barrow and Frank J Tipler, *The Anthropic Cosmological Principle,* Oxford, (1986) 1996, p 32

145.   See the interesting discussion in Paul Davies, *Are We Alone?*, London, 1995. He writes: 'I conclude from all these deliberations that consciousness, far from being a trivial accident, is a fundamental feature of the universe, ...'

146.   Stanislav Grof, *The Holotropic Mind*, Harper San Francisco, 1990, p 5

147.   *New Scientist*, 4 April 1998, p 3

148.   David Darling, *After Life*, London, 1995, p 96; and see also the extensive description of Libet and his team's experiments at www.Wikipedia.org under his name listing further references

149.   David Darling, op. cit,, p 99

150.   'Why honeybees never forget a face', *In brief, New Scientist*, 10 December 2005, p 22. See also Philip E. Ross, 'Half-Brained Schemes', in *Scientific American*, Vol. 294, 1 January 2006, p 15, describing small brained individuals, some even lacking a *corpus callosum*, with high IQ and the recently discovered *Homo floresiensis* making sophisticated tools with only a chimp sized brain.

151.   As described by Socrates/Plato
152.   Jeremy Campbell, *Grammatical Man*, Pelican Books, (1982) 1984, p 137
153.   See the quotation I used at the beginning of section 5.1.
154.   Barbara R. Rommer, *Blessing in Disguise*, St Paul, 2000, p 48
155.   Around September 2007 , John Davidson, *Subtle Energy*, *The Web of Life*, *The Secret of the Creative Vacuum*, C. W. Daniel, Saffron Walden,1987, 1988, 1989
156.   John Davidson, *The Secret of the Creative Vacuum*, C. W. Daniel, Saffron Walden, (1989) 1994, p 217ff

Chapter 9 What went wrong?

1.   Sun Chief, a Hopi Indian quoted in: T. C. McLuhan, *Touch the Earth* , London, 1982 (1972), p 108
2.   Dalai Lama, *The Little Book of Wisdom,* Random, 1997, p 37
3.   Meladoma Some, an African spiritual teacher, Quoted in Matthew Fox, *The Reinvention of Work,* New York, 1995, p 253
4.   Quoted in Gablik, *Reenchantment of Art,* p 57f
5.   Michael Wiederman, 'Why It's So Hard to Be Happy', *Scientific American*, February/March 2007, p 41
6.   Roland Peterson, Everyone Is Right, 1986, p 57
7.   Geoff Russel, letter to *New Scientist*, 14 April 2007, p 22
8.   Quoted in: Danielle Fanelli, 'Meat is murder on the environment', *New Scientist*, 21 July 2007. Also see the cover story by Bijal Trivedi, 'Dinner's dirty secret', *New Scientist*, 13 September 2008, p 28ff: 'One sure-fire way to reduce your carbon footprint is to go vegetarian'. Also quoting Cristopher Weber: "Plant based diets are safe, and are probably nutritionally superior to mixed diets deriving a large fraction of their calories from animals. ... but our planet's health would be better off if we just gave meat the chop'.
9.   Dean Inge, quoted in W T Palmes, *The Gods Within Us*, London, 1961, p 48
10.   Howard A. Rusk Quoted in Amital Etzioni, '"Shortcuts" to Social Change?', in *Man-Made Futures*, Open University, 1974, p 289
11.   Lila Bek and Philippa Pullar, *The Seven Levels of Healing*, Century, London, p 140
12.   Quoted in Rupert Sheldrake, *Seven Experiments That Could Change the World*, London, 1995, p 201

13. See e.g. Holger Kalweit, *Shamans, Healers and Medicine Men* , Shambala, 2000

14. Michael Gearing-Tosh, *Living Proof: a medical mutiny,* Scribner, 2002. He died on 29 July 2005 'of an unrelated blood infection', John Bagley, *the Guardian*, 6 August 2005, p 23

15. Carmen Wheatley, 'The Case of the .0005% Survivor', in Michael Gearing-Tosh, *Living Proof: a medical mutiny,* Scribner, 2002 p 267ff

16. Michio Kushi and Alex Jack, *The Gospel of Peace*, Tokyo, 1992, p 99

17. John Templeton on www.johntempleton.org

18. Hazel Courteney, *Divine Intervention*, London, 2005

19. Hazel Courteney, *The Evidence for the Sixth Sense*, London, 2005, p 246

20. Subtitle of Lynne McTaggart, *What Doctors Don't Tell You,* Thorsons, 1996

21. ibid., p 295

22. ibid., p 316

23. Victor Hugo, *Les Misérables*, quoted in Peter Lorie & Manuela Dunn Mascetti, *The Quotable Spirit*, London, 1996, p 206

24. Julia Cameron, *God is no Laughing Matter,* London, 2001, p 24

25. Rupert Sheldrake & Matthew Fox, *Natural Grace*, Bloomsbury, 1997, p 5

26. Stephan A. Hoeller, *The Gnostic Jung and Seven Sermons to the Dead*, Quest, 1982, p 14

27. Quoted in Rupert Sheldrake & Matthew Fox, *natural grace*, London, 1997, p 29

28. Quoted in Satish Kumar, *YOU ARE Therefore I AM*, Green Books, 2002, p 129

29. I have put civilisation deliberately between hyphens because of what Gandhi replied when he was asked what he thought of Western civilisation: 'That would be an excellent idea'.

30. Napoleon Bonaparte in a letter to Count Thibaudeau, 6 June 1801, Quoted in Peter Lorie & Manuela Dunn Mascetti, *The Quotable Spirit*, London, 1996, p 206

31. Such as the Trinity, Eucharist, Virgin birth, see e.g. Origen replying to attacks on the latter: 'In addressing Greeks, it is not out of place to quote [pagan] Greek stories, lest we should appear to be the only people to have related this incredible story'. Quoted together with other examples by: Frances Young, *Two Roots of a Tangled Mass?*, in John Hick (ed.), *The Myth of God Incarnate*, London, 1977, p 89ff

32. Fynn, *Anna's Book,* Collins, 1986, p 14; the text has been reproduced from Anna's own handwritten text.

33.   Fynn, *Anna and Mister God*, HarperCollins,London, 2004, p 187 and iii

34.   Michio Kushi and Alex Jack, *The Gospel of Peace*, Tokyo, 1992, p 18

35.   "Popery was portrayed as the great repository of 'ethnic superstitions' and most Catholic rites were regarded as thinly concealed mutations of earlier pagan ceremonies." Keith Thomas, *Religion and the decline of Magic* ,Penguin, 1984, p 74

36.   Luke 18: 23f

37.   Lin Yutang, *The Importance of Living*, in Jaroslav Pelikan (ed.), *The World Treasure of Modern Religious Thought*, Little, Brown and Co, 1990, p 408

38.   Aldous Huxley, *The Perennial Philosophy*, London, 1950, p 66

39.   Mark 10: 25 Some argue that 'camel' is a mistranslation for a substantial hawser, as used on a boat.

40.   Quoted in: Charles L. Harper, *Beginning to Explore an Infinite Cosmos of Living Worlds*, in: Robert L. Hermann (ed.), *God, Science & Humility*, Templeton Foundation Press, 2000, p 100

41.   Kingsley Weatherhead, *Leslie Weatherhead: a personal portrait*, London, 1975, p 60

42.   In the RC South of The Netherlands, it was often cynically joked that the agreement between the local vicar and factory owner was; 'You keep them stupid and I will keep them poor'. The Protestants often adhered to the same recipe: '... the Puritan clergy often came very near to endorsing the old Catholic view that ignorance was the mother of devotion'. In Keith Thomas, *Religion and the decline of Magic*, Penguin, 1984, p 437

43.   Rupert Sheldrake & Matthew Fox, op. cit., p 59

44.   William Johnston, *Christian Mysticism Today*, Collins, 1984, p 148

45.   Andrew Harvey, *Son of Man*, New York, 1999, p 75

46.   Laurens van der Post, *Testament to the Bushmen*, Viking, 1984

47.   Quoted in: T. C. McLuhan, *Touch the Earth* , London, 1982 (1972), p 110

48.   Although Peter Blake & Paul S. Blezard, in *The Arcadian Cipher* , London, 2000, claim to have found Jesus' grave in southern France, the thoroughly scientifically verified claim by Simcha Jacobovici & Charles Pellegrino, in *The Jesus Tomb*, HarperElement, London, 2007, to have found Jesus' family tomb near Jerusalem is much more credible

49.   John Hick (ed.), *The Myth of God Incarnate*, SCM, London, 1977

50.   Eric Butterworth, *Discover the Power within You*, Harper San Francisco, 1992, p 10

51.   Keith Thomas, *Religion and the decline of Magic* , Penguin, 1984, p 794

52.   In Dutch it was 'Ban des afsnijdings van de gemeente'.

53.   Holger Kersten, *Jesus lived in India*, (1994), Penguin India, 2001, p 232

54.   Hugh Montefiore, *On Being a Jewish Christian*, London, 1989, p 66

55.   Neale Donald Walsch, *The New Revelations: A Conversation with God*, London, 2002, p 47

56.   From *Red Writings and Jade Mysteries*, Quoted in Jennifer Oldstone-Moore, *Understanding Taoism*, London, 2003, p 60

57.   Quoted in Aldous Huxley, *The Perennial Philosophy*, London, 1950, p 237f

58.   Neale Donald Walsch, op. cit., p 46

59.   Eric Butterworth, *Discover the Power within You* , Harper San Francisco, 1992, p 227

60.   *The Essential Lenny Bruce,* Quoted in Peter Lorie and Manuela Dunn Mascetti (eds), *The Quotable Spirit*, London, 1996, p 210

61.   Joseph Campbell, *Myths to live by*, 1992, p 102

62.   Lao-tzu Quoted in Roland Peterson, *Everyone Is Right*, DeVorss, Marina del Rey, 1986, p 86

63.   Quoted in Nicholas Shrady, *Sacred Roads,* Viking, 1999, p 200

64.   David Heinemann, *Sufi Therapy of the Heart*, New Delhi, 2003, p 248

65.   Sergei Bramley, 1987, Quoted in Holger Kalweit, *Shamans, Healers and Medicine Men,* Shambala, 2000, p 78

66.   Much later I discovered that a similar message had been uttered by many others, take this for instance from Herbert Spencer in: 'The Reconciliation' from *First Principles*, London, 1887 (1862), p 99f: 'Of Religion then, we must always remember, that amid its many errors and corruptions it has asserted and diffused a supreme verity'.

67.   Mark 3:28-9

68.   Leslie Houlden, *The Creed of Experience*, in John Hick (ed.), *The Myth of God Incarnate*, London, 1977, p 125

69.   John Templeton on www.johntempleton.org

70.   C.G. Jung, *Psychology and Religion*, 1937, p 6

71.   ibid., p 113

72.   John 10:16

73.   Roland Peterson, *Everyone Is Right*, DeVorss, Marina del Rey, 1986, p 82

74.   R. K. Prabhu (ed.), *Truth is God*, 1955

75.   Roland Peterson, *Everyone Is Right*, DeVorss, Marina del
       Rey, 1986, p xi
76.   Matthew 19:14
77.   See Holger Kalweit, *Shamans, Healers and Medicine Men*,
       Shambala, 2000
78.   James E Twyman, *Emissary of Love: The Psychic Children
       Speak to the World* , Hampton Road, 2002; and James E
       Twyman, *Messages from Thomas: Raising Psychic Children*,
       Findhorn, 2003
79.   Quoted in Satish Kumar, *YOU ARE Therefore I AM*, Green
       Books, 2002, p 126
80.   Chiparopai, an old Yuma Indian, quoted in the very moving
       collection of Native Indian sayings and wisdom, collected
       by T. C. McLuhan in *Touch the Earth* , London, 1982
       (1972), p 113
81.   Rupert Sheldrake & Matthew Fox, *Natural Grace*, London,
       1997, p 4
82.   Holger Kalweit, op. cit., p 191f
83.   Helen Phillips, 'Mind-altering media', *New Scientist*, 21
       April 2007, p 37
84.   In a BBC Radio 4 press review on 6 March 2004, it was
       claimed that 200 of the UK's top football players are
       alcoholics.
85.   Aldous Huxley, *The Perennial Philosophy*, London, 1950, p
       250
86.   See e.g. the review article: Helen Phillips,op. cit., p 33ff
87.   In the USA suicide rates in the fifteen to nineteen age group
       have soared 400% between 1950 and 1990. See: David B.
       Larson and Susan S. Larson, *Health's Forgotten Factor,* in
       Robert L. Hermann (ed.), *God, Science & Humility,* Radnor,
       2000, p 264
88.   Editorial *New Scientist*, 21 April 2007, p 5
89.   *The Independent*, 14 February 2007, p 1ff. On p 2, an article
       by Jonathan Brown, 'Childhood in Britain', details results of
       the UNICEF Report: *An overview of child well-being in rich
       countries.*
90.   Peggy Mason & Ron Laing, *Sathya Sai Baba: The
       Embodiment of Love*, Pilgrim Books, 1987, p 202
91.   T. C. McLuhan, *Touch the Earth,* p 108
92.   BBC news report 'Today', Radio 4, 12 May 2006, 0725
       hrs and see the article by Maria Szalavitz, 'The K fix', *New
       Scientist*, 20 January 2007, p 38ff
93.   Quoted in Aldous Huxley, *The Perennial Philosophy*,
       London, 1950, p 88

Chapter 10 Listening to a different music

1. Quoted in Catherine Ingram, *In the Footsteps of Gandhi*, Berkeley (Ca), 1990, p 11
2. Quoted in Peter Plichta, *God's Secret Formula*, Element, Shaftesbury, 1997, p 126
3. Cary F. Baynes, Translator's Preface to Richard Wilhelm, *The Secret of the Golden Flower*, (1931) 1972, p viii
4. C. G. Jung in his Commentary on Richard Wilhelm, *The Secret of the Golden Flower*, (1931) 1972, p 85
5. Albert Einstein, *What Life means to Einstein*, Quoted in Robin Royston & Anne Humphries, *The Hidden Power of Dreams*, Bantam, London, 2007, p 65
6. Laurens van der Post, *The Heart of the Hunter*, Penguin, Harmondsworth, (1961) 1976, p 126
7. ibid., p 211
8. Peter Plichta, *God's Secret Formula*, Element, Shaftesbury, 1997, p 95
9. Lawrence LeShan, *Clairvoyant Reality* (formerly: *The Medium, The Mystic and the Physicist*), Turnstone Press Ltd, 1982 (1974), p xiii
10. ibid., p 11
11. David Icke, *The Robot's Rebellion*, Gateway, Bath, 1994, p 296
12. Jurij Moskvitin, *Essay on the Origin of Thought*, p 83
13. Gary Lachman, *A Secret History of Consciousness*, Lindisfarne Books, 2003, p 189f
14. Matthew Fox, *Creation Spirituality*, Harper San Francisco, 1991, p 131ff
15. *Alcoholics Anonymous*, New York, 1976
16. David B. Larson and Susan S. Larson, *Health's Forgotten Factor,* in Robert L. Hermann (ed.), *God, Science & Humility*, Radnor, 2000, p 266 referring to: H.A. Montgomery, W.R. Miller, and J.S. Tonigan, 'Does Alcoholics Anonymous Involvement Predict Treatment Outcome?', *Journal of Substance Abuse Treatment*, 12 April 1995, p 241-46
17. Margot Grey, *Return from Death*, 1986, p 108
18. Quoted in Aldous Huxley, *The Perennial Philosophy*, London, 1950, p 227
19. Quoted in Aldous Huxley, *op. cit.*, p 228
20. See estimate in chapter 9
21. Bernard Carter, 1962; this extract and the George Fox quotations are from the Quaker website.
22. John Main has written many books, and contacts all over the world are listed on 'The Community of Christian Meditation' website: www.wccm.org

23.   Described in detail by Isobel Jane Jeffery in her doctoral
        thesis: *The contemporary Influences of Muhyiddin Ibn 'Arabi
        in the West: The Beshara School and the Muhyiddin Ibn 'Arabi
        Society,* University of Exeter, February 2003; alternatively
        look on the Internet
24.   Many of the Dalai Lama's books can be found easily
25.   Werner Heisenberg writes similarly about our investigations
        in physics: We have to remember that what we observe is
        not nature in itself, but nature exposed to our method of
        questioning. In *Physics and Philosophy*, New York, 1958, p
        58
26.   Frithjof Schuon, *The Transcendent Unity of Religions*,
        Theosophical Publishing House, Wheaton (Ill), (1984)
        1993, p xii
27.   Sandy Cohen, 'Rabbi combines yoga with Hebrew mantras
        and teaches that "God is in each of us"', *Daily Breeze*, 23
        October 2004, see www.rickross.com/reference/general/
        general686.html
28.   On the Internet, some information on Miranda can be
        found, while for the amazing story of how such a young
        woman came to this step, see: Miranda Holden, *Boundless
        Love*, London, 2002.
29.   See e.g.: Susanna Stefanachi Macomb, *Joining Hands and
        Hearts: Interfaith, Intercultural Wedding Celebrations*, New
        York, 2003
30.   A very similar experience is described by Elmer Green,
        Quoted in Brian Inglis, *The Unknown Guest*, London, 1989,
        p 185.
31.   Our experiences were very much in parallel with those
        of the founders of the Findhorn Community: 'In the 60s
        the Community was a magical place, but one where the
        expectations were no less than a full day's work, seven days
        a week, and a serious-minded commitment to both work
        and spiritual practice'. see Alex Walker (ed.), *The Kingdom
        Within*, Findhorn Press, 1994, p 58
32.   'Halse' is local dialect for hazel, while 'combe' stands for
        valley; halse has several other appropriate meanings, such as
        'to call upon in the name of something divine or holy' (see
        Greater Oxford Dictionary).
33.   Richard Acland, *Hungry Sheep*, 1988, p 106
34.   Hazel Courteney, *The Evidence for the Sixth Sense*, London,
        2005, p 45
35.   Sallie McFague, *Super, Natural Christians: How we should
        love nature*, SCM Press, 1997, p 47
36.   Rolling Thunder's reply to the question: 'How could he be
        sure they were safe?' Cited by Stanley Krippner in a study of

shamanic states of consciousness, in Robin Royston & Anne Humphries, op. cit., p 280f

37. Lawrence LeShan, op. cit., p 131
38. Julie Chimes, *A Stranger in Paradise*, Bloomsbury, London, 1995, p 102
39. Robert L. Hermann (ed.), *God, Science & Humility*, Templeton Foundation Press, 2000, p 228ff
40. Quoted in David B. Larson and Susan S. Larson, *Health's Forgotten Factor,* in Robert L. Hermann (ed.), *God, Science & Humility*, Radnor, 2000, p 235
41. ibid., p 234
42. ibid., p 241
43. ibid., p 264
44. ibid., p 270
45. Harold K Schilling, *The New Consciousness in Science and Religion*, London, 1973, p 53
46. Carl R. Rogers and Barry Stevens, *Person to Person: The Problem of Being Human*, London, (1967) 1981, p 25
47. ibid., p 170
48. ibid., p 173
49. ibid., p 174
50. *Sacred Space,* Redmire, Mungrisdale, Cumbria CA11 0TB, England
51. 'A Conversation with Dr Larry Dossey MD', *Sacred Space,*, Vol 3, 1, 2002, p 17ff

Chapter 11 Summing up

1. Victor Hugo, *Les Misérables,* Book VII, ch VI
2. Adama & Naomi Doumbia, *the Way of the Elders*, St. Paul, MN, 2004, p 5
3. Quoted in Peter Plichta, *God's Secret Formula*, Element, Shaftesbury, 1997, p 126
4. Aldous Huxley, *The Perennial Philosophy*, London, 1950, p 5f
5. William James, *The Varieties of Religious Experience*, [1902], Penguin Classics, 1982, pp 378 & 388
6. Of which 26 per cent in the preceding year, see: Ann F. Garland Edward Zigler, 'Adolescent Suicide Prevention', *American Psychologist*, 48, 169ff; and read the shocking diagnosis in David R. Hawkins, M.D., Ph.D., *Power vs. Force: The Hidden Determinants of Human Behavior*, London, 2006, p 278
7. Aldous Huxley, op. cit., p 125

8.   Sylvia Cranston, *Reincarnation*, Theosophical University Press, Pasadena, 1994

9.   Glen Barclay, *Mind over Matter*, London, (1973) 1975, p 128

10.   C. G. Jung, *Modern Man in Search of a Soul*, London, (1933) 1985, p 224

11.   Harry R. Moody & David Carroll, *The Five Stages of the Soul*, Rider, London, 1998, p 20

12.   Quoted in William H. Shannon, *Thomas Merton in Dialogue with Eastern Religions*, in Patrick F. O'Connell (ed.), *The Vision of Thomas Merton*, 2003, p 215

13.   Daisetz Suzuki, *The Doctrine of Karma*

14.   Celeste Biever, 'Let's meet tomorrow in Second Life', *New Scientist*, 30 June 2007, p 26f. I am aware that the increase in autism has also been linked to vaccinations, see: Jim Giles in 'US vaccines on trial over link to autism', *New Scientist*, 23 June 2007, p 6f. In the same issue the editor stated that: '... in the US and Europe ... the prevalence of autism has leapt, perhaps tenfold over the last 20 years'.

15.   C. G. Jung, *Synchronicity: an Acausal Connecting Principle*

16.   Gary E. Schwartz, *The Afterlife Experiments*, Atria Books, New York, 2001

17.   Stephanie Matthews-Simonton, O. Carl Simonton and James L. Creighton, *Getting Well Again*, Bantam, 1984, pp 198 and 64

18.   Russell Targ and Hal Puthoff, *Mind-Reach*, New York, 1997; Russell Targ, *Limitless Mind*, New World Library, Novato (Ca), 2004

19.   Stanislav Grof, *The Holotropic Mind*, Harper San Francisco, 1990, p 139

20.   Gary E. Schwartz with William L. Simon, *The Afterlife Experiments*, Atria, New York, 2002, p 210

21.   ibid., p 216

22.   Fritjof Capra, *Uncommon Wisdom*, Flamingo, 1990, p 46

23.   Stanislav Grof, op. cit, p 196f

24.   Opinion Interview in *New Scientist*, 3.3.2001, p 46

25.   Institute of Electric and Electronic Engineers

26.   Harold Puthoff & Russell Targ, 'A Perceptual Channel for Information Transfer over Kilometer Distances. Historical Perspective and Recent Experiments', *Proc. IEEE*, Vol. 64, No. 3 (March 1976)

27.   Editorial in the *Proceedings of the IEEE*, Vol. 64, No.3 (March, 1976), p291

28.   Kahlil Gibran, *The Prophet*, London, (1926) 1992, p 74f

29.   Rumi, *Mathnavi*, quoted in Sophy Burnham, *The Ecstatic Journey*, Ballantine, 1997, p 49

30.   Anthony de Mello, *One Minute Wisdom*, New York, 1988

31.   Quoted in: R. C. Johnson, *Psychical Research*, London, 1955, p 45
32.   Harry R. Moody & David Carroll, op. cit., p 312
33.   Peggy Mason & Ron Laing, *Sathya Sai Baba:The Embodiment of Love*,Pilgrim, 1987 (1982), p 199
34.   Matthew Fox, *The Reinvention of Work,* New York, 1995, p 170
35.   Fritjof Capra, *Uncommon Wisdom*, Flamingo, 1990, p 34
36.   C. G. Jung, *Richard Wilhelm: In Memoriam*, in *The Collected Works*, Vol. 15, p 58
37.   see e.g. Barry Singer and Victor A. Benassi, 'Occult Beliefs', *American Scientist*, Vol. 69, p 49ff
38.   Lawrence LeShan, *Clairvoyant Reality* (Formerly *The Medium, The Mystic and the Physicist*), Turnstone Press Ltd, (1974)1982, p 197
39.   Matthew Fox, op. cit., p 188
40.   Eric Butterworth, *Discover the Power within You* , Harper San Francisco, 1992, p 75 (his italics)
41.   The amazing plant-growing experiences she had in Findhorn have also been reported by G. I. Gurdjieff about his teacher, Father Evlessi, in *Meetings with Remarkable Men*, London, (1963)1985, p 133. There are several books about the Findhorn Community, see www.findhorn.org.
42.   Machaelle Small Wright, *Behaving as if the God in all Life Mattered,* Warrenton, VA, (1983) 1997 or www.perelandra-ltd.com
43.   Quoted in Francis Younghusband, *Modern Mystics,* London, 1935, p 60
44.   ibid., p 85
45.   ibid., p 185
46.   ibid., p 254
47.   Quoted in Catherine Ingram, *In the Footsteps of Gandhi,* Berkeley (Ca), 1990, p 255
48.   William Blake expressed this poignantly: 'As a man is, so he sees'. And Anais Nin expressed this as, 'We don't see things as they are. We see things as we are'. Modern research has confirmed this fact in several experiments, see e.g. Max Velmans' writing in his review of several books on this subject: The 'standard model' of perception has got to be wrong, *New Scientist*, 25 March 2006, p 50f.
49.   Quoted in Russell Targ, *Limitless Mind*, New World Library, Novato (Ca), 2004, p xii
50.   E. F. Schumacher, *Good Work,* p 121
51.   *The Bhagavad Gita*, Juan Mascaro (transl.), Penguin, 1962, p 58f
52.   ibid., p 52
53.   Lao Tse, *Tao Te Ching*, Mitchell (transl.), p 53

54. Quoted by Matthew Fox in *The Reinvention of Work*, New York, 1995, p 83

55. There are so many different methods on offer; take for instance (although they all come from the Hindu tradition) the different approaches to meditation by Yogananda, Krishnamurti, Sat Baba, Maharishi and Osho.

56. Aldous Huxley, *The Perennial Philosophy*, London, 1950, p 137

57. William Johnston, *Christian Mysticism Today*, Collins, 1984, p 145f

58. Quoted in Aldous Huxley, op.cit., p 147

59. James William Coleman, *The New Buddhism*, Oxford University Press, New York, 2002, p 121

60. Harry R. Moody & David Carroll, op.cit., p 72

61. Dom Bede Griffiths, *River of Compassion,* Warwick NY, 187, p 7

62. Luke 16:15

63. Gospel of Thomas, *logion* 37

64. The website is www.sofn.org.uk, and my letter can be found as Annex 1

65. Adama & Naomi Doumbia, *The Way of the Elders*, St. Paul, MN, 2004, p 21

66. Quoted in Anthony Gottlieb, *The Dream of Reason,* London, 2000, p 314

67. Abraham Pais, *Einstein Lived Here*, Oxford University Press, 1994, p 253f

68. E. F. Schumacher, *Good Work*, Harper & Row, New York, 1979, p 32

69. Quoted in: Rhonda Byrne, *The Secret*, London, 2006, p 166

70. Harold K. Schilling, *The New Consciousness in Science and Religion*, London, 1973, p 232

71. Gary Zukav, *The Seat of the Soul*, London, 1990, p 243

72. Matthew Fox, *The Reinvention of Work,* New York, 1995, p 26

73. Quoted in Lawrence LeShan, *How to Meditate*, Thorsons, London, 1995, p 28f

74. Rachel Naomi Remen, *My Grandfather's Blessings,* HarperCollins, London, 2000, pp 376, 29, 91, 148 and 232 respectively

75. W. R. Inge, *Lay thoughts of a Dean*, London, Putnam, 1926

76. Susan Howatch, *Glamorous Power,* HarperCollins, 1996

77. Susan Howatch, *Mystical Paths*, HarperCollins, 1996, p 518

78. ibid., p 537

79. Susan Howatch, *Glamorous Power,* HarperCollins, 1996, p 218

80. Susan Howatch, *Mystical Paths,* HarperCollins, 1996, p 68

81. C. G. Jung, *The Secret of the Golden Flower*, London, 1931, p viii
82. quoted in A.W. Osborn, *The Expansion of Awareness*, Theosophical Publishing House, 1967, p 232
83. Carl Sagan, *The Demon Haunted World*, 1996, p 32
84. ibid., p 197f
85. ibid., p 20
86. ibid., p 40
87. Leonard Leibovici made this quite clear in the BMJ in a response to his critics: 'I believe it [the effect of prayer] should not be tested in controlled trials. ... empirical methods [cannot] be applied to questions that are completely outside the scientific model of the physical world'. Quoted in Lynne McTaggart, *The Intention Experiment*, Element, London, 2007, p 216
88. Called governors, teachers and checkers respectively
89. Russell Targ, *Limitless Mind*, New World Library, Novato (Ca), 2004, p 152
90. Konstantin Tsiolkovsky, quoted in Sheila Ostrander and Lynn Schroeder,*The ESP Papers* , Bantam, 1976, p 222
91. Quoted in D. E. Harding, *The Little Book of Life and Death*, Arkana, 1988, p 65
92. Quoted in W. Y. Evans-Wentz, *Tibet's Great Yogi Milarepa* , OUP, London, (1928)1976, p viii
93. Masami Saionji, *The Golden Key to Happiness*, Element, 1995, p 168
94. Antoine de Saint-Exupéry, *The Little Prince*, London, (1945) 1975, p 68
95. John Davidson, *The Web of Life*, Daniels, Saffron Walden, 1988, p 393
96. If you want that same point expressed with respectable academic authority, read the study report of the Harvard Research Center in Creative Altruism, quoted in Pitrim A Sorokin, *Integralism is my Philosophy*, in Whit Burnett (ed.), *This is my Philosophy*, London, 1958, p 187f
97. Christmas Humphreys, *Exploring Buddhism,* London, (1974) 1980, p 80
98. Swami Prabhavananda, *The Sermon on the Mount according to Vedanta*, Hollywood, 1963, p 22
99. Peggy Mason & Ron Laing, *Sathya Sai Baba:The Embodiment of Love*,Pilgrim, 1987 (1982), p 21
100. Norman Friedman, *Bridging Science and Spirit*, quoted in Russell Targ, *Limitless Mind*, New World Library, Novato (Ca), 2004, p 92
101. His Holiness the Dalai Lama, *The Little Book of Wisdom,* 1997, p 28

102.   Quoted in William H. Shannon, *Thomas Merton in Dialogue with Eastern Religions*, in Patrick F. O'Connell (ed.), *The Vision of Thomas Merton*, 2003, p 211

103.   Yu-Lan Fung, *The Spirit of Chinese Philosophy* in Jaroslav Pelikan (ed.), *The World Treasure of Modern Religious Thought*, Little, Brown and Co., 1990, p 582f

104.   His Holiness the Dalai Lama, op.cit., p 135

105.   See e.g.: http://www.artchive.com/artchive/H/hunt/hunt_light_of_world.jpg.html

106.   Quoted in Sophy Burnham, *The Ecstatic Journey*, Ballantine, 1997, p 276

107.   Quoted in Harry R. Moody and David Carroll, op.cit., p 352

108.   William James, *The Will to Believe,* in Jaroslav Pelikan (ed.), *The World Treasure of Modern Religious Thought*, Little, Brown and Co, 1990, p 101

109.   ibid., p 111

110.   Julie Rousseau, letter to *New Scientist*, 27 March 2005, p 30

111.   Quoted in Sylvia Cranston, *Reincarnation*, Theosophical University Press, Pasadena, 1994, p 386

112.   Marion Bowman, quoted in *Open Eye Magazine,* Spring 2004, p 10

113.   *Dhammapada,* quoted in Christmas Humphreys, *Exploring Buddhism,* London, (1974) 1980, p 172

114.   Roy Wilkinson, *On Growing Old*, privately published in May 2005 in the *Rudolf Steiner: Aspects of his Spiritual Worldview* series, Rudolf Steiner Press Ltd, Forest Row, East Sussex

115.   Thomas Keating, *Intimacy with God*, Crossroad Publishing, New York, 1994

116.   Mark 10:15

117.   Anna in Fynn, *Anna and the Black Knight*, Collins, London, 1990, p 102

Lightning Source UK Ltd.
Milton Keynes UK
18 September 2010

160070UK00001B/9/P